Cancelled

To Luca, who showed me that true love exists

and

To Carmen, Julie, and Pere, who showed me that true love is stronger than death.

Cancelled
The Left Way Back from Woke

UMUT ÖZKIRIMLI

polity

First published in 2023 by Polity Press

Polity Press
65 Bridge Street
Cambridge CB2 1UR, UK

Polity Press
111 River Street
Hoboken, NJ 07030, USA

ISBN-13: 978-1-5095-5091-3
ISBN-13: 978-1-5095-5092-0 (pb)

A catalogue record for this book is available from the British Library.

Library of Congress Control Number: 2022919724

Typeset in 11 on 14pt Warnock Pro
by Cheshire Typesetting Ltd, Cuddington, Cheshire
Printed and bound in Great Britain by TJ Books Ltd, Padstow, Cornwall

For further information on Polity, visit our website:
politybooks.com

Contents

Acknowledgments

This book is a lot of firsts for me. It is the first book I've written after the death of our five-and-a-half-year-old son Luca in 2018, following an epic struggle with neuroblastoma, a rare form of childhood cancer. It is the most personal book I've written so far, inspired and shaped by the lived experience of the last five years, and a great deal of soul-searching. And it is the first book I've written for the general public, unlike my previous books which catered to a more academic audience.

As such, it wasn't an easy book to write, and it wouldn't have seen the light of day if it weren't for the encouragement and endless patience of my editor Louise Knight who is in many ways the godmother of this book. I've had the chance to work with many inspiring editors in the past, but her unique blend of care, empathy, and professionalism made Louise the right person at the right time, and for this, I will always be indebted to her. The same goes for Polity for believing in this project in the first place. I am also grateful, in no particular order, to the anonymous reviewers of Polity, Elise Heslinga, Lars Trägårdh, and Julie Wark for reading through an earlier draft of this manuscript. It would not be an exaggeration to say that this is a better book thanks to their incisive and elaborate comments. And if the book is not good enough, it's me, not them. Special thanks are due to Julie Wark for her magical editing, Inès Boxman for her editorial assistance, Ian Tuttle for his meticulous copy editing, and to Julie Bindel, Craig Calhoun, Jo Phoenix, and Jean Wyllys for endorsing the book.

In a rare interview with Reuters in 2001, the Swedish film director and screenwriter Ingmar Bergman was asked about what inspired his art. Candidly referring to his inner demons, he said: "The demons are innumerable, arrive at the most inappropriate times and create panic and terror. But I have learned that if I can master the negative forces and harness them to my chariot, then they can work to my advantage." This book was written during a period when I had regular visits from my own demons, some more grim than others. I would not be able to resist their temptations, and channel their destructive power into creative energy, without the unwavering support and love of countless people. I cannot name them all here, but a few deserve special mention. I would like to thank Sebastian Scheiman, Özge Artık, and Suzan Türkarslan for believing in justice in an unjust world; my co-warrior Erika Larsson for being an amazing mother to our son and being there for me whenever I needed her wisdom and friendship; Marianne, Lars, and Gunilla for being part of "Team Luca," wandering around the world with us to keep him happy; Jan, Sergi, Anahi, and Charo for giving me a new family; my selfless, loving mother and my big-hearted aunt for suffering, crying, and laughing with me; and last, but certainly not least, my partner Bahar for – where should I begin? – giving me a second chance at the most inopportune time, patiently enduring my never-ending agonies, and offering me a love like no other (for what it's worth, I love you!).

Yet the list above has a glaring omission – well, three omissions. Julie, who wrote the following to be read at Luca's funeral: "Normally one thinks that kids take after their parents but, this time, at least as I see it, you take after Luca. He is so much a part of you I'll never be able to look at you again without seeing him in you"; Carmen and Pere who told me to "bring my shell" to Barcelona and greeted me at the airport, the day after the funeral, with a hug and a heartfelt "Welcome home!" Without them, I wouldn't be sitting here and writing these words. It is to my anchor, Luca, and to Carmen, Julie, and Pere that this book is dedicated.

Prologue

> "Would you tell me, please, which way I ought to go from
> here?"
> "That depends a good deal on where you want to get to," said
> the Cat.
> "I don't much care where –" said Alice.
> "Then it doesn't matter which way you go," said the Cat.
> "– so long as I get *somewhere*," Alice added as an explanation.
> "Oh, you're sure to do that," said the Cat, "if you only walk
> long enough."
>
> Lewis Carroll, *Alice in Wonderland*

It all started with a tweet.

Since it popped up in the midst of a meticulously planned and seamlessly executed pile-on, I probably wouldn't have noticed it if it hadn't been posted by a certain person of interest. "How telling it is that the person who enthusiastically shared the most TERF article (sic) of 2019 in 2020 also liked the repulsive and lie-ridden blog post some guy wrote . . . It handily helps us to separate out the good from the bad," the cryptic tweet read. Who was the target of these accusations? What on earth did TERF mean? Was it an acronym? A neologism deliberately capitalized to make a point? How did it relate to the pile-on and, more importantly, what did it have to do with being good or bad? I didn't have the slightest idea. In the end, I decided to let it go for I had other, more pressing, concerns to attend to. After all, as I would come to realize later, I was in the process of being "cancelled."[1]

I had forgotten about the enigmatic signifier TERF until July 16, 2020, when a historian posted a hefty thread on the issue, coming out as the person addressed in the mysterious tweet that had made the rounds 26 days earlier. Apparently, she was the one who recirculated "the most TERF article of 2019," though this wasn't what attracted the ire of the Furies. She also committed the unforgivable sin of liking a tweet by two friends of mine – self-professed "feminist dinosaurs" – who defiantly stood against the outrage mob, declaring "We value solidarity, truth, justice and integrity; we find nothing inspiring about lies and vindictiveness. Feminism is about justice, not about destroying people." Ironically enough, they didn't know what TERF stood for either.

I had to find out. This was my white rabbit with a waistcoat-pocket and a watch, and like Alice, I was burning with curiosity.[2]

Down the Rabbit Hole

So I googled it. TERF stood for "Trans-Exclusionary Radical Feminist," retrospectively attributed to a series of blog posts by the Australian writer and blogger Viv Smythe in 2008. The term was used disparagingly, often as a slur, to refer to feminists who hold "gender-critical" views, including the belief that biological sex is binary, immutable, and relevant, and should not be conflated with the sociological concept of gender – a view that trans rights activists consider as "transphobic." I now knew what TERF was, but I still didn't have a clue as to why the historian who liked my friends' tweet was called a

TERF. Even though I had never met her, as an avid follower of her popular Twitter account, I was aware that she described herself as a feminist. Did her feminism exclude transgender and non-binary people's rights? Was she transphobic? If so, why hadn't I noticed before? In any case, how did this relate to me and the cancel campaign that was fizzling out as abruptly as it began?

There was only one way to find out. I jumped down the rabbit hole. And I found myself in a parallel world, an alternate reality if you will, every bit as surreal as Alice's Wonderland. Truth is, I had never stopped following the debates in my areas of interest, above all identity politics and nationalism.[3] But as a proud leftist, it had never occurred to me to look around my own rabbit hole. Now that I was in, I might as well do some digging. I began reading. And listening. And learning. The more I learned, the more I was sucked in. There were times I wished, like Alice, "I hadn't gone down that rabbit-hole – and yet – and yet," it was rather eye-opening.

Woke

As it turned out, TERF was only the tip of a gigantic iceberg which had calved from the traditional Left – the universalist, egalitarian Left that I was committed to – and found itself a new name: "woke." The intransitive form of the verb "wake," the term took on a new meaning in the late 2000s, thanks to Erykah Badu's hit song *Master Teacher* with the refrain "I stay woke," and became closely associated with the Black Lives Matter movement which was rekindled in the aftermath of the fatal shooting of Michael Brown in Ferguson, Missouri, in 2014. This led the *Oxford English Dictionary* to expand its definition of "woke" in 2017 as an adjective used figuratively in the sense of "alert to racial or social discrimination and injustice; frequently in *stay woke* (often used as an exhortation)."[4]

Once out there, in the marketplace of idioms, it didn't take long for woke to be hijacked by the Right, which took it as a stand-in for their pet bogeyman "political correctness" and deployed it as an umbrella term depicting a set of ideological – in their view, quasi-religious – beliefs and their cult-like followers, bent on destroying all the values that were dear to the conservative heart and mind. The right-wing moral panic around woke was fueled by both politicians and prominent media personalities, including the provocateur-in-chief Donald Trump, who made it a key theme of the 2020 National Republican Convention. "[T]his election will decide whether we will defend the American Way of Life, or whether we allow a radical movement to completely dismantle and destroy it," the 45th president of the US said. "In the left's backward view, they do not see America as the most free, just, and exceptional nation on earth. Instead, they see a wicked nation that must be punished for its sins."[5]

But bar the term "woke" and its assorted derivatives – wokeness, wokedom, wokeism, among myriad others – all this was familiar territory. Once it was the "commies"; today it was the "wokies." And yet, those who tried to "cancel" me were not right-wing stooges; they were (supposedly) left-wing activists, with all the right credentials, feminists, trans rights support-ers, self-appointed spokespeople for marginalized minorities. In other words, they were on my side. Or so I thought. Was I missing something?

Cancelled

I felt Alice's confusion. "So many out-of-the-way things had happened lately," I thought like her, "that very few things indeed were really impossible." I wasn't perfect and I made some mistakes (though certainly not the ones they said I did); still, I couldn't fathom this sudden outburst of anger, by my erstwhile comrades no less. To make sense of it all, I had to dig deeper, and acquaint myself with other quirks of the rabbit hole, first and foremost the concepts of "cancelling" and "cancel culture."

The etymological trajectory of "cancelling" was as intriguing as that of "woke." First used as a line in the 1991 American crime thriller *New Jack City*, the term reached a wider audience with an episode of VH1's popular reality show *Love and Hip-Hop: New York*, aired on December 22, 2014 to 2.17 million viewers, in which one of the characters tells his girlfriend, "You're canceled!" during a heated outdoor fight. The term then seeped into Black Twitter, and from there the broader public where it morphed into a lexical weapon to galvanize opposition to perceived offense, in particular those committed by celebrities or other powerful figures, often accompanied with a call for boycotts. The final seal of approval came from the *Oxford English Dictionary* which introduced a new, colloquial, definition of the term "cancel" in March 2021, "To dismiss, reject, or get rid of (a person or thing). In later use, esp. in the context of social media: to publicly boycott, ostracize, or withdraw support from (a person, institution, etc.) thought to be promoting culturally unacceptable ideas" as well as an entry on "cancel culture," "the action or practice of publicly boycotting, ostracizing, or withdrawing support from a person, institution, etc., thought to be promoting culturally unacceptable ideas."[6]

Therein lay the rub. What were "culturally unacceptable ideas"? Who, or which authority, decided what was culturally acceptable and what wasn't? And what should be the proper Left stance vis-à-vis culturally unacceptable ideas, whatever they may be? This last question was the one that mattered most to me, for I didn't care much about the Right. In fact, the way it was defined by the *OED* and other sources, "cancel culture" seemed to be nothing more than the latest incarnation of censorship and witch hunts, the hallmarks of reactionary, conservative thinking throughout centuries. The problem was that both woke and cancelling hailed from progressive circles, in particular those who embraced some form of radical identity politics.

Spitting Images

I was slowly getting to the bottom of things. Certain ideas were culturally inappropriate, and it was up to the self-appointed guardians of the new orthodoxy to ensure that they remained inappropriate. "To publicly boycott, ostracize, or withdraw support from," or cancelling, was simply a means to a higher end, and especially here down the rabbit hole, the end always justified the means. The woke Left was a mirror image of the reactionary Right in its disdain for dissent, its bunker mentality, and Manichean simplicity.

It was not surprising in this context that asking questions about the legal and practical implications of the blurring of the boundaries between gender and sex made you a TERF, a "trans-exclusionary radical feminist," insidiously promoting a discourse with "racist undertones" to preserve the privileges of White "cis" women (yet another newly minted term to describe people who allegedly identify with the sex they are assigned at birth) from the "encroachments" of Black women, transgender, or non-binary people – and this not in *Vox*, *Slate*, *Salon*, *Buzzfeed*, *Daily Beast*, or *The Nation*, the official gazettes of the woke Left, but in legacy media and top academic journals in humanities and social sciences.[7]

It was also perfectly normal for the chief executive of Stonewall, the most powerful LGBTQ+ rights organization in the UK, to liken "gender-critical" beliefs to anti-Semitism;[8] or for trans rights activists to condone doxing, death and rape threats so long as they were directed, say, at J. K. Rowling.[9] In its effort to impose its own peculiar understanding of social justice, the woke Left didn't hesitate to borrow freely from far right repertoire. Any attempt to make a new Harry Potter series, *Vox* writer Aja Romano wrote, upon the rumors that some networks are exploring the options for bringing the franchise to TV, would mean "that trans people will be overlooked, will have their concerns and their sorrow pushed aside – by Rowling, by Hollywood, by anyone who continues to work with Rowling and promote or publish her works, and by the society that has yet to repudiate her into obsolescence."[10] After all, they said, "Anything that we respond to and love about a new Harry Potter series will still be something that ultimately came from J. K. Rowling – from the den mother who betrayed us."[11]

Now I had some idea about why the historian who happened to like a tweet was also called a TERF. Little did it matter that the tweet in question had nothing to do with transgender rights. She didn't toe the line, and that in itself was enough for the woke Left to write her off.

Who Am I?

It was time for a reckoning. If this was the Left, then I wasn't a leftist. It wasn't the so-called threats to free speech – the key talking point of the right-wing propaganda machine – that I was worried about. Few celebrities or public figures lost their platforms permanently due to cancel campaigns by social media vigilantes or woke activists; and in the few instances they did, they had either committed a crime and were convicted in court, or the evidence for their breach of moral codes was too glaring to ignore even if it slipped through the cracks of the ever not so perfect legal system. Then there is the Right's own eagerness to embrace cancel culture to push its conservative agenda or get rid of its most outspoken critics (ask the Cambridge academic Priyamvada Gopal who was exposed to a torrent of abuse over a misinterpreted tweet).[12] That was in fact my problem: the Left's readiness to mimic the Right's ways and its arrant, and self-blinding, sense of entitlement and self-righteousness. I couldn't take part in this spectacle of non-politics, the stifling intolerance, hasty condemnations, virtue-signaling, public shaming, bullying, and other trademarks of the reactionary Right, recycled in a glossy package along with a name tag that read the "woke Left."

Not that the woke would welcome me in their exclusive club either. Playing the TERF card wouldn't work, for I am not a woman, biologically speaking, but that doesn't rule out transphobia, homophobia, sexism, heterosexism, toxic masculinity, ableism, ageism, and a litany of other transgressions. Chances are I would also be diagnosed with "white fragility," a term invented by social and racial justice consultant Robin DiAngelo, to describe "a state in which even a minimal challenge to the white position becomes intolerable, triggering a range of defensive responses."[13] I may as well consider myself a progressive, but, alas, "it is the white progressive who can cause the most daily harm to people of color."[14] "A positive white identity is an impossible goal," DiAngelo would tell me; "white identity is inherently racist."[15] How can we break the cycle then, and join the fight for anti-racism? Well, we can't, if we are White. All we can do is to admit our complicity in perpetrating white supremacy, and embark on an infinite process of self-correction, reminding ourselves on a daily basis that "no one is ever done."[16]

And what if, on top of all that, I insist that woke strategy is defeatist, that radical identity politics is divisive, lacking a vision for coalition-building and a program based on shared values? In the best case, I would be branded as a "useful idiot," advancing or unwittingly enabling a right-wing agenda. In a less charitable, but more likely, scenario, I would be lumped together with evangelical Christians, far right groups or, let's not be coy, fascists.

So basically, I had two options. I could try to stay in the rabbit hole as a denizen, prepare a fancy CV along with some "sample activism work" and a list of hashtags I endorsed, and submit an application for the membership of the woke club, as many of my liberal and progressive (often male) colleagues have done. In the meantime, I could book a "Diversity, Equity and Inclusion" training course with Robin DiAngelo for $14,000 (the average fee in 2020 according to DiAngelo's official website)[17] and learn how to deal with my white guilt; I could familiarize myself with Stonewall's guidelines on gender-inclusive language, and hope for the best.

But this option was a no-go. I could remain forever stuck in precarious denizenship status, or even be demoted to a pariah, for I didn't fit the membership profile. As a White "cisgender" heterosexual middle-aged man, I was at the bottom of the inverted oppression pyramid with few, if any, chances to make amends, and get a citizenship certificate. What's worse, there was the risk of alienation and radicalization, especially if the waiting period was too long or my membership application was rejected. I was already feeling the effects of overexposure to the toxic atmosphere of the rabbit hole, notably a growing unease with the Left's endless victim-mongering and obsession with symbolic harm at the expense of more flagrant forms of injustice. I could even sense a sneaking empathy for centrist/liberal criticisms of woke activism – a feeling I knew I shared with most gender-critical feminists who were subject to the most heinous forms of online or real-world abuse day in day out.

But I didn't want to go down that road. I couldn't recant the ideals I've cherished all my life and connive with those who were determined to eradicate them. So I had to go for the second, more challenging, option: to find a way out of the rabbit hole and reclaim the Left from the woke Left. I didn't lack ideas, but needed guides and fellow travelers, people who couldn't be dismissed out of hand by the indigenous population of the rabbit hole for not possessing the right identity credentials.

That's when I found her.

Loretta

I first came across her name in a 2019 opinion piece in *The New York Times* called "I'm a Black Feminist. I Think Call-Out Culture Is Toxic."[18] The title in itself was intriguing enough, for I'd encountered few Black feminists who took on "call-out culture" (often a stepping stone to full cancellation) so forthrightly, but the author had more to offer than this statement that immediately caught my eye. "Can we avoid individualizing oppression and not use the movement as our personal therapy space?," she asked, without throwing the baby out with the bathwater, and acknowledging the usefulness of "call-outs" as a tactic to hold the powerful accountable. "But most public shaming is horizontal and done by those who believe they have greater integrity or more sophisticated analyses," she rightly noted – something that is all-too-easily overlooked by left-wing denialists. And this breeds a culture of fear which leads people to close off, and close ranks, hampering social justice work. Instead of "calling out," we should "call-in," she wrote, engaging "in debates with words and actions of healing and restoration, and without the self-indulgence of drama." Key to this process of "restorative justice" is the venerable framework of human rights which builds on the values we share simply by virtue of being human.

A Black feminist preaching universal human rights (at the expense of radical identity politics) in today's highly polarized world was somewhat unusual, to say the least, and she would have certainly been snubbed by the woke Left if she weren't an internationally renowned reproductive rights and anti-rape activist. Loretta J. Ross was the perfect source of inspiration for the troubled leftist, the glimmer of light at the bottom of the pitch-dark rabbit hole. I had to delve deeper into her life, find out about the "lived experience" which led her to a very different path from that of most contemporary activists.

Loretta J. Ross was born in Temple, Texas, in 1953. Her father was an immigrant from Jamaica and her mother came from a family of slaves on a peanut plantation near Selma, Alabama. As the daughter of an Army weapons specialist, she moved around quite a lot and attended integrated military schools. "We felt worldly, we felt cosmopolitan," Ross recalled in a long interview she gave in 2004–2005 as part of the *Voices of Feminism Oral History Project*; "we felt like all the little kids who never went anywhere were disadvantaged."[19]

Loretta's life took a dismal turn at the age of 11, when she was beaten and raped by a stranger. At 15, she was raped again, this time by a distant relative, and left pregnant. She gave birth to her son, Howard, in 1969. As she decided to keep her child, she lost her scholarship to Radcliffe College – a women's liberal arts college in Cambridge, Massachusetts, functioning as the female coordinate institution of the all-male Harvard College. She ended up enrolling at Howard University in 1970.

Her college life was no less eventful. Surviving a gang rape, a miscarriage and a late-term abortion with life-threatening complications, she finally decided to stop taking birth control pills and go for Dalkon Shield, an intrauterine device produced by the pharmaceutical company A. H. Robins, handed out gratis at the Howard University Health Services. Unlike most other users, she did not experience too many side effects at first, which led her to believe that she was blessed. Unfortunately, two to three years into her use of Dalkon Shield, her luck ran out and, after a series of misdiagnoses and "missed diagnoses," she woke up post-op in a hospital discovering that she'd just had a full hysterectomy. She was only 23 when the doctor told her she would never have children again. Furious, Loretta sued A. H. Robins and, even though she settled out of court, she opened the way – along with a few others – to a huge class-action suit against the company which filed for bankruptcy in 1985 after settling 9,500 cases.

Being a victim of "sterilization abuse" set the course of Loretta J. Ross's later activism. After a brief flirtation with Black nationalist politics, she soon moved on to reproductive rights and anti-violence activism. In 1979, she became director of the D.C. Rape Crisis Center, the only center at the time run primarily by and for women of color. One year later, she organized the first National Conference on Third World Women and Violence. Her activist career continued to flourish, first as Director of Women of Color Programs for the National Organization for Women, NOW (1985–9), then as Program Director for the National Black Women's Health Project (1989–90), and as National Program Research Director for the Center for Democratic Revival (formerly the National Anti-Klan Network) (1991–5). From the mid-1990s onwards, Ross expanded her activism into the area of human rights and set up the National Center for Human Rights Education. In 1997, she co-founded SisterSong Women of Color Reproductive Justice Collective and served as its National Coordinator from 2005 to 2012. She was among the first (women of color) to coin the term "reproductive justice," understood both as a theory and a model for activism based on "three interconnected human rights values: the right *not to have children* using safe birth control, abortion, or abstinence; the right *to have children* under the conditions we choose; and the right *to parent the children we have* in safe and healthy environments."[20]

As I was reading Loretta J. Ross's 355 page-long interview, I was overwhelmed with a torrent of emotions – guilt for not being aware of her work earlier; discomfort for my White-heterosexual-male-middle-class privileges; but also an empowering sense of hope, and will to fight for justice. The highlight of Ross's story, the watershed moment if you will, that changed the course of her activism, and setting her on a path that diverged radically from that of the woke Left, took place when she was working at the D.C. Rape Crisis Center.

One day Ross and her activist friend Yulanda Ward (who was later assassinated under suspicious circumstances according to Ross)[21] were contacted by a group of black prisoners at Lorton Reformatory, a former prison complex in Lorton, Virginia. The rest of the story should be quoted in full:

> This guy named William Fuller wrote us. William was a guy who was in prison for rape and murder. He'd been incarcerated for 15 years about that time, and he wrote this oh so moving letter, saying that while I was on the outside, I raped women. Now on the inside, I rape men. I want to stop raping. Can you help me? That's the essence of his letter. We went, Ah, ssshhh – talk about causing a controversy . . . What should we say to this guy? And um, we kind of made the decision that at least we would check him out because, I mean, you could bandage women up all you want to, but if you don't stop men from raping, what's the point? Better bandages?[22]

So Ross and Ward went to the prison to meet William. "I was scared of William," Ross recalled; "when he was 18, he raped, sodomized, and murdered this woman. He was 33 now, and he'd gotten hold of some feminist readings . . . and his argument was that, I believe that rape is a form of power and control, and I want to know how not to be a rapist." Ross and her friend set some ground rules, the most important being that they would only bring feminist literature to the prison. They then bought several copies of bell hooks's *Ain't I a Woman?* and, with five men, all rapists, they started a prison-based version of a group. Ross, Ward, and others went there every Friday for two years and spent the afternoon with them. In the end, William and his friends formed their own group called Prisoners Against Rape, which became a model for prison-based anti-rape programs.

"That caused a revolution in how we saw things," Ross told her interviewer in 2004, "because heretofore, we'd only worked with the victims of sexual assault, we had not talked about the perpetrators of sexual assault. And again, we had objectified them. If anybody had asked me, particularly given my own personal experiences, I don't think I would've predicted that I'd be in a prison teaching rapists."

This was what the woke Left and the many movements it propelled could not see: that cancelling or calling out are also about power and privilege; that radical identity politics is individualistic and narcissistic; that personal therapy is no substitute for collective political action; that performative outrage does not advance the cause of social justice.

Ross saw all this because, even as a victim of rape, gang rape, and incest, she could overcome her fears and confront rapists. She knew, after decades of hands-on activism, that there were more effective ways of building movements, and that "they happen in person, in real life":[23]

> [P]eople who really do the hard work of community organizing, crossing borders, smuggling health care drugs to save lives, door-knocking among apathetic neighbors ... and getting Black people to vote to save white folks from themselves, have no time for pretending we can solve our collective problems by ritualized practices that may be better suited for a mountaintop retreat chanting to become one with the universe. ... In some ways, this is just cultural appropriation run amok. In other ways, these are dangerous practices that suck up energy, time, resources, money, and importantly, trust. How can anyone who's life is in danger take us seriously when we spend our time as social justice dilettantes?[24]

Loretta J. Ross was the ideal guide for the disillusioned, *yes-privileged-yet-eager-to-learn* leftist. Her life, the tenacity with which she held to her faith in and love for her fellow human beings were a perfect reminder of the ideals that the Left had long forgotten. Armed with the compass Ross provided me, I began climbing back out of the rabbit hole.

This book could be read as a diary of this personal journey. It is also a call to all those disenchanted with reactionary populism and radical identity politics to break free from dogmatism and fanaticism, and adopt a new progressive agenda based on our common humanity while respecting our differences.

Roadmap

Navigating the alternate reality of the woke Left is no small feat. The hole is deep, and there are no signposts. All I can do is to stick to a path and leave a trail of breadcrumbs behind to make sure that readers can follow me or find their way back to reality in case they get lost. Each stage of my journey is marked by one such breadcrumb, a real-world example – a true story if you will – to set the scene for the discussion that follows. I begin in chapter 1 with a reflection on the radicalization of both the Right and the Left, or their colonization by exclusionary forms of identity politics. I argue that this is the result of a tectonic shift to the Right and a general retreat from liberalism, which led to the rise of White identity politics and populism on the Right, and a parochial, narcissistic form of "politics for identity" on the Left. In this chapter, I also outline the central thesis of the book and provide introductory remarks about the "great convergence" between Right and Left, followed by an account of the key concepts that will guide my analysis in the remainder of the book. The following two chapters are devoted to a more detailed overview of identity politics on the Right and the Left, respectively, in the context of the broader crisis of democracy and growing polarization around issues of national identity, immigration, race, gender, and sexuality – the bread-and-butter of the so-called culture wars. The aim of the fourth, and longest, chapter is to substantiate the main argument of the book, which is that the woke Left has much more in common with right-wing illiberal populism than both sides would like to admit. In this context, I contend that the dominant forms of identity politics today constitute a radical departure from the original, anti-capitalist, vision of Black feminist lesbian activists who first coined the term in 1977. This is followed by a discussion of the subversion of progressive politics by neoliberal globalization, in particular the overriding logic of marketization that turns everything, even "identity," into a commodity that can be bought and sold. This chapter also problematizes the use of identity as a weapon of individual empowerment which manifests itself most visibly in what has come to be called "cancel culture." The fifth, and final, chapter is a call for a return to a universalist progressive politics dedicated to community activism and coalition-building. In this chapter, I outline an alternative vision for the Left which seeks to reclaim social justice and to make it the foundation of a political program that promotes redistribution, recognition, and participation within the framework of a democratic socialist welfare state.

1

A Rude Awakening

The Women's March on Washington

On November 8, 2016, hours after Donald Trump declared his victory as the 45th President of the United States, Teresa Shook, a retired lawyer in Hawaii, took to Facebook to vent her frustration. She created a private event page in "Pantsuit Nation," a Facebook group devoted to mobilizing Hillary Clinton supporters, which she shared with a mere 40 friends. The underlying message was short but to the point: "We have to march!" When she woke up the next day, her page had gone viral. Over 10,000 people sent RSVPs, with another 10,000 showing some interest. Overwhelmed, Shook reached out to two strangers, Evvie Harmon and Fontaine Pearson, who replied to her initial post. "I picked people at random," she later told *The New York Times*. "My message box was full. I had no time to vet anyone."[1]

Neither Shook nor others who created similar Facebook pages to meet the cascading demand could foresee that hundreds of thousands of women would flock to the National Mall in Washington, D.C., on January 21, 2017, the day after the president's inauguration. The Women's March was likely the largest single-day demonstration in recorded US history, according to estimates by political scientists Erica Chenoweth and Jeremy Pressman. There were 653 reported marches across the country, involving between 3,267,134 and 5,246,670 people (their best guess was 4,157,894). That corresponded to 1–1.6 percent of the US population, they wrote, noting that the combined armed forces of the US military comprised just over 2 million people.[2] This was an impressive show of unity in the face of arguably one of the most serious threats to liberal democracy in recent years, as Trump's later performance would go on to prove. Women had shown the world that it was possible to rally behind progressive causes, and had sown the seeds of a transnational movement of solidarity with sister marches taking place in at least 261 locales outside the US, from Antarctica to Zimbabwe.

But, like other American dreams, this one was destined for a rude awakening. And it was not the Right which was going to lead to its undoing. From the beginning, the Women's March was riddled with controversies, and endless bickering over issues of inclusion and exclusion which pitted various feminist groups against each other. The organizers had attracted criticism already in November, when they tried to name the event after The Million Woman March, a 1997 protest organized by African American women in Benjamin Franklin Parkway, Philadelphia. "I thought it was important that people acknowledge that there had been a Million Woman March in the past," said Nyasha Junior, a writer and religion professor at Temple University, "and acknowledge the work that black women had done."[3] This led Vanessa Wruble, one of the influential members of the original organizing committee, to change the name to the Women's March. "I knew it would be a disaster if it was only white women marching on Washington," Wruble later said. "We had to correct wrongs in the past and ensure that there was leadership of color."[4]

And this is precisely what she set out to do, contacting Carmen Perez and Tamika Mallory. Perez was a Chicana activist working on issues of civil rights, and the President and CEO of The Gathering for Justice, a nonprofit founded by Harry Belafonte; Tamika Mallory was a Black activist and a longtime advocate against gun violence and police brutality. They were later joined by Linda Sarsour, a Muslim of Palestinian descent and the former executive director of the Arab American Association in New York. Together with the American fashion designer Bob Bland, Perez, Mallory and Sarsour became the face of the Women's March and profiled in *Time* magazine's "100 Most Influential People" list in 2017.

But this meticulously "diversified" organizing committee and the Unity Principles that were released on January 12 were not enough to forestall the criticisms. One particularly thorny issue was the knitted pink pussy hats worn by most participants during the Women's March on Washington. The pussy hat was created by Krista Suh and Jayna Zweiman in reaction to Donald Trump's "locker room talk" in the leaked *Access Hollywood* tape. "You know I'm automatically attracted to beautiful – I just start kissing them," the former president infamously said. "It's like a magnet. Just kiss. I don't even wait. And when you're a star, they let you do it. You can do anything. Grab 'em by the pussy. You can do anything."[5] The creators of the hat wanted to reclaim the word and turn it into an empowering symbol for the protestors. Yet the choice was spurned by LGBTQ+ activists for excluding and offending transgender women and gender non-conforming people, and women of color who might not possess pink genitalia. The color pink was chosen as it is the most "associated with femininity," Suh and Zweiman explained; "It does not matter if you have a vulva or what color your vulva may be. If a participant wants to create a Pussyhat™ that reflects the color of her vulva, we support her choice."[6]

Not everybody was convinced. In the days leading up to the 2018 Women's March, the organizers of the Pensacola, Florida protests posted a powerful rebuke on the group's Facebook page, asking the participants not to wear the hats in respect of marginalized groups: "The Pink P*ssy Hat reinforces the notion that woman = vagina and vagina = woman, and both of these are incorrect," they claimed. "Additionally, the Pink P*ssy Hat is white-focused and Eurocentric in that it assumed that all vaginas are pink; this is also an incorrect assertion." So the charge was double-barreled; the pink pussy hats were not only transphobic but also racist.[7] "Your genitals do not define your gender and it's time that we scrap the all-too-TERFy (Trans Exclusionary Radical Feminist) pussy hat to make room for our trans siblings in our fights for equality and justice," a non-binary activist wrote in 2019.[8] For others, the hat was the symbol of a selfish feminism, "the type of upper-middle-class white privileged feminism where women show up to the march as a big exciting event and then don't return home to their local Black Lives Matter demonstrations."[9] Even knitting was a serious source of contention. Some saw the act of knitting the hats, to be given out free, as a cathartic and spiritually unifying experience. Others, like anthropologist Jamie E. Shenton, pointed to the contested history of knitting which was used to advance political causes or simply for fun by upper-class White women in the nineteenth century, while it remained as a means of livelihood by women belonging to marginalized groups.[10]

Perhaps somewhat ironically, White women didn't feel welcome either. This was what led a 50-year-old wedding minister from South Carolina to cancel her trip to Washington, reported Farah Stockman of *The New York Times*. "This is a women's march," she said. "We're supposed to be allies in equal pay, marriage, adoption. Why is it now about, 'White women don't understand black women'?" The same sense of bitterness characterized some of the responses to the posts on the march's Facebook page. White women who might have been victims of rape and abuse were now being "asked to check their privilege," a young White woman from Baltimore wrote, in one of the examples quoted in *The New York Times* story.[11]

Racial and ideological divides were more visible on issues related to reproductive rights and abortion, the perennial thorn in the side of US politics. The co-organizers included the right to access abortion and birth control in their Unity Principles, and had Planned Parenthood, one of the largest nonprofit organizations dedicated to the provision of reproductive healthcare in the US, as one of the sponsors of the Women's March. Some members of pro-life organizations were uneasy about these choices, despite considering themselves as "feminists first and foremost." Their concern was not completely unfounded; when word got out that official partnership status was granted to two anti-choice organizations, the reaction of the pro-choice camp was swift and uncompromising. Women's March organizers immediately released a statement, reaffirming that the march had always been pro-choice. Still, this did not deter some anti-choice groups from attending the march, with banners like "Abortion Betrays Women." "It was brutal," said Kristina Hernandez, Director of Communications for the pro-life Students for Life of America, when she described their experience to *Vox*. "We had marchers screaming at us, ripping up our signs, one spit on us." Not everybody was hostile, though, Hernandez added. One group with pro-choice signs "shouted at us, 'We still love you!' I almost ran over and hugged them."[12]

But the coup de grâce for Women's March and its co-organizers came on December 11, 2018, when *Tablet*, a daily online magazine of "Jewish news, ideas, and culture," published an explosive article accusing Tamika Mallory and Carmen Perez of anti-Semitism. Mallory had already come under criticism for attending an event which featured Nation of Islam leader Louis Farrakhan, where he reportedly said "powerful Jews are my enemy."[13] Refusing to publicly disavow Farrakhan, she responded to the criticisms in an article she wrote for *NewsOne*, explaining that her activism required her to "go into difficult spaces" and that, "It is impossible for me to agree with every statement or share every viewpoint of the many people who I have worked with or will work with in the future."[14] Yet the *Tablet* story went further. It presented evidence which showed that Nation of Islam members acted as security guards and drivers for the co-organizers of the march; it raised question marks over the group's finances, in particular about whether donations were handled properly. Worse still, it alleged that the co-organizers themselves made anti-Semitic remarks. According to Leah McSweeney and Jacob Siegel writing in the *Tablet*, it was in the first meeting, less than a week after the idea for a march was aired, that Tamika Mallory and Carmen Perez "allegedly first asserted that Jewish people bore a special collective responsibility as exploiters of black and brown people."[15] Anti-Jewish remarks were also allegedly made at a January meeting which took place after the march. In their turn, Tamika Mallory, Bob Bland, and Cassady Fendlay (the Women's March communications director) denied that such remarks were ever made, either in the first meeting or later in Mallory's apartment: "there was no particular conversation about Jewish women, or any particular group of people," Mallory told the *Tablet*.[16]

The effects of the article were devastating. The Women's March co-organizers had already been called on to step down by Teresa Shook, whose Facebook post sparked the march, a month before the article was published. "Bob Bland, Tamika Mallory, Linda Sarsour and Carmen Perez of Women's March, Inc. have steered the Movement away from its true course," she wrote. "In opposition to our Unity Principles, they have allowed anti-Semitism, anti-LBGTQIA sentiment and hateful, racist rhetoric to become a part of the platform by their refusal to separate themselves from groups that espouse these racist, hateful beliefs."[17] After the *Tablet* article, critical media coverage increased, on both the Right and the Left. Despite these misgivings, the Women's March 2018 went ahead on January 20, with 1.8–2.6 million protestors.[18] The numbers dropped significantly on the second anniversary of the original march. The Women's March 2019, which took place on January 19, managed to attract between 665,324 and 735,978 people to various US locations.[19]

Many on the Left chose to focus on the achievements of the marches, turning a blind eye to the various controversies that had plagued the movement since day one, or explaining them away as leadership infighting. The impact of the first Women's March on Washington was indeed monumental, and unprecedented. Leaving aside the sheer size of the protests, the march introduced the concept of "intersectionality" – coined by law professor Kimberlé W. Crenshaw to denote the manifold ways in which race and gender interact to shape Black women's experiences – into the mainstream with its Unity Principles which proclaimed that "We must create a society in which women – in particular Black women, Native women, poor women, immigrant women, Muslim women, and queer and trans women – are free and able to care for and nurture their families, however they are formed, in safe and healthy environments free from structural impediments."[20] It also encouraged more women to run for office, and get elected. A record number of women obtained seats in the Virginia House of Delegates in November 2017, for example, including the state's first Latina, transgender, and Asian-American female delegates.[21]

These achievements – and the subsequent disintegration of the movement – are precisely why we need to stand firm against the excesses of radical identity politics, and renounce partisan whitewashing or fence-sitting. Obsessively preoccupied with right-wing propaganda about high profile cases of campus activism, many on the Left sleepwalk into the booby trap set by their adversaries, directly contributing to the "culture wars" whose very existence they take pains to deny. Yet university campuses or social media are neither the only, nor the most important, battlegrounds in the fight for justice. The streets, by contrast, are; elections are. And that's where the Left is losing the battle.

Nothing is more emblematic of the woke Left's narcissism than the Women's March's two-year-long predicament. How could an organizing committee which included Black, Latina, Muslim-American and, yes, White women – in addition to 200 women who worked as conveners, 500 partners, 24 women involved in drafting the Unity Principles – be more inclusive? Is it possible to come up with a single symbol that unites all women, or any other diverse grouping for that matter? What's wrong with the pink pussy hat so long as it's not imperative to wear it and those who dislike its message and stick to a different symbol are welcome? What are we to make of trans women of color who didn't mind wearing the pussy hat, saying "they never once felt excluded for [their] trans-ness or [their] woman of color-ness" at the March on Washington?[22] Do intentions always matter over impact? And who are we to police intentions? By which authority? What chance does a Left so fixated on the inclusiveness of one single symbol stand against a Right which has a plethora of symbols to rally around, from national flags and religious traditions to invented histories, and real or imagined homelands? Do all potential protestors need to provide an inventory of their privileges in order to join the fight for justice? Isn't there room for making mistakes? Could we disagree with the march co-organizer Bob Bland who once said, in response to various criticisms, that the Women's March "was just the beginning of a learning process we all had to go through. Women are not a monolith and a lot of the issues we're dealing with are longstanding issues between communities that will not get solved today or tomorrow." Are we supposed to rank oppressions, and make a bigot out of every dissenter? Notwithstanding the merits of the allegations against her, was Tamika Mallory wrong when she wrote, "Where my people are is where I must also be. Coalition work is not easy . . . My work requires an operational unity that is sometimes extremely painful and uncomfortable, even for me. But I push forward even when I am personally conflicted because our people are more important"?[23] And isn't this true of other individuals and groups whom we consider as "enemies"? Shouldn't we talk to White male working-class voters of Trump, pro-life women or gender-critical feminists, and try to understand them? Don't they also fall under the remit of intersectionality even if we believe they might not be as marginalized as, say, a trans woman of color who has no option but to work as a sex worker?

On the surface, these are all rhetorical questions. We all know that both the Right and dominant sections of the Left have tailormade answers to each one of them. And contrary to what both sides believe, the answers are very similar. But at a deeper level, these are complicated questions which require well-thought-out and nuanced answers. Real inclusiveness requires *dialogue, solidarity,* and *coalition-building,* not calling out, cancelling, and squabbling over the right pronouns or minor verbal offenses transmogrified into existential threats – tactics perfected and effectively deployed by the Right. The Left deserves more than being a copycat. It needs a unifying vision, and its own response to the much-talked-about crisis of liberal democracy to which it wittingly or unwittingly contributes. That vision needs to start with and build on our shared predicament as fellow human beings. As Loretta J. Ross reminds us – echoing one of the slogans of the 2017 Women's March on Washington, "Women's Rights are Human Rights and Human Rights are Women's Rights" – "Intersectionality is our process; human rights are our goal. We must allow everyone to have the space for their own unique journeys of self-discovery through understanding intersectionality, but we won't stop the Freedom Train while you debate the price of the ticket."[24]

The Retreat from Liberalism

Few would disagree today that liberal democracy is in crisis. And this is not simply a catchphrase, or the latest academic fad propped up by media hype, but a well-documented long-term trend. "The long democratic recession is deepening," Sarah Repucci and Amy Slipowitz wrote in their overview of the Freedom House's latest annual report *Freedom in the World 2021: Democracy under Siege.* Evaluating the state of freedom in 195 countries and 15 territories through a series of 25 indicators, 2021 marked the 15th consecutive year of decline in global freedom, the report noted. This affected the world's most populous democracy, India, which dropped from the "Free" to "Partly Free" category in 2021 and, perhaps not so surprisingly, the US, which narrowly survived the most egregious attack on its democracy, the Capitol Hill riot on January 6, 2021. Overall, "less than 20 percent of the world's population lives in a Free country," the report concludes, "the smallest proportion since 1995."[25]

The Economist Intelligence Unit and Varieties of Democracy project (V-Dem), two other widely used democracy indexes, confirm these findings. *The Democracy Index* of the former, which rates the state of democracy across 167 countries on the basis of five measures – electoral process and pluralism, the functioning of government, political participation, democratic political culture, and civil liberties – finds that only 8.4 percent of the world's population lives in a "full democracy," whereas more than a third live under authoritarian rule.[26] V-Dem on its part asserts that "the level of democracy enjoyed by the average global citizen in 2020 is down to levels last found around 1990." This corresponds to 87 states out of 202, which in turn means that approximately 68 percent of the world's population lives under some form of autocracy.[27]

Yet the consensus on the crisis of liberal democracy crumbles once we move past this scientifically backed observation and start discussing the nature of the crisis. For some, this is a crisis of liberalism marked by the rise of populism or radical identity politics which cuts across the Left–Right spectrum. For others, it is a crisis of democracy characterized by declining levels of trust in the political system, either caused or precipitated by neoliberal globalism and the concomitant erosion of national sovereignty. Still others talk about a dual crisis, the parallel development of illiberal and undemocratic tendencies, which pits the two pillars of the current political order against each other. As in all periods of crises, when "the old is dying and the new cannot be born," to use Gramsci's memorable adage, there is a rush to come up with neologisms that would best describe the times we live in, most of them preceded by the prefix "post" to suggest that we have already left something behind, whether it be "post-liberalism" or "post-democracy." Irrespective of one's choice of terms and ideological affinities, the list of symptoms linked to our political malady are more or less the same: apathy, atomization, polarization, resentment, and, above all, anger, which all too often manifests itself in outbreaks of outrage, either online or in the streets.

Although I also take the crisis of liberal democracy as my point of departure, I do not intend to contribute to an already overcrowded market of eschatological neologisms or the-day-after scenarios, for I do not believe that we have left either liberalism or democracy behind. Crises do not always lead to tragic endings; they also provide opportunities for change and betterment. I will therefore refrain from overdramatizing our problems and try to put things into perspective, arguing that the present crisis was a long time in the making, and that we are not the first generation of scholars or pundits looking for solutions to circumvent it.

I argue, then, that what we are witnessing today is more a question of *a retreat from liberalism* than anything else, for procedural democracy and elections are still the only game in town, however contested and imperfect they may be. This is what prompted the various democracy indexes mentioned above to diversify their categories, and use terms like "electoral autocracy," to better capture the nuances of hybrid regimes which still hold regular and relatively competitive elections. In fact, as the vast literature on democracy and democratization shows, most problems associated with what political scientists call "democratic backsliding" (electoral manipulation, institutional tinkering, restrictions on basic rights and freedoms, the dismantling of checks and balances, and judicial scrutiny) are intrinsically related to the retreat from liberalism. Populist, authoritarian leaders still enjoy the support of large chunks of their populations and, even though that may well be the result of tampering with electoral processes as is obviously the case in Putin's Russia, Erdoğan's Turkey or Orbán's Hungary, it certainly is not the reason why well over 74 million people voted for Trump for a second time in the 2020 US elections. The main reason, I contend, is a deliberate retreat from liberalism.

My starting premise is simple, if somewhat controversial, at least at first glance. The retreat from liberalism affects both the Right and the Left. Put differently, the Right and the Left have much more in common than both sides would like to admit. Populism is one form of identity politics, and radical identity politics is the mirror image of populism. The idea of the post-liberal consensus some commentators talk about, such as the "left on the economy and right on the culture" vision of the UK's Blue Labour movement, is nothing but a slightly toned-down version of the hegemonic neoliberal project, in particular when it comes to issues of culture, immigration, and security. This is due partly to the mainstreaming of far right discourses by center-right and center-left parties to improve their electoral fortunes, but also to the readiness of the woke Left to adopt the illiberal tactics and strategies of their opponents, often to suppress internal dissent. As a result of this tectonic shift to the Right, the center is vacated, and politics is reduced to a zero-sum game with two increasingly similar players – a sibling rivalry between the modern-day Romulus and Remus.

Drawing attention to the growing convergence between populism and radical identity politics does not mean that the Left is on a par with the Right, or that woke dogmatism poses a greater threat to liberal democracy than reactionary conservatism. Far from it. The Right clearly dominates the political (not only by winning elections or becoming part of ruling coalitions but, more importantly, by framing the agenda) and the economic (the global financial system and much of the wealth it produces), whereas the Left claims the cultural (and even there, its reign is rapidly waning). Largely ousted from the realms of political and economic power, the Left is pretty much confined to a war of trenches in the cultural sphere, notably in university campuses and media, taking politics to cyberspace and, less successfully as we've seen earlier, the streets, aping the "Us" versus "Them" mentality of the Right, and countering state-sponsored violence and structural inequalities with ad hoc protest movements, keyboard activism, and language policing.

It is striking in this context that, despite a lively academic and political debate on right-wing populism and other forms of White identity politics, there are very few critiques of radical identity politics *from within the Left* today, compared to the 1990s when there was a rigorous, yet empathetic debate between defenders of race- or gender-oriented identity politics and the Marxist Left. As we'll see in more detail later, veteran critics of what was then called "left identitarianism," such as Todd Gitlin, Adolph Reed, Jr., William Julius Wilson, and Walter Benn Michaels, continued to swim against the current well into the twenty-first century, defending class-based universalism on the pages of a handful of socialist or progressive journals, including *Jacobin, Endnotes, Counterpunch, Common Dreams, Monthly Review*, to name a few. But the tide of woke activism got stronger, and swept away those who disputed established dogmas on race, gender, and sexuality. Nothing is more emblematic of the ascendancy of woke sensibilities than the outrage caused by the invitation extended to Adolph Reed, Jr., to address the Democratic Socialists of America's (DSA) New York City and Philadelphia chapters in May 2020. On the morning of the talk, the organization's Afrosocialists and Socialists of Color Caucus formally asked the New York City chapter to "unendorse" the event, stating that the idea of inviting Reed was "reactionary, class reductionist and at best, tone deaf."[28] Amidst rumors that protestors might crash the Zoom talk, Reed and DSA leaders cancelled the talk – "a striking moment as perhaps the nation's most powerful Socialist organization rejected a Black Marxist professor's talk because of his views on race," in the words of Michael Powell writing in *The New York Times*.[29]

The silencing of critical voices and the general atmosphere of fear this created in progressive circles have led to an intellectual vacuum that was rapidly filled with a flurry of right-wing accounts, some polemical and overtly partisan, others trying to project an aura of objectivity with the alleged aim of protecting "viewpoint diversity" in the "marketplace of ideas," an analogy first used by Justice Oliver Wendell Holmes Jr. in his dissenting opinion in the *Abrams v United States* case (1919). As I argue in the next chapter, these accounts broadly reiterate populist talking points, emphasizing the purportedly growing gap between ordinary "people" and distant "elites" or, as catchy metaphors would have it, the "Somewheres" and the "Anywheres," the "back rows" and the "front rows," drawing attention to the "legitimate grievances" of the "left behind" in a world of rapid change, growing diversity, and loss of "cherished" national identities and traditional values. Some add an ethnic dimension to the story and underline the need to talk about Whiteness, calling for a new politics that would restore White majorities' hopes in the future. The common denominator of these accounts is a livid contempt for the Left which they hold responsible for the retreat from liberalism and the growing polarization that cripple democracies. Their response is some version of the "faith, family, flag" catechism which invariably reflects conservative White majority values. Women often figure as supporting actresses in these scenarios, invoked mainly against foreign "Others" (e.g., Muslim immigrants) or so-called social justice warriors (as the recent surge of right-wing interest in gender-critical feminism shows). More often than not, they end up whitewashing or amplifying the message of right-wing populists and far right movements.

These accounts are fiercely, and rightly, criticized by liberals and the Left for lacking academic rigor and promoting a reactionary agenda. Oddly, this is also where most of them stop.

To Boldly Go Where No Leftist Wants to Go

And herein lies the thorniest challenge facing liberals and the Left. It is inconceivable that so many distinguished minds populating university campuses, corporate boardrooms, or newspaper editorial boards, do not notice the absurdity of balaclava-clad trans rights activists blocking access to the Emmeline Pankhurst statue in Manchester (the founder of the UK Suffragette movement, herself from Manchester),[30] the controversial concept of "cotton ceiling" used to refer to the difficulty some trans women might encounter when seeking relationships or sex with biological women,[31] or the dangers of ignoring, even mocking, credible death threats to prominent writers such as J. K. Rowling – all in the name of progressive activism.[32] The fact that they remain silent, or worse egg on, out of fear of getting "cancelled" themselves shows that there is something rotten in the state of the Left today, a kind of moral cowardice that needs to be tackled head-on.

And this is what this book sets out to do. I am aware that the subtitle I chose for this section is not fully accurate. As alluded to before, there were many Captain Kirks who explored "strange new worlds" and sought out "new civilizations" before I was even born. I know that I am neither the first nor probably the last leftist who dares to go to places that no one has been before, though it would not be inaccurate to say that none of us has reached the "final frontier" yet. On the contrary. We have probably never been further away from it than today – all the more reason to take up the challenge.

I will thus venture into the minefield most liberals and the Left dodge, either by denying it exists or downplaying its importance. My aim is (i) to offer an alternative account of the retreat from liberalism, with a particular focus on radical identity politics and the ways in which it colludes with various forms of right-wing identity politics, from populism and nativism to White nationalism and supremacism, and (ii) to propose a universalist vision of progressive politics, one that is predicated on dialogue, solidarity, and coalition-building within a framework of justice and equality for all. It should be clear by now that I am more concerned with identity politics on the Left than its right-wing counterparts, even though the latter poses a greater threat to liberal democracy as such. And it is precisely for this reason that I believe there is a pressing need to provide a critique of woke identity politics from within the Left, i.e., to end the vicious internecine conflicts that plague social justice activism in order to create a united front against the real foe, the behemoth that is called the Right, and to address more effectively our collective woes, from climate change to soaring inequalities and global poverty, from racism, misogyny, and other forms of identity-based discrimination to the broader war on dignity.

The bone of contention here is not free speech or academic freedom per se, as far right provocateurs and "anti-Left entrepreneurs" claim (though admittedly, this is also part of the problem). In any case, the Right cannot be taken seriously on this given its selective and duplicitous approach to real or perceived breaches of free speech. After all, call-outs and

cancelling do not make it to the headlines of right-wing publications when progressive intellectuals are the victims of, say,
pro-Israeli and ultra-conservative lobbies, or wealthy donors.
This does not change the fact that radical identity politics
today, or what is called the woke Left, is way more intolerant and exclusionary than its predecessors, notably the civil
rights movement of the 1960s or the multiculturalism of the
1990s. I am, of course, fully aware that these observations,
and more generally my incursion into the minefield, following in the footsteps of liberal and progressive trailblazers, will
not be welcome by many on the woke Left which holds firm
to the belief that widely circulated concepts such as "cancel
culture" or "culture wars" are no more than rhetorical tools to
discredit new forms of identity-based activism and, perhaps
more importantly, to divert attention from the real dangers
posed by the reactionary Right. In any case, denialists and
apologists will hasten to add, it is wrong to compare brazen
acts of violence as witnessed in Capitol Hill, Charlottesville,
Christchurch with "relatively harmless" acts of campus censorship or de-platforming.

These two potential objections should not be conflated. So
far as the second objection is concerned, it is worth reiterating
that I do not claim to compare like with like, overlooking the
structural imbalances between the Right, which wields enor-
mous political and economic power, and the Left, which tries
to challenge the conservative hegemony through a cultural
"war of position" in the sense in which Gramsci uses the term,
i.e., a protracted intellectual struggle to transform hegemonic
beliefs and values. I do not believe, however, that existing
power disparities inoculate the Left against criticism. It is possible, in fact quite urgent, to provide a candid account of the
ways in which the Left suffers from the global shift to the Right
and contributes to the retreat from liberalism, and to issue a
warning against the perils of seemingly innocuous adulations
of violence ("Punch a Nazi"),[33] misogyny ("I punch TERFS";

"Stab your local TERF"),[34] or acts of vandalism and physical violence (book burning, physical harassment of "unwanted" speakers or protestors) without feeding into the idea of a false equivalence.

On the other hand, as might be evident from what I've written so far, I am firmly against cancel culture denialism or apologism. "Cancel culture" may have been an example of a "moral panic" instigated by the Right in the sense in which sociologist Stanley Cohen defined the term, a condition or episode that is perceived as a threat to societal values and interests. But as Cohen notes, "calling something a 'moral panic' does not imply that this something does not exist or happened at all and that reaction is based on fantasy, hysteria, delusion and illusion or being duped by the powerful."[35] And while it is true that the Right exaggerates the seriousness and extent of the "harm" caused by cancel campaigns, we should not forget that they are wielded by the woke Left as a weapon to impose internal ideological conformity. At a time when conflicts within the Left are frequently more ferocious than the traditional tug-of-war between the Left and the Right, and fellow progressives are accused of being on "the wrong side of history" or "in league with the far right" simply for questioning woke orthodoxies, denialism can only lead to atrophy.[36] A better action plan, one that Cohen himself advocates, is to encourage or stir up moral panics about other political problems and "expose the strategies of denial deployed to prevent the acknowledgement of these realities."[37] "All of us cultural workers," he writes, are in the business of "constructing social problems, making claims and setting public agendas," thinking that "we are stirring up 'good' moral panics." Perhaps we could purposely recreate the conditions that make a particular moral panic successful and try to overcome "the barriers of denial, passivity and indifference" that blind us to human cruelty and suffering – or to problems, I would argue, that affect each and every one of us as human beings.[38]

The Right, the Left, and the Liberal

So far I've been writing about the Right and the Left as if they were two giant ideological monoliths acting in perfect synchrony, and sucked into a perennial conflict with each other. Needless to say, this is simply a narrative sleight of hand, the deliberate oversimplification of a much more complicated reality, designed to keep the reader engaged in what will be a long and winding ride. Inspired by Ian Haney López, Chief Justice Earl Warren Professor of Public Law at Berkeley, I use the terms "Right" and "Left" to talk about "competing constellations of ideas" about culture and identity, broadly construed, since this book is concerned mainly with different versions of identity politics.[39] These partly dovetail with established definitions of "Right" and "Left" in that the former is more preoccupied with individual rights and liberties, favors a small state, and holds conservative principles, in particular a commitment to the nation, traditional family, and religious values, whereas the latter focuses on collective good, social justice, and equality, envisaging a greater role for the state to achieve these. I say "partly" because both political labels involve a great deal of policy choices, different priorities and strategies, and are also constantly shifting. Like López, I will also use the terms "conservative" and "reactionary" as a loose synonym for the Right, and "progressive" for the Left.

These preliminary observations need to be qualified in four ways. First, when necessary, I distinguish between the moderate and extremist versions of the Right, and refer to the latter as "far right," sticking to the simple dictionary definition of the term, i.e., designating a dogmatic or hardline faction within a movement or political spectrum – though, admittedly, the lines separating the two are increasingly blurred in the current political landscape. I do not use the term "far left," not because it doesn't exist, but because in ordinary parlance, this often corresponds to what I call radical identity politics or the woke Left.

Second, the way I define them, the terms "Right" and "Left" do not neatly overlap with existing political parties across the world which continue, or aspire, to be broad churches bringing together a wide range of ideas and policy choices in order to succeed at the ballot box. To take a few well-known examples, the Republican and Democratic parties in the US consist of at least two factions, a centrist and more mainstream faction vying for power with more extremist elements. The Republican Party that Donald Trump and the likes of Florida governor Ron DeSantis or Texas senator Ted Cruz have in mind is openly far right the way I define it, and probably not something others, say, representative Liz Cheney or the former presidential nominee John McCain are comfortable with. Likewise, the Democratic Party is not defined by the more radical ideas of "The Squad," led by representative Alexandria Ocasio-Cortez, though their policy proposals sometimes make it to the mainstream. The Labour Party of the UK was much more left-leaning under Jeremy Corbyn than under Tony Blair or Keir Starmer. The political movements led by authoritarian populist leaders such as Putin, Erdoğan, Bolsonaro, and Orbán could be described as far right in view of their aversion to democratic mechanisms and common disdain for ethnic, religious, national minorities, and non-conforming identity groups, in particular LGBTQ+ people. However, the same is true for the People's Republic of China or North Korea, where there are no anti-discrimination protections for LGBTQ+ people, and neither country legally recognizes same-sex marriage, civil unions, or domestic partnerships – not to mention their treatment of ethnic and national minorities. In short, any attempt at labeling a movement or a person politically is bound to be subjective and arbitrary, but heuristically speaking, it is also indispensable.

This brings me to the third problem. It is almost certain that the various academics, pundits, or activists I mention in the following chapters as representatives of particular political

movements and strands of thought will object to their clas-
sification as "Right" or "Left" (and all that comes with it). It is
equally certain that some – though hopefully not most! – readers will agree with them, objecting to my account, or arguing
that these depictions are too broad and abstract to provide an
accurate representation of the realities on the ground. There
is more than a grain of truth in this last point. Many people,
and I am no exception, are only imperfectly committed to the
ideals associated with conventional understandings of "Right"
and "Left," economically, politically, or, indeed, culturally.
What's more, our ideals and priorities are not cast in stone,
and evolve in response to changing circumstances. We may
get more or less radical over time, as our threat perceptions
and our "Others" shift. Given this apparent lack of a perfect
solution, I simply stick to López's apt metaphor and treat
the contest between the Right and the Left as "more akin to
clashing weather fronts that pack tremendous power yet are
composed of millions of air particles and rain drops swirling in
cross-cutting currents."[40]

The final qualification, or better, clarification concerns the
huge elephant in the room: how does liberalism fit into this
picture? And what do I mean when I talk about the "retreat
from liberalism"? It needs to be stated up front that a full
account of the relationship between liberalism and various
strands of the Right and the Left is well beyond the confines of
this book. Suffice to say that as a political doctrine and a moral
philosophy, liberalism entails support for (i) individual rights
and liberties, (ii) freedom from bias, prejudice, or bigotry, and
(iii) a limited government, i.e., necessary only to protect individual freedoms. Beyond this bare minimum, trying to define
liberalism is very much like building castles in the air, as it
straddles the division between the Right and the Left, taking
its color from the political and historical context in which it
develops. The retreat from liberalism refers to the first and
second aspects of this core definition, a shying away from or

a willful abandonment of fundamental rights and freedoms, including freedom of speech, freedom of belief, freedom from fear, and freedom from want – Franklin D. Roosevelt's famous "four freedoms" which are also enshrined in the Universal Declaration of Human Rights and the subsequent covenants on civil, political, economic, and social rights.[41]

The starting premise of this book is a belief that contemporary forms of identity politics constitute a deviation from basic liberal norms, in the sense in which the nineteenth-century English philosopher John Stuart Mill defined them in his classic *On Liberty*: "If all mankind minus one were of one opinion, mankind would be no more justified in silencing that one person than he, if he had the power, would be justified in silencing mankind."[42] On the other hand, the kind of progressive vision I identify myself most with is better described as "democratic socialism," for it is resolutely anti-neoliberal, and roots for a politics of redistribution and an interventionist, welfare state that I suspect few on the Right would be thrilled about. But that's a topic for later.

2

Identity Politics on the Right

The Capitol Hill Riot

On January 6, 2021, just a few weeks before the fourth anniversary of the Women's March, Washington, D.C. was once again the epicenter of protests. The crowd was much smaller than four years ago, around 2,000 people according to the estimates by the FBI, and certainly more united in its goals. Nobody was wearing pink pussy hats, though there were many who donned red MAGA caps, and a handful going for a more "exotic" fashion style that included animal pelts, fox-hide hoods, and fur hats with horns. Despite its modest size and glaring absurdities, the Capitol Hill riot was no less consequential than the anti-Trump protests of January 2017, and it probably posed the most serious threat to the constitutional order in the US since the Civil War – this in a country which presents itself as the beacon of liberal democracy.

Not that it was unexpected. *The New York Times* reported that, according to media insights company Zignal Labs, the term "Storm the Capitol" was mentioned 100,000 times on various social media platforms in the month leading up to the riot.[1] The FBI did its job too and released an internal situation report the day before the attack, warning the US Capitol Police that armed extremists were planning to travel to Washington to wreak violence. "An online thread discussed specific calls for violence," the report said, including "Be ready to fight. Congress needs to hear glass breaking, doors being kicked in, and blood from their BLM and Pantifa slave soldiers being spilled. Get violent. Stop calling this a march, or rally, or a protest. Go there ready for war. We get our President or we die. NOTHING else will achieve this goal" (BLM was a reference to Black Lives Matter and Pantifa was a derogatory term used for the anti-fascist movement Antifa).[2] Despite these early signs and numerous warnings, the security forces were caught off guard, leading even President-elect Joe Biden to confess to the double standards used by law enforcement in its treatment of White and Black protestors.

The chain of events that set off the attack began the night before, at the "Rally to Save America" called by Donald Trump, who refused to concede the results of the 2020 presidential elections. "We will never give up. We will never concede. It doesn't happen," the outgoing president said in his usual inflammatory style. "You don't concede when there's theft involved. Our country has had enough. We will not take it anymore, and that is what this is all about." The speech, delivered to a jittery mob of supporters, ended with what was interpreted by many as a clear incitement to violence. "You will have an illegitimate president. That is what you will have, and we can't let that happen. These are the facts that you won't hear from the fake news media. It's all part of the suppression effort . . . We fight like hell, and if you don't fight like hell, you're not going to have a country anymore."[3]

Later, when the investigation into the events progressed, it turned out that Trump actually had a plan. Devised by John Eastman, a conservative lawyer who was working as part of the then-President's legal team, the six-point plan provided a roadmap for the former Vice President Mike Pence to overturn the election results. According to the plan published in the recent book *Peril* by journalists Bob Woodward and Robert Costa, Pence, who would preside over the joint session of Congress to count electoral votes that would formalize Biden's victory, was supposed to open the ballots by going through the states in alphabetical order, and announce when he reached Arizona that they had "multiple slate of electors," and thus the decision on those would be deferred until he finished counting the other states. Repeating the same procedure for six other swing states and using the 12th Amendment as a legal sleight-of-hand, Pence would then overturn the election results and declare Trump as re-elected.[4] "We know there was fraud," Eastman said in his address to the crowd at Trump's rally. "All we are demanding of Vice President Pence is this afternoon at 1 o'clock, he let the legislatures of the state look into this so we get to the bottom of it and the American people know whether we have a control of the direction of our government or not."[5]

But the Vice President did not cave in. Once this news was leaked, a sizeable group of protestors broke away from the crowd, and began marching on Capitol Hill where the electoral vote count was happening. The rest was pandemonium. Hundreds of people breached the security perimeter and entered the buildings in the Capitol Complex, assaulted police officers and reporters, vandalized and looted the offices of House Speaker Nancy Pelosi and other members of Congress who had by then been evacuated by the security. Outside, the rioters built gallows, chanting "Hang Mike Pence." Meanwhile, Trump resisted calls to send in the National Guard, and posted a video on Twitter at 16:13 local time, saying "I know your pain, I know you're hurt. We had an election that was stolen from us. But you have to go home now." The Capitol was cleared of rioters; the electoral vote count resumed, and Mike Pence declared Joe Biden and Kamala Harris as victors – the climax to a long and chaotic day which left five people dead, including a police officer and a protestor shot by Capitol police, and many injured.

White Identity Politics on Steroids

For many, the Capitol Hill riot was a White supremacist insurrection. Front pages of major newspapers and online news platforms were filled with soundbites on far right militias and their insignias, who were considered to be the driving force behind the violent attack on American democracy.[6] In a limited sense, this was true. The riot was the culmination of a process that had started roughly in the 1980s, the gradual yet steady general shift to the right which made itself felt first in electoral politics. During this initial phase, which lasted until the 2000s, according to political scientist Cas Mudde, far right parties were confined to the political fringes, as they were generally excluded from ruling coalitions. But the picture started to change in the twenty-first century.[7] Claiming and eventually getting a greater slice of the electoral pie, they became a regular fixture of the political landscape, either directly, as part of governing alliances, or indirectly, through the infiltration of their ideas into the mainstream, in particular on issues related to immigration and security. For the Right, this was an inevitable and welcome development. What was once regarded as marginal was rebranded as "populist" and presented as the voice of the losers of rapid globalization, above all those who felt threatened by the weakening of national sovereignty and increasing levels of immigration. The "people" wanted to be heard, we were told, and we'd better listen, if we were to avert a more lasting damage to liberal democracy.

The problem is, the people had *already* spoken, and elected a right-wing populist who ran on an isolationist platform as president of the US in 2016. During his four-year rule, Trump adopted what he called an "America First" policy, and started building a wall along the border with Mexico allegedly to stop illegal immigration, signed an executive order banning people from six Muslim-majority countries from entering the US, and pulled the US out of a number of key international agreements, including the Paris climate agreement. And yet lasting damage to liberal democracy could not be averted, as January 6 has painfully shown. Apparently, some people wanted to continue to talk, and were ready to overturn the results of a democratic election to make sure their voices were heard.

But who were they? In hindsight, we know that the majority did not have any connections to White supremacist groups, contrary to what liberals and many on the Left initially believed. According to a report by the University of Chicago Project on Security and Threats, 716 individuals have been arrested or charged for storming the Capitol as of January 1, 2022. Of the 215 who have also been charged with acts of actual or threatened violence, only 14 percent were members of far right groups or militias such as the Proud Boys, the Oath Keepers or the Three Percenters; 86 percent had no affiliation. And despite all being pro-Trump activists, most rioters did not match the stereotypes presented in mainstream media. More than half worked as CEOs, shop owners, doctors, lawyers, IT specialists and accountants and, as such, had a lot to lose. Most hailed from counties that Biden won, including large pools from urban parts of "blue" states such as New York and California, and none came from "reddest" states such as North Dakota, South Dakota, Nebraska, and Wyoming. "The insurrectionists closely reflect the US electorate on most socio-economic vari-ables," the report concluded, and "come from the mainstream, not just the fringe of society."[8]

The rioters were not formal supremacists – to the extent that this could be established on the basis of available information – but they were overwhelmingly White (93%) and male (85%). And they shared a common vision. A subsequent report on the political mindset of the rioters found that out of the 398 people who made public statements on their motive for entering the Capitol, 80 percent declared one of five political motives: patriotic duty (41%), anti-government animus (38%), stolen election (36%), loyalty to Trump (23%), and fear of losing rights (12%).[9] The mentality of the January 6 rioters, the report claimed, could be called "Patriotic Counter-Revolutionary," one that asserts that "support for the US Constitution requires anti-government violent action – not for the purpose of destroying democratic institutions, but to preserve them in the face of imminent threat."[10]

I believe this is too gracious a definition, considering the rioters' understanding of patriotism, which included, as the report documents, "community defense, and preservation of the American way of life." The stress on the "American way of life," combined with the detailed profile of selected individual participants, indicates that a better term to describe the political motives of January 6 insurrectionists – and one that corresponds with existing research on the issue – would be "White identity politics." As political scientist Ashley Jardina argues in her compelling analysis of emerging patterns of White identity and collective political behavior, Whiteness is now a salient component of American politics. Whites are motivated not merely by prejudice or racial animus, but by what she calls "in-group favoritism," which is rooted in perceptions about their group's status and its potential loss of power and privileges.[11] Those who have high levels of group consciousness, she writes, are more likely to espouse exclusionary views about what it means to be American; "'True' Americans, in their minds, are not just more likely to feel American, have American citizenship, or respect America's institutions; they are also those that are English-speaking, Christian, and white."[12] This often comes with an incongruous sense of entitlement. On the one hand, they are aware of their privileged position in the racial hierarchy, and scared to lose it; on the other hand, they want to imitate the tools used by other, less privileged, racial and ethnic groups "to demand equality." If Blacks, Latinos, and Asians can organize around race and ethnicity, Whites say, why can't we? And this is precisely where the Right comes in. Their aim is not only to understand the conditions that led to the emergence of this sense of entitlement, but to affirm and legitimize it, downplaying the risks it poses to core values of liberalism. It is no surprise that the early warnings against Trump were readily dismissed by the Right as "polemical speculation rather than careful analysis," or for focusing too much on what could happen rather than what is actually happening.[13] Populism was a revolt of the "left behind," and it had serious long-term potential. It had won over a substantial amount of fairly loyal support, political scientists Roger Eatwell and Matthew Goodwin wrote, "from people who share coherent, deeply felt and in some cases legitimate concerns about how their nations and the West more generally are changing."[14] This could be construed as part of a broader challenge to liberalism but it was, as noted at the beginning of this section, an inevitable and welcome development. And if populists eventually failed at the ballot box, it would be because they have succeeded in general terms, by making the mainstream look and sound like them.[15]

Eatwell and Goodwin were not the only ones expressing their sympathies. "Racial Self-Interest is not Racism," another political scientist Eric Kaufmann wrote, in a report he prepared for the think tank Policy Exchange in March 2017,[16] anticipating the observation Ashley Jardina made in *White Identity Politics.* The overall thrust of the argument is correct. A desire to slow down immigration or to preserve national sovereignty is not in itself racist. But, as Kaufmann himself shows in his report, this desire is often associated with a yearning to maintain the Whites' privileged demographic position.[17] The challenge here, journalist and commentator David Goodhart notes, "is to distinguish between white racism and white identity politics. The latter may be clannish and insular, but it is not the same as irrational hatred, fear or contempt for another group – the normal definition of racism."[18]

I beg to differ. This is not a matter of choosing the right label for those who want to defend their in-group interests; after all, all kinds of groupings – ethnic, national, religious, or gender-based; majority or minority – act in a way that would maximize benefits for their own group. In other words, a certain level of clannishness and insularity is unavoidable. The problem is the tendency to disregard the power inequalities that exist between different groups. The aspiration to retain a group's privileged status is not the same as demanding equality for all. This is a major difference, one that Goodhart acknowledges when he says, "majority rights are uncharted territory for liberal democracies," though he does not elaborate on this, even though the Capitol Hill riot may have already given us an answer.[19] When privileges are (perceived to be) at stake, rejection of the rule of law becomes acceptable, and liberal values can be waived. Violent action, as the Chicago report shows us, ceases to be a threat and turns into a means of safeguarding democratic institutions in the face of perceived imminent threat.

It is interesting that none of the commentators named above has tried to offer an explanation for the Capitol Hill riot, how it fits into their narratives of "legitimate grievances" and the "left behind," or the implications of White identity politics for the future of liberal norms or democratic institutions. Eric Kaufmann and David Goodhart quickly distanced themselves from Trump, simply saying they've never been Trump supporters, while Matthew Goodwin shifted the blame to "loonies," revising his definition of Trump from a "national populist" to someone "closer to illiberal populism."[20] This stood in sharp contrast to what they had written before. Until January 6, 2021, the election of Trump, Brexit, and similar victories in other countries heralded, for them, the dawning of a new era in which "Western liberal hegemony" will fade into insignificance and differences between the populist Right and the mainstream will disappear (we've got to hand it to them that they were right on this second point).[21] The Right was not trying to respond to the crisis of liberal democracy for, as far as they were concerned, there was no crisis to respond to – or if there was one, that would be sorted out by itself, through the invisible hand of populism. Their job was to be interlocutors, to speak *for* the people or, rather, *as* the people. It was not easy to fit scenes of hundreds of rioters swarming the barricades, smashing windows with flag poles and desecrating the offices of democratically elected lawmakers at the Capitol into this idyllic picture, so the Right chose to remain silent, and divert the focus. Yes, there was indeed a threat to liberal democracy; but no, it did not come from White identity politics or its more extreme, supremacist, versions. Rather, it was the specter of American-style "culture wars," the last-ditch attempt by globalist elites to stifle *vox populi* and restore the status quo.

The danger was most acutely felt in post-Brexit Britain. Traditionally, "British didn't do ideology," wrote Matthew Goodwin; they are "hard-wired to feel proud of their institutions and traditions, to instinctively see the best in their country and to be skeptical of radicals whose shrill, dogmatic, messianic and angry politics were seen to threaten this precious inheritance."[22] Alas, things have changed; today's Britain is "a more hospitable place for foreign ideologies" imported from the US. And people are more worried about immigration, multiculturalism, Britishness, Englishness, Islam than their income, Goodwin says. What's more, for the first time in history, "one of Britain's mainstream parties has become a vessel for an ideology which encourages people to, put simply, dislike their own country." Labour has embraced "wokeism," and turned away from culturally conservative voters. The country needs unifying narratives, he concludes, built around the values that define Britishness, above all "tradition, consensus, moderation, tolerance, compromise and pluralism."[23]

But what exactly are these unifying narratives, and how are they supposed to mend fences in societies divided not only along ethnic, racial, and religious lines, but also markedly different value systems, as the Brexit referendum and the Capitol Hill riot have bitterly exposed?

Decent Populism

One particularly well-received answer to this question is "decent populism." The term is coined by journalist David Goodhart. The founder of the British current affairs magazine *Prospect*, Goodhart remained its editor until 2010, when he left this position to join the London-based think tank Demos. He had already become a controversial figure for many on the Left by 2004, after publishing an essay called "Too Diverse?," a critique of multiculturalism which he believed to be the enemy of the mutual obligations that sustain a good society and the welfare state. "It is one thing to welcome smart, aspiring Indians or east Asians," wrote Goodhart, "but it is not clear to many people why it is such a good idea to welcome people from poor parts of the developing world with little experience of urbanisation, secularism or western values."[24] These were hardly the anodyne musings of a concerned liberal. As Trevor Phillips, then Chairman of the Commission for Racial Equality, noted at the time, xenophobes come in different shapes and sizes, and some, like Goodhart, are "liberal Powellites" (referring to the infamous "Rivers of Blood" speech by British Conservative MP and former Minister of Health Enoch Powell). "What really bothers them is race and culture," Phillips said. "If today's immigrants were white people from the old Commonwealth, Goodhart and his friends would say that they pose no threat because they share Anglo-Saxon values. They may not even object to Anglophile Indians – as long as they aren't Muslims."[25]

This is, indeed, the main thrust of Goodhart's *The Road to Somewhere: The Populist Revolt and the Future of Politics*, first published in 2017.[26] The book begins by iterating a common right-wing populist trope, that Britain no longer feels like home. "For several years now," Goodhart says, "more than half of British people have agreed with [the] statement: 'Britain has changed in recent times beyond recognition, it sometimes feels like a foreign country and this makes me feel uncomfortable'." This feeling of alienation is at the heart of the "great value divide" in British society today, not along the Right–Left axis, or class and economic interest, but "between the people who see the world from Anywhere and the people who see it from Somewhere."[27]

Anywheres are driven by an ideology Goodhart calls "progressive individualism." This worldview prioritizes "autonomy, mobility and novelty" over "group identity, tradition and national social contracts (faith, flag and family)." Somewheres, by contrast, are socially conservative and communitarian. They are not "hard authoritarians" or "consistent xenophobes," he hastens to add, but do not feel comfortable about certain aspects of cultural change, "such as mass immigration, an achievement society in which they struggle to achieve, the reduced status of non-graduate employment and more fluid gender roles."

The typical Anywhere is a "liberally-inclined graduate" who embraces egalitarian and meritocratic attitudes toward race, sexuality, and gender. The average Somewhere, on the other hand, is a middle- or low-income small-town/suburbia dweller, often without a university degree. Somewheres represent a larger portion of society than Anywheres. They are nostalgic for a lost Britain; they place a high value on security and strong group attachments. And this is where populism enters the picture. For Goodhart, populism can be seen as a result of the breaking down of the liberal democratic consensus over matters of culture and identity. It is "a normal reaction to Anywhere liberal over-reach, a change of political tone as much as a backlash."

This is in keeping with the view that "at least part of Trump's success came through appealing to a hitherto latent white identity politics." Even though he is not a White supremacist, we are told, he did nod toward "white America's anti-integrationist, anti-black traditions" and, more legitimately, "he did start to address lower income whites as a group with their own interests and concerns overlooked by the country's elites."[28]

Goodhart's proposed solution to the current political impasse is to embrace the Somewhere worldview, or what he calls "decent populism." Decent populists do not fit the old categories, he says. Most British Somewheres who voted for Brexit would support "minority and gay rights while also rejecting European integration and mass immigration." They may have reservations about modern liberalism, but "they are not, in the main, illiberal." "Shorn of the Hard Authoritarians decent populism is a fundamentally mainstream worldview representing a large part of the centre ground of British politics."[29]

A similar answer is provided by Roger Eatwell and Matthew Goodwin in their *National Populism: The Revolt Against Liberal Democracy*, published one year after Goodhart's passionate defense of decent populism. Well-known for his work on fascism and the far right, Roger Eatwell, an emeritus professor of Politics at the University of Bath, was Matthew Goodwin's PhD supervisor at the same university. A professor of Politics at the University of Kent and the director of the UK's leading pro-Brexit think tank Legatum Institute's Centre for UK Prosperity, Goodwin is more of a household name for the British public, thanks to his regular media appearances which include an amusing episode where he ate pages from his own book on live TV after underestimating Jeremy Corbyn's performance in the 2017 general elections.[30]

Eatwell and Goodwin prefer the term "national populism" to describe the challenge to mainstream politics and liberal values in the West. This challenge is not anti-democratic, they claim; on the contrary, most national populists want more democracy and control over the decisions that affect their lives. Just like Goodhart's decent populists, they feel uneasy with the way in which elites (Anywheres) have become more and more detached from the lives of ordinary people (Somewheres). They are particularly concerned with increasing rates of immigration and "hyper ethnic change," and question whether "the state should accord priority in employment and welfare to people who have spent their lives paying into the national pot." They are also wary of religions that do not accept key aspects of Western culture, such as "equality and respect for women and LGBT communities."[31]

National populism reflects four deep-seated societal changes, the authors tell us. The first is "the way in which the elitist nature of liberal democracy has promoted distrust of politicians and institutions." The second is growing anxiety about the future of the national group's identity and historical ways of life due to unparalleled levels of immigration and rapid demographic change. The third is the feeling of relative deprivation triggered by neoliberal globalization. And the fourth is partisan dealignment, or the weakening of the bond between traditional mainstream parties and the people. Eatwell and Goodwin's recipe is not dissimilar to Goodhart's:

> to reassert the primacy of the nation over distant and unaccountable international organizations; to reassert cherished and rooted national identities over rootless and diffuse transnational ones; to reassert the importance of stability and conformity over the never-ending and disruptive instability that flows from globalization and rapid ethnic change; and to reassert the will of the people over those of elitist liberal democrats who appear increasingly detached from the life experiences and outlooks of the average citizen.[32]

Populism lies at the heart of the UK's "post-liberal" Blue Labour movement as well. Launched by Maurice Glasman, a close friend of the former Labour Party leader Ed Miliband, in 2009, Blue Labour was a reaction to Tony Blair's New Labour, in particular its free-market fundamentalism and top-down managerialism. The aim of the movement was to create a small-c conservative critique of neoliberal globalism. "Labour is seen as a transferable commodity that moves around the world seeking higher wages, and no thought is given to the fact that these are human beings with families and relationships," Glasman told *The Guardian* in 2011. "We also haven't given enough thought to the people who live here, whose wages have been forced down. Immigration has been a de facto wages policy for the past 30 years."[33] Perhaps the clearest exposition of Blue Labour populism can be found in Paul Embery's recent manifesto *Despised: Why the Modern Left Loathes the Working Classes*.[34] A former firefighter and pro-Brexit trade union activist, Embery is the quintessential example of a populist interlocutor speaking *for* the people and *as* the people (in this specific case, of the borough of Barking and Dagenham in Essex, part of Greater London, where he grew up).

"Treat people like cattle, and you'll get kicked," Embery tells us in the opening pages of his book. "The people of Barking and Dagenham had been treated like cattle for years. Patronised, neglected, dismissed," and now they are rightly feeling resentful against the educated, professional classes, or those who left them behind. The Brexit referendum was simply an opportunity for them to vent their "festering anger." The seeds of Brexit and the wider polarization of British society were sown back in the 1960s, says Embery. His depiction of the "seismic shift" that shook the nation is worth quoting in full:

> Old-fashioned concepts such as patriotism, self-discipline, conscience, religious belief, marriage and the centrality of family, manners, respect for tradition, personal morality, and a belief in free will – all of which had, over many generations, become so firmly embedded in British society, not least as a conse-

quence of the country's deep roots in Christianity – were being rejected wholesale. And in their place came the beginnings of a new age of free love, drugs, self-gratification, individualism, divorce, contempt for tradition, and disdain for the concept of personal responsibility for one's own actions.[35]

So what do the people want? Embery responds: they want a more egalitarian economy through redistribution of wealth, progressive income tax, a higher minimum wage, and so on. But they do not want only economic security; they also long for more cultural security. They want the politicians to respect their "way of life and sense of place"; they want them "to start speaking the language of home, place, family, relationships, work and nation – concrete things that really matter to them – instead of hammering on about modish concepts such as 'diversity', 'inclusivity' and 'equality'."[36]

As this brief outline shows, Goodhart, Eatwell, Goodwin, Embery, and other like-minded pundits are not telling us anything different from what right-wing populist politicians have been saying for decades: a society divided between "the good people" and "the bad elites," and a pressing need to challenge the establishment and give power back to ordinary people, or submit to the "general will" (a concept developed by eighteenth-century French philosopher Jean-Jacques Rousseau to refer to the collectively held will of the people). But the resemblances do not end there.

First, despite the best efforts of its advocates to sugar the pill, decent populism is distinctly nativist. Somewheres are seldom opposed to immigration, Goodhart writes, but they are definitely "anti-mass-immigration." They are not nativists or nationalists – terms which carry negative connotations – but they subscribe to a more "'fellow citizens first' view of national identity," and lament the erosion of "national citizen favouritism." Eatwell and Goodwin are not shy about using the term native when they emphasize "important debates" about immigration, asking "should such immigrants have immediate access to benefits on the same terms as native people?," but they are quick to invoke the hackneyed distinction between patriotism (love of one's country) and nationalism (which they define as "nativist boundary-setting") to absolve populists of the charge of nativism. "Few are nativist in the sense of the US nineteenth-century Know Nothings who defined the people on a narrow Protestant ethnic basis," they argue. In fact, the people's widespread desire to reduce immigration has nothing to do with any ethnically "totally closed conception of the nation."[37] In the same way, Embery's supposedly "post-liberal" formula takes its cue from the sense of "national dispossession" felt by "the English," and promotes a vision based on "the human instinct for solidarity and belonging."[38]

The picture becomes clearer once we start probing deeper into the type of immigration that causes populist unease. High levels of immigration and ethnic diversity reduce trust, "especially when the people arriving come from places that are culturally distant," says Goodhart; after all, "absorbing 100,000 Australians is very different to 100,000 Afghans." Britain feels like a foreign country when White symbols and priorities no longer "automatically dominate" a neighborhood – "as the pub closes and the Polish shop or Halal butcher opens." "Should what many see as symbols of women's oppression like the niqab be banned in public?," ask Eatwell and Goodwin, and should "Muslim schools be expected to teach Western values openly and fairly?" Perhaps we need a points-based system of immigration, Embery suggests, which ranks applicants not only in terms of skills and qualifications, but also proficiency in English.[39]

And this is not simply a question of culture, as defenders of decent populism would have us believe; rather, this is the language of evolutionary psychology, that of instincts, natural selection, and adaptive mechanisms, and as such, it is bound to exclude. "Group attachments are hard-wired into us," says

Goodhart; "the British are hard-wired to feel proud of their institutions and traditions," writes Goodwin; "we are social and parochial beings with a profound attachment to place and a desire to belong," declares Embery.[40] If such feelings are "hard-wired" into us, how could we expect others, be it immigrants or simply people who do not share the same values, to assimilate or integrate into "our" cultures? Are non-White Somewheres part of the decent populist majority? How are, say, Afro-Caribbean, Bangladeshi or indeed Scottish, Irish, and progressive Somewheres (after all, not all inhabitants of post-industrial, small towns are "small-c conservatives") supposed to identify with the unequivocally White, English, and Christian traditions of majority Somewheres? What makes Australians more prone to "re-hard-wiring" than Afghans? These are all rhetorical questions, of course, and decent populists probably know all the answers. Are they too coy to say it out loud?

There is a second way in which defenders of decent populism feed into the discourses of right-wing populist politicians, and that relates to matters of family and gender, the final tenet of the "faith, flag, family" catechism. Here Goodhart, Eatwell and Goodwin, and Embery move uncomfortably close to far right politicians and demagogues who do not hesitate to deploy women's and LGBTQ+ rights instrumentally, namely to point to the incompatibility of Islam with Western/Christian values. It is in this context that Eatwell and Goodwin refer to the French far right leader Marine Le Pen who, they claim, "anchors her hostility towards Islam and rapidly growing Muslim communities in a defense of women's and LGBT rights," often presenting herself "as a twice-divorced single mother who was successful in her own right as a lawyer"[41] – a very charitable description of a politician who regularly talks about "*ensauvagement*," or descent into savagery, to refer to the alleged links between criminal violence and mass migration in France.[42] Or maybe it is their own dislike of new ways of "doing gender" that lurks beneath the allegedly liberal surface.

"If middle class women are now as financially self-sufficient as men, and many working class women are supported by the state," asks Goodhart, "what is the place for the male provider?" "The traditional notion of making men good citizens through family duties has largely disappeared," he then notes.[43] Embery takes it even further, telling us "there is an overwhelming body of evidence to show that children who are raised with two parents in a stable family unit have better outcomes than those who aren't," he writes, without citing a single source to back up this claim. Still, he continues: "The whole of society pays when families break up."[44]

But how could a vision based on such a narrowly defined set of values unify a society that is already split over every single value in question? The answer lies in numbers. In a way, decent populists attribute mystical powers to majorities, even the narrowest ones. The number 52 is not only numerically bigger than 48, but also morally superior; 52–48 is not simply a percentage, but a political statement, a declaration of the will of the people. And when people speak, we need to listen.

White Nationalism

The second, increasingly more popular, unifying narrative is nothing but a blast from the past: nationalism, and not the civic, liberal type. The kind of nationalism advocated by the proponents of this narrative is ethnic and openly illiberal. It is based on a distinctive model of ethnicity which treats Whites as an endangered species. It seeks to limit the cultural influence of the woke Left in university campuses through direct government intervention. It proposes to protect free speech by clamping down on particular forms of speech. And it does all this by claiming to pursue a purportedly evidence-based, scientifically rigorous policy agenda, while actually pushing for a reactionary, "race-conscious" ideology.

The best-known advocate of the nationalist narrative is Eric Kaufmann, a professor of Politics at Birkbeck University in London, who skyrocketed to fame with his 2018 book *Whiteshift: Populism, Immigration and the Future of White Majorities*. Kaufmann is no stranger to controversy. He was one of the participants in a 2018 debate titled "Is Rising Ethnic Diversity a Threat to the West?," which was renamed following social media backlash and an open letter accusing the organizers and participants of the event of framing immigration and multiculturalism "as a problem to be fixed."[45] His anti-Left activism and regular appearances on right-wing media led several Birkbeck students to start a campaign asking for the university administration to take action, and eventually prompting one member of faculty to resign in protest.[46]

Kaufmann begins his analysis with a simple, if somewhat provocative, statement. "We need to talk about white identity," he says; not as a fabrication to maintain power, but as "an ethnic identity like any other." "The big question of our time is less 'What does it mean to be British' than 'What does it mean to be white British'."[47] And that meaning has been changing due to faster immigration and increasing rates of intermarriage. In two centuries, Kaufmann notes, "few people living in urban areas of the West will have an unmixed racial background" – hence the term "Whiteshift," which refers to this process of ethnic mixing and "the declining white share of the population in Western countries." This shift is undermining the self-confidence of White majorities, and breeds a kind of tribal populism fueled by existential insecurity. Kaufmann opposes this to another form of tribalism, that of the "religious anti-racist left." If these two types of tribalism had equal resources (contrary to conventional wisdom, he thinks that it's the Left that has the institutional upper hand), "white nationalism" would win over the majority because "it resonates slightly better with our instincts."[48]

According to Kaufmann, the main factor that causes the rise of the populist right is White majority concerns over immigration. Demography and culture, not economic interests, are key to understanding the populist moment. "Ethnic change – the size and nature of the immigrant inflow and its capacity to challenge ethnic boundaries – is the story."[49] But the Left, or what he prefers to call "left-modernism," does not get this. Sticking to a theory of White ethno-racial oppression, exponents of left-modernism are seeking "to consecrate the university campus as a sacred space devoted to the mission of replacing 'whiteness' with diversity." The dominant ideology of the Left is "moralistic and imperialistic"; it aims to institutionalize itself in law and policy, and turn liberalism into a worldview which not only tolerates, but mandates, diversity, in particular when it comes to issues of race, gender, and sexuality, the "trinity of sacred values."[50]

This is a battle the Left is bound to lose, because we all are "hard-wired" to be tribal. Right-wing populism, which champions the cultural interests of White majorities, has already subverted "the multicultural consensus which held sway between the 1960s and the 1990s," but this came at the cost of growing polarization between the Right and the Left. What we need now is "a new vision that gives conservative members of white majorities hope for their group's future while permitting cosmopolitans the freedom to celebrate diversity." This new vision is what Kaufmann calls "ethno-traditional nationalism." Civic forms of nationalism based on universal ideals or shared goals are not enough because they cannot provide "deep identity in everyday life." Ethno-traditional nationalism, on the other hand, cherishes the ethnic majority as an important component of the nation alongside other groups. It favors "slower immigration in order to permit enough immigrants to voluntarily assimilate into the ethnic majority, maintaining the white ethnotradition." The goal, Kaufmann concludes, is not to assimilate all diversity but to keep "an enduring white-Christian tradition" alive and kicking.[51]

Another fervent warrior of the nationalist cause is political commentator and author Douglas Murray. An associate editor of the British right-wing magazine *The Spectator*, Murray is widely known for his reactionary views[52] and his proximity to prominent figures of the international far right, best illustrated by a much-talked-about photo with Steve Bannon and the Hungarian Prime Minister Viktor Orbán, whose immigration policies he applauds.[53]

Douglas Murray's *The Strange Death of Europe: Immigration, Identity, Islam* is probably the most mainstream iteration of the French far right conspiracy theorist Renaud Camus's ill-famed "great replacement theory," which promotes the idea of a global conspiracy against the White population of Europe to replace them with non-European peoples.[54] "Europe is committing suicide," writes Murray; "or at least its leaders have decided to commit suicide." As a result of this decision, in a not-so-distant future, "Europe will not be Europe and the peoples of Europe will have lost the only place in the world [they] call home."[55]

There are several reasons for "the present sickness." By far the most important of these is mass immigration, i.e., "the replacement of large parts of the European populations by other people." At this point, Murray gives a nod to the "Rivers of Blood" speech, which he thinks was "filled with prophetic foreboding."[56] People who arrive for the first time in a host country will chip away at the welfare system in the form of housing, schooling, and other benefits without themselves contributing to it, at least for some time. Then there is the cultural decay; "Places dominated by Pakistani immigrants [resemble] Pakistan in everything but their location," he bemoans, "with the recent arrivals and their children eating the food of their place of origin, speaking the language of their place of origin and worshipping the religion of their place of origin. Streets in the cold and rainy northern towns of Europe filled with people dressed for the foothills of Pakistan or the sandstorms of Arabia."[57]

There is only one way to avoid this dystopian scenario, according to Murray. Europe should stop being a place anybody in the world can move to and call home. Europeans are not obliged to take care of everybody fleeing war or looking for better standards of living. Instead, those in power should try to keep these people in the vicinity of the country they are escaping from; this might prevent potential cultural clashes that might occur in more distant territories, and make it easier for them to return home when things go back to normal. This requires, first and foremost, inviting "thoughtful and clearly non-fascist parties" to the national conversation and a search for broader consensus.

The difference between decent populism and White nationalism, the two "unifying narratives" proposed by the Right to counteract the woke Left threat to liberal democracy, is one of degree and, we should perhaps add, level of honesty. Kaufmann, Murray, and other aficionados of White identity politics do not beat about the bush, or try to hide their messages in a haystack of euphemisms to come across as more moderate or tolerant. They are not only nativists, in the sense of favoring the interests of native-born citizens over immigrants; they are also White nationalists in the dictionary sense of the term, i.e., "advocacy of or support for the primacy and dominance of the white population and its perceived culture, identity, etc., within a particular nation."[58] Of course, White nationalism is not the same thing as White supremacism. But some expressions of the latter, we are told, for example the White genocide theory – the idea that low White birth rates, non-White immigration, and race-mixing will lead to the extinction of the White race in the West – are not entirely false. It is important to address these issues because "refusing to discuss the fine points of white genocide theory can only give the impression of a cover-up and provide oxygen to these ideas."[59] It is okay for members of dominant groups to be interested in their cultural traditions and organize around them; and while Whites are not facing imminent extinction, there is some truth in the claim that "liberals intend to transform white societies into non-white ones through immigration and race-mixing."[60] At the end of the day, this is what "Whiteshift" is all about. "Whites are already a minority in most major cities of North America"; "Together with New Zealand, North America is projected to be 'majority minority' by 2050, with Western Europe and Australia following suit later in the century."[61] This view treats Whites as if they are an endangered species, facing the threat of extinction due to the size and nature of the immigrant inflow. They are also becoming less homogeneous through demographic change, in particular dropping fertility rates. "In 1950 there were 3.5 Europeans and North Americans for every African," Kaufmann notes; "the UN's medium projection tells us that by 2050 there will be two Africans for every Westerner, and four Africans per Westerner in 2100."[62] But the process of extinction can be halted, even reversed, through slower immigration, voluntary assimilation, and intermarriage. The key policy challenge here is to enable Whites to see a future for themselves.[63]

What separates this particular vision, or what Kaufmann calls ethno-traditional nationalism, from White nationalism? The answer is easy: nothing. The model is explicitly "White-centric" in that the aim is to maintain an enduring White-Christian tradition. Immigrants are welcome so long as they are willing to assimilate into the dominant culture, which should remain, at least in principle, open. But openness does not necessarily mean inclusiveness. "Only those with some European background can be members, just as only those with some African background can be African American. White archetypes would form part of the symbol system of the new white group, despite its mixed heritage."[64]

Kaufmann's intentions become clearer if we consider his other writings. Take the above-mentioned 2017 report titled "Racial Self-Interest is not Racism." Here, Kaufmann draws a clear line between racism and racial self-interest, which is equated with "ethnic self-interest" – on a par with individual self-interest. The difference between the two lies in motivations. Racists "fear, hate or look down upon those of other ethnic backgrounds"; immigration sceptics, on the other hand, are "majority ethnic partisans," acting out of racial self-interest to maximize the demographic advantage of their group.[65] The problem today, he argues, is the Left's insistence on calling anyone who identifies loosely with her own ethnic group "racist."

And this brings us to another trait shared by decent populists and White nationalists, namely a deep aversion to the Left. Once again, White nationalists are much more forthright than decent populists who target more abstract enemy figures like liberals or globalist elites. Douglas Murray, for instance, takes no prisoners in his *The Madness of Crowds: Gender, Race and Identity*, published two years after his anti-immigration rant. The problems we are experiencing today are not the consequence of a presidential election or a referendum; they are brought about by the collapse of grand narratives that gave meaning to our lives, and the vacuum that this created which was filled by a "new religion" hailing from the "obscurest fringes of the academia." "The interpretation of the world through the lens of 'social justice', 'identity group politics' and 'intersectionalism' is probably the most audacious and comprehensive effort since the end of the Cold War at creating a new ideology," according to Murray. If we do not fight back, we face "not just a future of ever-greater atomization, rage and violence, but a future in which the possibility of a backlash against all rights advances – including the good ones – grows more likely."[66]

It is important to remember here that Murray himself is not hailing from the "obscurest fringes" of the media. He is the associate editor of the oldest right-wing magazine in the UK (*The Spectator*, edited by none other than the former Prime Minister Boris Johnson between 1999 and 2005), a frequent contributor to major newspapers like *The Times*, *The Telegraph*, *The Daily Mail*, and *The Sun*, among others, and a highly sought-after speaker in various platforms. And it is not only Murray. Eric Kaufmann is equally relentless in his attacks on the Left. "Only government can break the spell of woke activists over our universities," he declares in a 2021 article, celebrating the appointment of a free speech director in the Office for Students – an independent public body which reports to Parliament through the Department for Education.[67] The roots of "progressive censorship" can be found in the unconstitutional speech codes developed in American universities nearly 40 years ago which have since found their way to Britain. Administrators are unwilling to defend freedom of speech against these intrusive trends, he argues, for fear of appearing reactionary or insensitive on issues of racism, sexism, and transphobia, which are powerful taboos in modern society. "All of which means that when the woke sorcerers cast their equity and diversity spell, the decent majority are immobilised," concludes Kaufmann. Thanks to the white paper, though, "we can all breathe a little easier."[68]

Alas, this is also where rational analysis and debate end, for how can we argue with someone who speaks about "woke sorcerers" or "woke Taliban"?[69] We cannot know or speculate about whether decent populists and White nationalists are opportunists or true believers; but at any rate, it doesn't matter. We can still deduce from their writings what their operating system is, which is nothing more than an updated version of a much older model – culture wars.

Culture Wars

On the face of it, the Right's claims are not totally unfounded. The populist backlash is as much about culture and identity as economics; states should have control over their borders and the fate of their citizens; and solidarity does require a greater degree of cohesion and sense of collective belonging than an unmitigated universalism could provide, and so on – nothing that a centrist or liberal would not agree to. But that is just part of a bigger story. Whether decent populist or White nationalist, the right-wing accounts I have outlined in this chapter are not only trying to understand the rise of anti-systemic, in most cases illiberal and authoritarian, movements; they also seem to be interested in justifying and amplifying them. They are advancing a perilously nativist, White-majority-oriented agenda, while downplaying the far right threat to liberal democracy. The success of their project depends on the invention of a useful ideological nemesis, and what better candidate for this role than the woke Left, in the absence of more traditional enemies like, say, old-style communists or socialists?

British pundits take great pains to show that neither the woke Left nor their "progressive authoritarianism" is native to the British soil. Hence according to Matthew Goodwin, "Post-Brexit Britain is rapidly following America into the abyss of highly-polarised culture wars over populism and wokeism."[70] Everything changed the day Britain voted for Brexit:

> I was no Brexiteer but, in a world where just one in ten academics backed a Brexit decision that more than half of the country supported, merely accepting the result was more than enough to make me an outcast. For the next four years, I faced a constant wave of criticism that at times bordered on harassment . . . Which is why, over the past year, a group of rebel academics began meeting to share ideas about how to push back against

this illiberalism. I am proud to be a founding member of that secretive group.[71]

This imagery of martyrdom, of joining a secretive resistance movement against wokeism, is a tad rich coming from someone writing in *The Daily Mail* or *The Sunday Times*, two of the highest circulated daily newspapers in the UK, not to mention frequent appearances on the main national and international news channels. But why refer to "culture wars" as a specifically American concept, a foreign virus wreaking havoc on the otherwise healthy British body? Oddly enough, despite its ubiquitous presence, there is, in all the work I've discussed so far, only one passing reference to the concept of culture wars as it is used in the American context, and that particular reference hardly does any justice to the way in which the concept is defined by the US sociologist James Davison Hunter who gave the term its popular currency in his influential 1991 book *Culture Wars: The Struggle to Define America.*[72] For Hunter, the key contention of the culture war thesis is the belief that there had been a realignment in American public culture that had affected all major institutions, from special interest organizations and political parties to competing media outlets and professional associations, "and the elites whose ideals, interests, and actions give all of these organizations direction and leadership."[73] And here the British Right's reluctance to discuss the origins of the concept starts to make sense. Culture war is not the abstract pursuit of detached left-wing intellectuals, confined to the privileged life of university campuses or corporate boardrooms. Rather, it is "a competition to define social reality," a "matter of social morality." Hunter distinguishes between two broad camps in contemporary culture war: the orthodox and the progressive. Orthodoxy requires a commitment to an external, definable, and transcendental authority. For progressives, by contrast, moral authority is defined by the spirit of the modern age, "a spirit of rationalism and subjectivism." Hunter does not attribute a normative value to either orthodoxy or progressivism. These are merely "competing understandings of the good and how the good is grounded and legitimated." Perhaps more importantly, these understandings are not mutually exclusive; "at the heart of the new cultural realignment are the pragmatic alliances" being formed across opposing traditions.[74]

Hunter revisits his culture war thesis in 2006, and stresses once again that this is not simply a matter of "noisy extremists" or activists shouting from their ivory towers. "If the culture war is a myth and the real story is about the consensus that exists in 'the middle'," he asks, "then why is it that the middle cannot put forward, much less elect, a moderate who represents that consensus? If the center is so vital, then why is it that the extremes are overrepresented in the structures of power?" Whatever the merits and limitations of Hunter's overall thesis, his question is spot on. Culture war is indeed real; it is a manifestation of the structural inequalities produced by late-stage capitalism (or neoliberal globalization) and the cultural-political polarization the latter feeds into. And it will remain real for there is a whole industry of experts-cum-entrepreneurs, both on the Right and the Left, which is invested in it. This is what is missing in the Right's response to the crisis of liberal democracy, and its astonishing blame shifting. By singling out the woke Left, the Right tries to conceal its own moralistic agenda, and its commitment to a transcendental authority, that of the flag, the faith, and the family. Defenders of right-wing populism are not the passive victims/observers of a culture war perpetrated by the woke Left. They are active participants in it. In many ways, then, culture war is not only an operating system; it is also a business model.

And a business model that simply does not, or could not, work – a point that James Davison Hunter himself underscored in an interview he gave five months after the Capitol Hill riot. There are two factors that complicate the original culture war thesis, Hunter said. First, the Great Recession of 2008 drove a wedge between the White middle and working classes and the highly trained managers, technocrats, and intellectuals. As a result, class differences were overlaid on cultural differences, turning culture wars into "a kind of class-culture" conflict. And second, "race" replaced abortion as the main critical issue that animates culture wars, as reflected in the ways in which progressives speak about them. These are ominous signs for Hunter:

> I'm beginning to see signs of the justification for violence on both sides. Obviously, on January 6, we not only saw an act of violence – I mean, talk about a transgression – but one that the people who were involved were capable of justifying. That's an extraordinary thing . . . the argument I made [in the book that followed *Culture Wars*] was that culture wars always precede shooting wars. They don't *necessarily* lead to a shooting war, but you never have a shooting war without a culture war prior to it, because culture provides the justifications for violence. And I think that's where we are. The climatological indications are pretty worrisome.[75]

Regrettably, it is not only the Right which is invested in this business model.

3

Identity Politics on the Left

The Combahee River Collective

"I think our goal first of all was to make a political place for people like ourselves," said Boston-based independent scholar and Black feminist activist Barbara Smith in 2017, which marked the 40th anniversary of the seminal Combahee River Collective Statement. "We were marginalized in the Black movement . . . And we were marginalized in the white feminist movement, for different reasons. One of the reasons we were marginalized in the Black movement, besides sexism and misogyny, was also homophobia. A lot of us were indeed lesbians, and we – including myself, at this time I was coming out."[1]

Combahee River Collective (CRC) was a Black feminist lesbian socialist organization active in Boston from 1974 to 1980. The Collective got its name from a military expedition at the Combahee River in South Carolina planned and carried out by the abolitionist Harriet Tubman on June 2, 1863. The raid, which freed 750 slaves at the time, was the first and only military campaign in American history led by a woman. "There were women's groups all over the country named for

Harriet Tubman and Smith wanted to do something different," Demita Frazier, another co-founder of the CRC, later recalled; "[Barbara] liked the idea of naming the group for a collective action, as opposed to one heroic person's feats."[2] In addition to weekly meetings at the Women's Center in Cambridge, Massachusetts, the Collective held a number of retreats between 1977 and 1979. "It was really about – first of all – to get Black feminists together so we could talk about what it was we were trying to do. It was to address the isolation that we faced as Black feminists," Smith said. The first retreat, which had 20 participants including the famed Black feminist poet and activist Audre Lorde, took place on July 8–10, 1977, at a private home in South Hadley, Massachusetts. The participants were asked to bring written material to the retreat, to share with the rest of the group. "We would have a literature table," Smith recalled. "And literature in those days was xeroxes. And even mimeographed. That's what literature was for Black women who were interested in feminism or in politics that included a gender analysis. There were no books."[3] The Collective held seven retreats in total, after the publication of the Combahee River Collective Statement in April 1977.

The statement, penned by Barbara Smith, her sister Beverly Smith, and Demita Frazier, is credited to be the first text where the term "identity politics" is used. "Our politics initially sprang from the shared belief that Black women are inherently valuable," the statement proclaimed:

> This focusing upon our own oppression is embodied in the concept of identity politics. We believe that the most profound and potentially most radical politics come directly out of our own identity, as opposed to working to end somebody else's oppression. In the case of Black women this is a particularly repugnant, dangerous, threatening, and therefore revolutionary concept because it is obvious from looking at all the political movements that have preceded us that anyone is more worthy

of liberation than ourselves. We reject pedestals, queenhood, and walking ten paces behind. To be recognized as human, levelly human, is enough.[4]

According to Keeanga-Yamahtta Taylor, a professor of African-American Studies at Northwestern University, the authors of the Combahee Statement meant two things by identity politics. First, oppression on the basis of identity, whether it is race, gender, class, or sexual orientation, is a source of political mobilization and radicalization. "The most general statement of our politics at the present time would be that we are actively committed to struggling against racial, sexual, heterosexual, and class oppression, and see as our particular task the development of integrated analysis and practice based upon the fact that the major systems of oppression are interlocking."[5] But, and that was the second meaning, "identity politics was not just about who you were; it was also what you could do to confront the oppression you were facing." This required cooperation and coalition-building; "we also drew many women of color who were not Black to us," said Beverly Smith. "We had connections with Latinas. We had connections with Asian women. We did draw women of color, and I'm so glad. And they drew us too. Because it wasn't just like one way ... I just think it's really important to have that piece, because it wasn't just that we were connecting with white women. We were connecting with all kinds of women."[6]

The Combahee women were also the first to refer to "interlocking systems of oppression," long before the term "intersectionality" was coined. "I have to talk to the young woman – Kimberlé Crenshaw ... who says that she coined the term intersectionality," Demita Frazier said in an interview; "I always laugh when I read that because I remember the day we were sitting at the women's center in Cambridge, drafting our probably third or fourth draft of the statement, I said, 'You know, we stand at the intersection where our identities are indivisible.' There is no separation."[7] Barbara Smith confirmed: "we have a right as people who are not just female, who are not solely Black, who are not just lesbians, who are not just working class, or workers – that we are people who embody all of these identities, and we have a right to build and define political theory and practice based upon that reality."[8]

This was indeed a very different understanding of identity politics, conceived at the height of the Civil Rights Movement, one and a half decades after the 1963 March on Washington (where Martin Luther King Jr. delivered his iconic "I Have a Dream" speech) and the signing of the Civil Rights Act by President Lyndon B. Johnson. It advanced a radical progressive agenda focused on the many exclusions of the Civil Rights Movement, Black nationalism and White feminism – not only the racism, sexism, and homophobia inherent in these movements, but also the lack of an internationalist and anti-capitalist perspective. The members of the Collective were actively involved in the antiwar movement, for they considered themselves to be, in the words of Barbara Smith, "third world women." "We saw ourselves in solidarity and in struggle with all third world people around the globe."[9] Growing out of the organized Left, they defined themselves as socialists, and believed, as the CRC statement put it, "that work must be organized for the collective benefit of those who do the work and create the products, and not for the profit of the bosses."

Till Identity Do Us Part

But times have changed, and not for the better. "It is difficult to explain what we were up against in the late 1970s," said Barbara Smith, reflecting on the impact of their statement four decades later, at a time when "gay people can get married, and Beyoncé says she's a feminist." There is evidence that the work we did on violence against women has been maintained, she continued. Still, when asked whether there is a revival of interest in Black feminism, "I don't know. I really don't know," she replied. "I can't tell you much about the state of Black feminism at the present time. And I'm not even clear that there's a Black feminist resurgence."[10]

Demita Frazier was more pessimistic. "So much of what brought us together was the unique combination at that intersection of our lives ... and that made us uninterested in adhering to what people decided was their dogma, their theory, their whatever." Part of what caused the current situation, Frazier believed, is "the commodification of everything," including identity politics which was completely detached from its anti-capitalist origins. This was because of the way it was co-opted by academics, she said; "I wouldn't say co-opted if it weren't for the fact that there's still this big divide between practice and theory, right? I mean, I'm glad that the children and the young'uns are getting educated, but it looks like a factory to me right now."[11]

Barbara Smith expressed similar views, complaining about the ways in which identity politics was reconfigured by the Left. "We didn't mean that if you're not the same as us, you're nothing," she said. "It's a real misapprehension of what we meant by it. And I don't know why people skip it. I mean, to me, all the explanation that's needed is in the Combahee River Collective statement, about what it is we stand for, and who we think we should be working with." Smith also blamed academics who "have a partial understanding of what the depths of [identity politics] would be." "Trigger warnings and safe spaces and microaggressions – those are all real, but the thing is, that's not what we were focused upon." Like other groups of Black women who were organizing around Black feminism, Combahee was "community-activist based. Focusing on looking at real issues affecting all Black women, which includes poor Black women."[12]

This brief excursion into history, and the reflections of the veteran activists of the Combahee River Collective on the legacy of their statement, provide several insights into the problems that plague current understandings of identity politics. Their vision was intersectionalist yet inclusive, open to the idea of working across differences. It drew its strength from the lived experiences and oppression suffered by its members, but it did not preclude solidarity with others suffering from different kinds of oppression. It inspired political work on a variety of issues from lesbian politics to sterilization abuse and abortion rights. Finally, and perhaps most importantly, it was part of a radical political program that was explicitly anti-capitalist. "The reason Combahee's Black feminism is so powerful," Barbara Smith said, "is because it's anticapitalist. One would expect Black feminism to be antiracist and opposed to sexism. Anticapitalism is what gives it the sharpness, the edge, the thoroughness, the revolutionary potential."[13]

A detailed discussion of the causes and dynamics of the transformation of a once radically progressive concept into a faint shadow of its former self in such a short span of time is beyond the scope of this book. Suffice to say that from the 1980s on, there were quite a few visionaries who tried to warn us against the growing tribalization and insulation of the Left, and the implications of this for the future of progressive politics. Predictably, the most consistent critics of identity politics were classical Marxists, many of whom were Black, who believed that the Left was too focused on race and not enough on economic class. The tone was set as early as 1978, when sociologist William Julius Wilson published his *The Declining Significance of Race: Blacks and Changing American Institutions*. The original argument was not that race is no longer significant, Wilson later recalled. "Rather, in comparing the contemporary situation of African Americans to their situation in the past, the diverging experiences of blacks along class lines indicate that race is no longer the primary determinant of life chances for blacks (in the way it had been historically)."[14] Political scientist Adolph L. Reed Jr. picked up where Wilson left off and, in a series of books and articles that span several decades, provided an in-depth analysis of the historical and structural conditions that led to a turning away from class politics and, above all, the failure of pragmatic political activism and changing intellectual sensibilities which created a reaction against "large-scale social theories of any kind and rejection of any form of centralizing power or notion of objective truth."[15]

Yet perhaps the loudest critic of identity politics from a universalist perspective was American sociologist and cultural commentator Todd Gitlin (a former president of the leading New Left national student organization, Students for a Democratic Society). Gitlin was aghast at the constant infighting that pitted various social justice movements against each other. "It is hard to grasp," Gitlin wrote in his 1995 book *The Twilight of Common Dreams: Why America is Wracked by Culture Wars*, "why people who care about justice strike so venomously against those who, whatever their differences, stand closest to them."[16] It was clear to him that the Left had abandoned its commitment to universal values. "What has become of the ideal of a Left," he asked, "that federates people of different races, genders, sexualities, or for that matter, religions and classes"?[17] Such a vision could only be achieved through reaching out to others as allies, if not friends. Instead, the Left was immersed in endless culture wars (Gitlin did in fact use the term "culture wars"), and became "like their counterparts on the Right, more adept at vituperation against their enemies than at reflecting upon, let alone practicing, human arrangements that would make life more supportable and dignified for humanity at large."[18]

Gitlin's own, "class-first," solution to this dilemma may be somewhat outmoded, but his diagnosis of the state of the Left, first adumbrated a quarter of a century ago, was eerily prophetic. Identity politics has always been rooted in the recognition of identity-based discrimination, as Gitlin also noted, but the Combahee River Collective carved out an emancipatory model of politics from collective hurt; whereas in more contemporary versions, this feeling led to "a 'culture' of exultation and victimization (exultation *through* victimization)." "Diversity insists that everyone march in lockstep while proclaiming how different they are," Gitlin wrote. That left us with a rather bleak picture: "While the Right was occupying the heights of the political system, the assemblage of groups identified with the Left were marching on the English department."[19]

But discontent was not limited to the Marxist Left. Writing a year after Gitlin, the American philosopher Martha Nussbaum provided an even more scathing critique of identity politics, with a particular focus on feminist theory and activism. In a polemical article titled "The Professor of Parody," Nussbaum pointed to a new "disquieting trend" in academic feminism in America. "It is not only that feminist theory pays relatively little attention to the struggles of women outside the United States," she wrote. "Something more insidious than provincialism has come to prominence in the American academy. It is the virtually complete turning from the material side of life, toward a type of verbal and symbolic politics that makes only the flimsiest of connections with the real situation of real women." Nussbaum's withering description of this new form of activism is worth quoting in full:

> The way to do feminist politics is to use words in a subversive way, in academic publications of lofty obscurity and disdainful abstractness. These symbolic gestures, it is believed, are themselves a form of political resistance; and so one need not engage with messy things such as legislatures and movements in order to act daringly. All that we can hope to do is to find spaces within the structures of power in which to parody them, to poke fun at them, to transgress them in speech.[20]

In the end, the Marxists and the liberals concurred. "The great tragedy in the new feminist theory in America is the loss of a sense of public commitment," Nussbaum wrote, prefiguring what Reed wrote in 2014: "the terms 'left' and 'progressive' ... now signify a cultural sensibility rather than a reasoned critique of the existing social order. Because only the right proceeds from a clear, practical utopian vision, 'left' has come to mean little more than 'not right'."[21]

Sadly, these warnings were not heeded by the Left, which was already in the beginning stages of its metamorphosis. The form of radical identity politics that emerged from the chrysalis differs from the original formulations in several respects.

On a moral level, *it is individualistic and absolutist.* The concept of harm is extended to include subjective experiences of any kind, individual or group-based. In such a scheme, perceived individual offenses are given as much importance as historical or structural injustices that are collectively experienced. And paradoxically, this subjective sense of harm is absolute in the philosophical sense of the term; it possesses an objective and unquestionable value. Even though they may be hard to measure, subjective feelings of oppression are real, and only those who have been subject to a particular form of oppression can speak about, let alone partake in the fight against, it.

On a political level, *it is particularist and narcissistic.* The idea of universal values is, it is claimed, itself a tool for domination, invented by the powerful to maintain the status quo (note the similarity with the Right's critique of the so-called globalist elites). In the absence of shared values, community becomes a chimera, or a shorthand for a patchwork of communities organized around disparate and ever-changing identities. "To be recognized as human, levelly human," the end goal of the Combahee model of identity politics, is not enough for there is no common human condition beyond the unique lived experiences of individuals who stand at the crossroads of myriad "interlocking systems of oppression." In this context, the analytical concept of intersectionality becomes an ideological slogan, or in the words of Black feminist activist Loretta J. Ross, "a buzzword, hip lingo, or an accusation you can lob at those who you feel like calling out for not being as 'woke' as you are."[22]

On a strategic level, *it is divisive and symbolist*. Infused with various strands of deconstructivist theory, which give pride of place to language and linguistic expression, younger generations of activists lay special emphasis on symbolic change, often at the expense of more substantive legal or institutional reforms. The new radicalism is more interested in policing and purifying speech than changing the mental codes that generate this speech. Impact trumps intention, but we are not told how we can achieve lasting change without directly addressing or altering intentions. Such a rigid and narrow understanding of activism rules out solidarity and coalition-building other than with those who share the same lived experience. It therefore fragments the struggle for justice and weakens the Left vis-à-vis the already superior Right.

Unfortunately, however, this is not the whole story. One of the most overlooked, or deliberately ignored, aspects of radical identity politics, and the woke Left in general, is its similarity with the Right. This is more than a "family resemblance" in the sense in which the Austrian-British philosopher Ludwig Wittgenstein used the term, i.e., the ensemble of characteristics members of the same family have without necessarily sharing all of them. The woke Left and the Right are Siamese twins when it comes to political tactics and strategies, as I hope to show in more detail in the next chapter. Of course, the Right itself makes much of this similarity, accusing the woke Left of being "authoritarian" or "totalitarian" – to wit, a "new religion." This is at best a typical example of psychological projection and at worst sheer hypocrisy given the Right's own track record on moral absolutism and sanctification of conservative values. But we do not need right-wing panic-mongers to notice the Left's fateful slip into illiberalism, tribalism, and intolerance, especially on issues of race, gender, and sexuality. The woke Left's understanding of identity politics is a travesty of the original Combahee model. And it counters the Right's "faith, family, flag" with its own catechism, "diversity, equity, inclusion" (DEI), by far the most popular way of tackling identity-based prejudice and discrimination in the twenty-first century.

Once a White, Always a White

"Diversity, Equity, Inclusion" or, "Equity, Diversity, Inclusion" (EDI) as it is known in some circles, is more than a motto, or a glib way of performing wokeness; it is an industry – part of the larger economy of culture wars. It is estimated that companies spend $8 billion a year on diversity efforts in the US alone, according to a 2003 study by MIT professor Thomas Kochan and his colleagues (which, though dated, is the largest field-based research project on the impact of diversity efforts on business performance). Much of this is wasted, the study noted, because it is spent on programs for awareness and valuing diversity that do not give people the skills they need.[23] One of the consequences of this, adds Laura Liswood, senior advisor to Goldman Sachs on diversity issues and a scholar at the University of Maryland's Academy of Leadership, is that the most serious discrimination issues may be trivialized. "Lapel pins and slogans on the wall may encourage people to think that diversity is just the special of the week," says Liswood. "Diversity requires real mind-set and cultural change."[24]

Curiously enough, a 2017 McKinsey report prepared by Iris Bohnet, co-director of the Women and Public Policy Program at Harvard Kennedy School, noted that the amount spent on diversity training had not changed much since 2003. "I tried very hard to find any evidence I could," said Bohnet in an interview on her report. "I did not find a single study that found that diversity training in fact leads to more diversity. Now, that's disappointing, discouraging, but maybe when we unpack it is also understandable." And the unpacking shows that "it is actually very hard to change mind-sets."[25]

Still, as Pamela Kirk informs us in her 2019 book *Diversity, Inc. The Failed Promise of a Billion-Dollar Business*, DEI continues to be the go-to formula to address implicit bias and lack of diversity.[26] Almost all Fortune 500 companies have training programs, and nearly two-thirds of colleges and universities in the US have training for faculty according to a survey of 670 schools carried out by Frank Dobbin and Alexandra Kalev, of Harvard and Tel-Aviv University, respectively.[27] Interest in DEI skyrocketed in the wake of Trump's election and the emergence of movements like #MeToo and Black Lives Matter. "A 2019 survey of 234 companies in the S&P 500 found that 63 percent of the diversity professionals had been appointed or promoted to their roles during the past three years," reports *Time* magazine, and this despite the fact that People of Color, who make up nearly 40 percent of the US population, continue to remain underrepresented in most influential sectors.[28]

But why does diversity training fail to achieve its objectives? And, more importantly, why is it still such a lucrative industry given the existence of a substantial corpus of work which documents its limitations? Dobbin and Kalev suggest five possible reasons in their oft-cited article. First, short-term interventions in general do not change people. Second, antibias training may activate stereotypes. Third, training "inspires unrealistic confidence in antidiscrimination programs, making employees complacent about their own biases." Fourth, this training may leave Whites feeling left out. And fifth, a large body of organizational research suggests that people react negatively to efforts to control them.[29] The best way to assess the merits of these arguments is to take a closer look at the DEI model that has come to dominate the Left's thinking on issues of race, gender, and sexuality in the twenty-first century, focusing in particular on the works of the gurus of the field of "anti-racism training," Robin DiAngelo and Ibram X. Kendi.

Robin DiAngelo is White. It may seem cynical to start an overview of someone's work with a reference to an irrelevant phenotypic characteristic, but this is the first thing that catches the eye of any visitor to Robin DiAngelo's official website. It is as if she needs us to "see" that she is White, but the right kind of White, or a White who teaches other Whites how not to be White. Under the tab "About Me," we read not only about DiAngelo's academic and professional qualifications, but also a snippet from an article on her personal background which seems to have been inserted there for the sole purpose of explaining away her Whiteness. "I grew up poor and White," says DiAngelo. "While my class oppression has been relatively visible to me, my race privilege has not." Discovering how her different identities have led her "to collude with racism," DiAngelo decided to distinguish between class and race for, she says, "my experience of poverty would have been different had I not been white."[30] This led her to embark on a career in consultancy and training on issues of racial and social justice. She is the author of *White Fragility: Why It's So Hard for White People to Talk About Racism*, which became a *New York Times* bestseller in the wake of George Floyd's brutal murder by a police officer in Minneapolis on May 25, 2020, reaching Amazon's No. 1 spot with 1.6 million copies sold.[31] The follow-up to *White Fragility* came three years later, with a deliberately provocative title, *Nice Racism: How Progressive White People Perpetuate Racial Harm*.

DiAngelo declares from the outset that her book is "unapologetically rooted in identity politics."[32] The arguments are then presented in first-person plural; "we" the Whites are socialized into a deeply internalized sense of superiority that we are either unaware of or reluctant to admit. As a result, we become fragile in conversations about race. DiAngelo calls this sense of unease "white fragility." White fragility may be triggered by discomfort or anxiety, she writes, but its roots lie in a sense of superiority and entitlement; it is an instrument of "white racial control and the protection of white advantage."[33]

This sets the pace of the following discussion on racism in the US. DiAngelo's observations on the relationship between racism and the power/domination nexus are trite. We already know, thanks to a long line of research and activism, that the projected self-image of America as a melting pot is just an illusion that is used to cover up an ugly reality, that of a racially organized society where Whiteness is the norm for human. We also know that People of Color are still considered by many to be a deviation from that norm, hence more expendable than Whites. It is when DiAngelo moves on to issues of White supremacy and privilege that things get messier.

White supremacy refers not only to the idea that Whites are superior to People of Color, she tells us; it also includes the above-mentioned belief that Whiteness is the default for being human. Color blindness, which is promoted as a remedy to racism, is simply another strategy to conceal White supremacy and maintain the racial hierarchy. In this sense, teaching color blindness, or telling a child not to say things that are overtly racist, does not put an end to racism. In fact, "a racism-free upbringing is not possible, because racism is a social system embedded in culture" and "white supremacy is a form of trauma that is stored in our collective bodies."[34]

Unsurprisingly, then, "so-called progressive whites" are not immune to racism or white fragility either. Even a minimum amount of racial stress triggers a variety of defensive responses – anger, withdrawal, guilt, or cognitive dissonance. White fragility impedes any meaningful discussion on race, and "functions as a form of bullying." DiAngelo's "progressive-bashing" reaches a whole new level in her second book, *Nice Racism*. The term "white progressive" is used as a stand-in for a particular type of Whiteness, we are told, to refer to "white people who see themselves as racially progressive, well-meaning, nice." They might even call themselves "woke."[35] Alas, they are the ones who cause the most harm to People of Color. But how? Well, "our" racism is not blatant of course, DiAngelo says, switching again to first person plural. "We employ more subtle methods: racial insensitivity, ignorance, and arrogance." Not clear enough? Here are some examples (this is just a small sample from a list of 35 – BIPOC stands for Black, Indigenous and People of Color):

- Repeating/rewording/explaining what a BIPOC person just said.
- Calling a Black person articulate; expressing surprise at their intelligence, credentials, or class status.
- Making a point of letting people know that you are married to a BIPOC person or have BIPOC people in your family.
- Insisting that your equity team address every other possible form of oppression, resulting in racism not getting addressed in depth or at all ("It's really about class").
- Loving and recommending films about racism that feature white saviors.
- Asking how to start a diversity consulting business because you attended a talk and found it interesting.

And the final blow:

- Not understanding why something on this list is problematic, and rather than seeking to educate yourself further, dismiss it as invalid.[36]

Given the examples DiAngelo provides, hardly anyone would be spared the label of racist. "Even white people involved in racial justice activism – the far end of the progressive spectrum – perpetrate racism," she writes.[37] And it is not only our racism;

we carry the burden of all the other White people who have hurt their friends of color.

How do we deal with our racism then? How can we atone, and work toward building racial justice – other than buying DiAngelo's books or attending her seminars of course? The answer is, we can't. We can of course build stamina, and face up to the suffering our racism causes. Or we can try to be "less white," and no, DiAngelo is not referring to tanning creams and skin-darkening moisturizers here, but to countering our socialization into Whiteness. What matters most at the end of the day is to learn to be "less racially oppressive, less racially ignorant and less arrogant in our ignorance, less defensive and silent."[38]

It is hard to engage with DiAngelo's views, and the particular model of identity politics she embraces, without sinking into the personal domain. Then again, DiAngelo's project *is* personal, and imperiously so. She professes to know what White progressives actually think, pretending to ventriloquize their irrevocably racist inner psyche. But human beings are not ventriloquist dummies following a fixed script. And even when they do, that does not mean they are almost always bolstering racism, let alone White supremacy. In any event, what is so startling about being defensive, especially when confronted with accusations of racism? After all, defense mechanisms are universally accepted unconscious thought processes that function to protect someone from anxiety and other stress-inducing factors, and they are considered to be pathological only if their persistent use leads to maladaptive behavior or poor mental health. This is, in fact, what DiAngelo herself does, becoming overly defensive in response to various criticisms leveled against her work. In a section on "Accountability" recently added to her website, she provides an extended summary of her academic achievements, the details of her annual income, and a list of donations she makes to racial justice organizations in order to "defend" herself against the accusation that she is "monetizing the Black experience and profiting from

Black pain/death." And this is a perfectly reasonable reaction to such serious allegations. Why would anyone else behave differently, in particular if they are accused of being racist? As a self-defined White progressive, my first reaction to reading DiAngelo's books was disbelief (is this real?), followed by anger (how could anyone be so opinionated and arrogant, yet unaware of this at the same time?). This turned into sheer outrage when I listened to a conversation DiAngelo had with Michelle Martin on Christiane Amanpour's program on PBS on August 4, 2021. Expressing her frustration with White people who claim they cannot be racists as they are married to Black people, DiAngelo says: "You know, Harvey Weinstein was around women all the time, he was married to a woman, did that mean he couldn't have misogynistic orientation to the world and that while he didn't assault all women, I imagine if I was around him, uh, I would pick up on it."[39] What is the implication here? That a White progressive who is married to a Black person is no different than Harvey Weinstein, a convicted serial sex offender, and has a racist "orientation to the world"? And how could someone who draws such a wild analogy on national TV tell us that "nice racism" is not a moral issue, or about being good or bad?

Even if we admit, for the sake of argument, that defensiveness is dysfunctional, and hinders constructive self-reflection, what is the best way of countering it? Tell them to get used to it, and build up stamina? "Proper tone is crucial – feedback must be given calmly," DiAngelo cautions us. But her own strategy is the exact opposite; it is provocative and condescending. Let's recall the list of subtle forms of racism she provides in *Nice Racism* and presume that a participant does not understand what is racist about, say, "Asking how to start a diversity consulting business because you attended a talk and found it interesting." And what if that participant also says, "This looks to me that you're more interested in eliminating business competition than exposing someone's racism." How would DiAngelo reply? The answer is already provided: "Not understanding why something on this list is problematic, and rather than seeking to educate yourself further, dismiss it as invalid." We are not even allowed to question a list of random examples of subtle racism compiled by a "White" DEI consultant, for doing so makes us racist. Who is the "white savior" here: the person who likes movies featuring White saviors, or the one who acts like a White savior?

All other flaws, and there are many, pale into insignificance in comparison with DiAngelo's obsession with White progressives, or the "nice racists," who need to be taught how to think and what to do to overcome their racism. Yet, what is the point of training if racism is a "trauma" stored in our collective bodies? Why should people attend DiAngelo's workshops given that "A positive white identity is an impossible goal. White identity is inherently racist" – unless compelled by their bosses or they enjoy masochistic psychological abuse?

The model of identity politics DiAngelo is relying on is the radical version minted at university campuses; it is essentialist, and deeply fatalistic. The language of traumas, fixed and unfixable identities is no different from the Right's evolutionary psychology-inspired talk of hard-wired group attachments. As such, it is antithetical to the original identity politics of the Combahee women, painstakingly woven into a progressive political program; it is an affront to generations of Black feminists, from Sojourner Truth, Harriet Tubman, Anna Julia Cooper, Ida B. Wells, Mary Church Terrell, Frances Harper to Barbara Smith, Beverly Smith, Demita Frazier, Angela Davis, Patricia Hill Collins, bell hooks, Audre Lorde, and Loretta J. Ross, who have spent their entire lives trying to build bridges and work together with, not only other progressives – of all colors – but also pro-life, conservative and, yes, overtly racist people to achieve a modicum of change. If only DiAngelo had listened to Alicia Garza, one of the co-founders of the Black Lives Matter movement, who once said:

To build the kind of movement that we need to get the things we deserve, we can't be afraid to establish a base that is larger than the people we feel comfortable with . . . We have to reach beyond the choir and take seriously the task of organizing the unorganized – the people who don't already speak the same language, the people who don't eat, sleep, and breathe social justice.[40]

Instead, DiAngelo asks people attending her workshops to turn to one another and share their reflections on the following question: "On a weekly basis, during what percentage of your day do you feel racial shame?"[41]

Anti-Racist Babies

"Antiracist is bred, *not* born / Antiracist baby is raised / to make society transform," says the rhyming opening lines of the National Book Award Winner Ibram X. Kendi's 2020 children's book, *Antiracist Baby*.[42] Take these nine steps and make "equity a reality," the readers are told. Keep your eyes open to all skin colors; don't blame people for being racist, but confess to your own racism; and grow to be an anti-racist. No doubt, the effort is laudable, and the end product playfully crafted (here the credit goes to Ashley Lukashevsky who illustrated the book). But in the parallel universe of the woke Left, it is the impact that counts, not intentions. And if the aim is to introduce "the youngest readers and the grown-ups" to the concept of anti-racism, as the blurb on the publisher's website states, expecting them "to knock down the stack of cultural blocks" or to "confess when being racist" does not seem to be a realistic starting point.

The "pop-theoretician of antiracism," according to the *New York Magazine*,[43] Ibram X. Kendi, or IXK as he likes to present himself (possibly a nod to Martin Luther King's MLK),

is the Andrew W. Mellon Professor in the Humanities and
the Founding Director of the Boston University Center for
Antiracist Research. He was named one of the 100 most influential people in the world by *Time* magazine in 2020 and listed
as the tenth most influential African American between the
ages of 25 and 45 by *The Root* 100 in 2021. Kendi is the author
of *Stamped from the Beginning: The Definitive History of Racist
Ideas in America* (with Jason Reynolds) and #1 *New York Times*
bestseller *How to Be an Antiracist*.[44]

In contrast to Robin DiAngelo's monochromatic worldview,
which consists only of shades of white, Kendi's understanding
of racism is bicolor, or rather black-and-white: you are either
racist or anti-racist. "Not racist" is not an option, because it
signifies neutrality, and there is no neutrality in the struggle
against racism. One either endorses the idea of a racial hierarchy as a racist, or opposes it as an anti-racist, Kendi tells us.
There is no in-between space: "not racist" is a cover for racism.
The same holds for color blindness; by failing to notice color, it
also fails to see race – ergo it is also racist. But what exactly is
racism then? According to Kendi, it is a "combination of racist
policies and racist ideas that produces and normalizes racial
inequities."[45] Racist policies and ideas are policies and ideas
that sustain racial inequity. And racial inequity is when "two
or more racial groups are not standing on approximately equal
footing."[46] Circular? Yes. Confused? Then, buckle up, this is
just the beginning.

We should not use terms like "institutional racism," "structural racism," or "systemic racism," Kendi says, for racism is
by nature institutional, structural, and systemic. Likewise,
we should steer clear of focusing on "racial discrimination"
because it diverts our attention away from the real agents of
racism, i.e., racist policy and racist policymakers, or what Kendi
calls "racist power." In any case, not all racial discrimination is
racist. If discrimination is creating equity, then it is anti-racist.
The rest is an endless loop of tautologies:

A racist is someone who is supporting a racist policy by their actions or inaction or expressing a racist idea. An antiracist is someone who is supporting an antiracist policy by their actions or expressing an antiracist idea.

Poor people are a class, Black people a race. Black poor people are a race-class.

Women are a gender. Black people are a race. When we identify Black women, we identify a race-gender.

When a policy produces inequities between race-genders, it is gendered racism, or gender racism for short.

Capitalism is essentially racist; racism is essentially capitalist.[47]

Kendi agrees with DiAngelo that the real danger to racial equity comes from the progressives. "The most threatening racist movement" is not the far right, but "the regular American's" drive for race neutrality, all the more so as it feeds White nationalists' sense of victimhood and creates a backlash to affirmative action which the Right regards as "reverse discrimination." Kendi also objects to the use of the term "microaggression"; persistent daily abuse is not minor, he says, and aggression is not as stringent as abuse. So what other people call microaggression, he calls "racist abuse." And how do we resist the temptations of the twin evils of race neutrality and racist abuse? Here, too, Kendi joins hands with DiAngelo: by embracing anti-racism, which in turn requires "persistent self-awareness, constant self-criticism, and regular self-examination."[48]

It is important to note at this point that the model of identity politics that underpins the writings of DiAngelo or Kendi is neither uniquely American nor limited to DEI/EDI trainers. Another example is the British journalist and author Reni Eddo-Lodge's debut non-fiction book *Why I'm No Longer Talking to White People About Race*, which made her the first Black

British woman to top UK book charts.[49] By now, you probably know the tune. Covert, often unnoticed, racism of highly educated, high-earning White men (landlords, bosses, CEOs, head teachers, or university vice chancellors) – "the silently raised eyebrows, the implicit biases, snap judgements," "the flick of a wrist that tosses a CV in the bin because the applicant has a foreign-sounding name" – play a more important role in upholding structural racism than overt racism; White denialism and color blindness thwart any attempt to address racism, and so on.[50] Another common theme that runs through antiracism scholarship is the question of privilege. It is not easy to describe White privilege, Eddo-Lodge writes, since it is an absence – "an absence of the consequences of racism." It refers to the fact that being White "will almost certainly positively impact your life's trajectory in some way" without you even noticing it. And it is all-pervasive, "a manipulative, suffocating blanket of power that envelops everything we know, like a snowy day," forcing us into silence for fear of losing our job, our flat, or our loved ones. A key mechanism in this process of silencing is what Eddo-Lodge calls "white victimhood" (a form of White fragility), the effort "to divert conversations about the effects of structural racism in order to shield whiteness from much-needed rigorous criticism." Obviously, it is progressives who most acutely feel white victimhood. "I have often had white people get in touch with me, using the words of civil rights leader Martin Luther King, Jr.," she says, "in attempts to prove to me that my work is misguided, that I am doing it wrong." But, she continues, Martin Luther King Jr. also wrote in 1963 that "the Negro's great stumbling block in the stride toward freedom is not the White Citizen's Counciler or the Ku Klux Klanner, but the white moderate who is more devoted to 'order' than to justice," "who paternalistically feels he can set the timetable for another man's freedom ... and who constantly advises the Negro to wait until a 'more convenient season'."[51] Eddo-Lodge uses King's words as a launching pad to hit back at left-wing criticisms of her work. "Even now, when I talk about racism," she says, "the response from white people is to shift the focus away from their complicity and on to a conversation about what it means to be black, and about 'black identity'." Instead of engaging in meaningful conversation, she continues, they complain about identity politics, and claim that we all belong to one race, "the human race." And yet "discussing racism is not the same thing as discussing 'black identity'"; rather it is about "discussing white identity. It's about white anxiety."[52]

The irony of talking about the need for having meaningful conversations in a book titled *Why I'm No Longer Talking to White People About Race* should not be lost on anyone. This is indeed the fundamental paradox at the heart of the anti-racist enterprise on both sides of the Atlantic. Their diagnosis of the current racial order is fundamentally correct. Structural racism continues to be the main domestic threat to justice and equality in the US, the UK, and beyond. Whiteness is still the entrenched norm for being human, and any discussion of racism should indeed begin by exposing the power dynamics that have led to the general acceptance of this historically constituted racial hierarchy. Problems start once we move past the diagnosis stage, and start discussing the causes and remedies of the current situation. The anti-racist message is plain and simple: we need to talk, but we'll do the talking. You should listen, and confess to your and your ancestors' sins. Don't question, for asking questions is racist.

To begin with, this message is based upon an uncompromisingly Manichean way of thinking, which sees everything through a black-and-white moral lens. The various disclaimers inserted into the narrative ("this isn't about good and bad people," Eddo-Lodge; "I am not saying that you are immoral," Robin DiAngelo; "we will find good and bad . . . in all spaces, no matter how poor or rich, Black or non-Black," Kendi) are no more than a fig leaf to cover this problematic dualism. And here I am not talking about issues of power. It is true that White people, as the historically dominant group, should be largely responsible for dismantling racial inequalities. But this does not say much about the identities in question. Being oppressed does not make any identity virtuous or morally superior to another, just as being born or socialized into the oppressor group does not make anyone automatically or necessarily complicit in some abstract notion of White guilt.

This simplistic view is partly caused by anti-racists' strong penchant for overgeneralization, and tendency to see Whiteness or Blackness as monolithic categories. In this regard, the anti-racist project as a whole is as essentialist as – if slightly more veiled than – DiAngelo's DEI manual. Eddo-Lodge does not go so far as to tell us that "white identity is inherently racist," but the idea sneaks in through the concept of White privilege which she believes leads to a "dull, grinding complacency" in White people to confront their complicity in racial inequality. Black people can be prejudiced but not racist, because racism is prejudice plus power, and "there simply aren't enough black people in positions of power to enact racism against White people on the kind of grand scale it currently operates at against black people."[53] Kendi is more nonchalant about the use of terms like White, Black, or "Latinx" (the woke version of Latino or Latina), as if they are neatly separated categories with no intermingling, and this in a country where the rates of intermarriages have risen from 7 percent in 1980 to 17 percent in 2015 for all newlyweds.[54] And, as an astute critic observes in the *New York Magazine*, Kendi never mentions intra-racial inequalities when he discusses, say, the racial wealth gap.[55] It is true, of course, that the latter is immense due to a number of historical and structural reasons; the typical White family has eight times the wealth of the typical Black family and five times the wealth of the typical Hispanic family, according to the findings of the Survey of Consumer Finances carried out by the Federal Reserve in 2019.[56] But the same survey also shows that the richest 10 percent of Blacks owned 75.3 percent of all Black wealth in 2016. Rather than focusing on the factors that cause these disparities, Kendi throws around such terms as "race class" and "class racism," topped up with slogans – "To love capitalism is to end up loving racism. To love racism is to end up loving capitalism" – without providing any explanation of why, for example, capitalism and racism reinforce each other.

Finally, the anti-racist project, true to the self-help tradition of which it forms a part, engages liberally in what is known as "conceptual stretching" in political science, which occurs when an existing concept does not fit new cases, and is extended or simply distorted to fit additional phenomena.[57] The best example of this is, of course, the concept of racism itself, which becomes a catch-all term that includes everything from everyday slights and insults, a smirky smile on a face, and raised eyebrows, through to police brutality, the prison industrial complex, and ghettoization. In the case of DiAngelo, this conceptual sleight-of-hand extends even to "White supremacy," which now covers "the multitude of ways our society elevates white people as the human ideal and norm for humanity."[58] Once concepts are stretched like this, it is no wonder that everyone is racist, irrespective of intentions or, we should add, impact, for there is no objective way of determining the harm caused by a particular word, gesture, or decision (institutional or individual) for those who happen to be on the receiving end of the interaction. By dividing the world into racists and anti-racists, and redefining the former in such a way as to include everyone who isn't anti-racist according to the particular definition adopted by the DEI trainer or anti-racist self-help kit provider, the likes of DiAngelo, Kendi, and Eddo-Lodge sabotage any chance of building a racially just society right from the start, demonizing even their closest allies, above all White progressives and Black conservatives.

Virtue Peddlers

Both the "Diversity, Equity, Inclusion" movement and the anti-racism self-help literature take their cue from what's called Critical Whiteness Studies, a "field of scholarship whose aim is to reveal the invisible structures that produce and reproduce white supremacy and privilege."[59] Even though the origins of critical thinking on Whiteness go back to the early twentieth century, in particular the works of W. E. B. Du Bois, James Baldwin, and, later, Theodore W. Allen, the field came of age in the early 1990s, in the wake of the publication of a provocative short essay titled "White Privilege: Unpacking the Invisible Knapsack" by American feminist and anti-racism activist Peggy McIntosh. At the heart of McIntosh's writings is the idea of the invisibility of Whiteness. Hence McIntosh defines White privilege as "an invisible weightless knapsack of special provisions, maps, passports, codebooks, visas, clothes, tools and blank checks."[60]

According to Barbara Applebaum, a professor of Philosophy of Education at Syracuse University, an important objective of Critical Whiteness Studies is to make Whiteness visible in order to disrupt the norms that dominate White society. Redefining the concept of "White supremacy" is key to this objective. White supremacy does not refer to explicitly racist groups like the Ku Klux Klan, but to a "continual pattern of widespread, everyday practices and policies that are made invisible through normalization." In that sense, "white supremacy is to race what patriarchy is to gender."[61] We have already seen where this path leads in our discussion of the works of DiAngelo, Kendi, and Eddo-Lodge. White supremacy is often hidden behind the cloak of good intentions or color blindness, and reproduced by well-meaning references to common humanity, which makes it difficult to acknowledge one's complicity in structural racism. We should refrain from framing this in terms of good and bad, Applebaum tells us – joining the chorus, since this "recenters white interests and needs over the needs and concerns of People of Color." "Even when white teachers are committed to diversity and multiculturalism, if they do not deconstruct their own investments in whiteness, they will not be able to understand how their good intentions might be detrimental to their students of color."[62] White privilege pedagogy should thus focus on personal awareness, confession, and renouncing privilege, the only way for White students to be comfortable with their Whiteness. In other words, no salvation without self-flagellation!

One may of course object to the drawing of a straight line between Critical Whiteness Studies and contemporary DEI and the anti-racism industry.[63] But the problematization of White privilege or supremacy does not necessarily entail the reification of the social construct of "Whiteness," or the imputation of guilt against those who possess a particular skin color. That is precisely why Theodore W. Allen, a pioneering figure in the study of White identity and the author of the two-volume *The Invention of the White Race*, insisted on using "Whiteness" in quotation marks, noting that it is just an abstraction, and "an attribute of some people, it's not the role they play."[64] Despite its heuristic value, he said elsewhere, the term is "an insufficient basis for refutation of white-supremacist apologetics."[65]

In the absence of a historically based critique of capitalism and its uneven impact on various class formations, Whiteness is nothing but an "empty signifier" without a referent and a commonly agreed upon meaning. It is not possible to forge a full-fledged political program out of individual self-flagellation. Anti-racist struggle is not an Alcoholics Anonymous meeting where racists stand up and say, "Hi! My name is John and I am a racist." And, let's not forget, even that takes a great deal of courage and willingness that few among us possess. The moderators of these meetings do not tell you, after you've introduced yourself, that, as an addict, you are responsible for every fatal incident of drink driving, past and present. Owning up to your racism, acknowledging your privilege are extremely complicated issues, and call for a higher level of self-awareness than, say, substance abuse. But those who are in the business of DEI or anti-racist training are more interested in shaming us from their lavishly funded pulpits than motivating us. They deliberately pick on White progressives for they know they are the only ones who would offer them a pulpit. And an expensive one at that. How many people could afford to pay $65 to $160 for a three-and-a-half-hour sermon?[66] Only middle/upper-middle-class progressives who do not need to bother with the angst of making ends meet, or their managers who want to show off their impeccable woke credentials. So, it is not surprising that DiAngelo's "partial list of clients" include Amazon, The Bill & Melinda Gates Foundation, The Hollywood Writers Guild, the YMCA, and Unilever, among many others, according to her own website.

The key word here is "client." For most diversity trainers, people are clients, not fellow human beings who need to be guided through a difficult process of introspection or potential allies in the fight for racial justice. Hence, various contracts obtained through public records requests show that Ibram X. Kendi's fee to speak at a one-hour virtual event ranged between $20,000 and $25,000 in 2020 and 2021.[67] Needless to say, no one is expecting Kendi to do his work for free. But how can someone preach about the mutually beneficial relationship between racism and capitalism, while making a small fortune by the very system he so decries?[68]

The radical identity politics of DEI trainers and anti-racism gurus is everything that the identity politics of the Combahee River Collective is not. To recap what I said earlier, the woke upgrade focuses on perceived individual harm and subjective experience at the expense of collective, structural injustice; it dismisses the idea of common humanity by resuscitating the theological concept of "eternal sin," which is then imputed to all White people who are expected to spend a certain percentage of their everyday life feeling racial shame; it interjects the term "intersectionality" here and there as a catchphrase, but treats identities, White, Black or People of Color, as if they are fixed, insulated categories with no internal hierarchies; it seeks to sanitize language without changing mindsets; neutralize impact without taking intentions into account; and tackle smirky smiles without problematizing institutional and sociocultural processes which enable those smiles in the first place.

For the Combahee women, identity politics was about *politics*, and identity was one way of doing politics and challenging hierarchies and – true to the spirit of intersectionality – not only "racial" hierarchies, but all kinds of hierarchies. For the woke Left, identity politics is about *identity*, and identity is *beyond* politics. It is a sacred value that needs to be preserved intact, at all costs. The questions of who defines a particular identity or what causes harm are left unanswered. In that sense, early critics of radical identity politics, Marxists and liberals alike, were right, but only partially. It is true that for the campus Left (the term "woke" did not have much currency back then), "symbolic verbal politics" was the only form of politics that was possible. Today, even verbal politics is out of bounds. Terms are not discussed but dictated; and truth, in an ironic twist, is no longer relative but absolute. Woke Left politics is *anti-politics*, not only in the conventional sense of alienation from and distrust in mainstream politics and institutions – often associated with various types of populism – but also in the broader sense of how we understand "the political." Here, I am relying on a distinction between "politics" as a set of decisions, policies, and institutions, and "the political" as the existence of a space of disagreement.[69] "An action is political," says political geographer Andrew Barry, "to the extent it opens up possibility of disagreement." In that sense, politics can be profoundly anti-political in its effects, suppressing potential spaces of contestation or placing limits on the possibilities for debate and confrontation:

> A democratic society is one which places particular value on the right to dissent and to contest, but the defence of this political norm should exist in conjunction with the protection and enhancement of other cultural, economic and political rights. In such a society, legislation is not grounded in reason, and rarely in a consensus, but may be justified in relation to the needs of the collective to reach agreement on matters of common interest, while recognizing the necessary existence of continuing disagreement about what the collective is, what its needs are and what is of common interest.[70]

The anti-politics of the woke Left rejects the idea of common interest. It sees no allies, and it seeks no allies. In such a scheme, White progressives or the regular Americans who pretend to be, perhaps mistakenly, color blind are more harmful to People of Color than explicitly racist modern day Ku Klux Klanners. It may well be so. But what does this mean, politically speaking? Are we not supposed to reach out to White progressives or regular Americans, and explain to them that in a society built on White values, color blindness may not be the best way to achieve racial equality? And if we cannot even speak to the progressives, how are we going to convince the conservatives, reactionaries, or overt racists who still constitute a substantial part of any given society?

The Black queer feminists who coined the term identity politics knew the answers to these questions because they were doing political work and consciousness-raising in the real world, with women of all colors and walks of life, not peddling virtue in sterilized boardrooms or slick vodcasts. They were guided by the motto "This Bridge Called my Back" (which was later to become the title of a groundbreaking feminist anthology edited by Cherrie Moraga and Gloria E. Anzaldúa), which they saw as the key to success. "The only way that we can win – and before winning, the only way we can survive," said Barbara Smith, "is by working with each other, and not seeing each other as enemies."[71]

4

The Left Meets the Right

Burning Books

Jack Dempsey Brock (1927–2020) was "sacrificially committed and supernaturally called to serve and reach people with the gospel of Jesus Christ," said an obituary in *Alamogordo Daily News*. After spending much of his youth as a traveling evangelist, Brock and his wife Sharon had settled in Alamogordo, a city with some 69,000 inhabitants located at the western base of the Sacramento Mountains in New Mexico where he founded Christ Community Church in 1973 and continued as its pastor until his death on April 3, 2020.[1] According to his obituary, his greatest accomplishment was his 70+ years of teaching the Word of God. Yet, it was not dedication to the gospel that earned Jack Brock a place in international headlines. On December 26, 2001, Pastor Brock announced that he would hold a bonfire to burn Harry Potter books because the famous series of fantasy novels by British author J. K. Rowling about a teenage wizard was "an abomination to God and to me." However, he also admitted he hadn't read any of them. "These books teach children how they can get into witchcraft and become a witch, wizard or warlock . . . Behind that innocent face is the power of satanic darkness," he told his congregation in a sermon delivered on the night of Sunday December 30. The sermon was followed by a ceremony of book burning, where Brock threw some 30 Harry Potter books into the fire while members sang "Amazing Grace" with their faces lit by the glow of the flames.[2]

Jack Brock was not the only evangelist who felt threatened by Rowling's hugely popular young wizard Harry Potter and his friends, Hermione Granger and Ron Weasley. Another was Reverend Doug Taylor of Jesus Party Church, a Pentecostal congregation in Lewiston, Maine, whose attempt to burn the Potter books was thwarted by the city's refusal to grant him a burning permit. Instead, Taylor went ahead by staging a "book-cutting" event: "Everybody's going to have scissors, and we're going to cut those four [Harry Potter] books up right into the trash."[3] "It's no secret that I enjoy what I'm doing right now," Taylor said while he shredded Rowling's book, as one of his flock shouted "Hallelujah."[4]

Since the release of the first movie adaptation of the series, *Harry Potter and the Philosopher's Stone*, in 2001, there have been at least six public burnings of Harry Potter books in the US alone, for allegedly promoting witchcraft and Satanism.[5] The numbers swelled when Donald Trump supporters jumped on the bandwagon, after Rowling's public condemnation of Trump's immigration ban on citizens from Muslim-majority countries in 2017. "Just burned all my Harry Potter books after being a fan for 17 years . . . You embarrassed me, disgusted me, and I will never read your work again," an angry user tweeted at J. K. Rowling who replied: "Guess it's true what they say: you can lead a girl to books about the rise and fall of an autocrat, but you still can't make her think."[6]

As a seasoned writer, Rowling was probably aware that despite her growing notoriety among far right pyrophiles, she was far from being the first or the most hounded author whose books were being ceremonially incinerated to protect gullible readers from the corrupting influence of the written word. Book burning, or the deliberate and ritual destruction by fire of books, is a centuries-old tradition whose origins go back to the Chinese Qin Dynasty (213–210 BC). Since then, there have been countless instances of public book burnings, by both religious orders and secular authorities, from the expurgations of Jewish and Christian scriptures by Ancient Greeks and Romans to the burning of Voltaire and Rousseau's books in Paris and Geneva. Book burning fell from grace with the Enlightenment, only to be rekindled in the runup to and during the First World War, first by "patriotic fires," which involved the burning of pro-German and pacifist writings, then the burning of the library at Louvain University by German occupying forces in August 1914. International outrage caused by this act of wanton violence led the German government to produce a report absolving its military command of any deliberate intent, but the report was dismissed elsewhere and, with hindsight, could even be read as an ominous portent for things to come.[7]

Almost two decades later, on the night of May 10, 1933, some 40,000 students, backed up by uniformed brown shirts of the paramilitary SA, gathered in the Opernplatz (now the Bebelplatz) in the Mitte district of Berlin to celebrate the "Action against the Un-German Spirit," a nationwide campaign to purify the German language and literature launched by the Nazi German Students' Association's Main Office for Press and Propaganda.[8] Amidst cheers, joyful singing, and fire oaths (the so-called *Feuersprüche*), a group of students marched up to the bonfire carrying the bust of the Jewish founder of the Institute for Sexual Science, Magnus Hirschfeld, and threw it on top of thousands of volumes from the institute's library, along with other books by Jewish and "un-German" writers.[9] The fire was surrounded by rows of young people in Nazi uniforms giving the Heil Hitler salute, while listening to the speech delivered by Hitler's Minister of Propaganda Joseph Goebbels who orchestrated the whole event:

> No to decadence and moral corruption! Yes to decency and
> morality in family and state! . . . The future German man will
> not just be a man of books, but a man of character. It is to this
> end that we want to educate you . . . You do well to commit to
> the flames the evil spirit of the past. This is a strong, great and
> symbolic deed.[10]

That night, students in 34 university towns across Germany
burned over 25,000 books by more than 75 German and foreign authors. Among the many authors whose books were
burned was the famous nineteenth-century German poet
and playwright Heinrich Heine who had written the horri-
bly prescient words almost a century earlier, in his 1821 play
Almansor: "Where they burn books, they will, in the end, also
burn people."[11]

The burnings of May 10 were just a drop in the ocean, as
Bodley's librarian Richard Ovenden notes in his magisterial
*Burning the Books: A History of the Deliberate Destruction of
Knowledge*: "over 100 million books were destroyed during
the Holocaust, in the twelve years from the period of Nazi
dominance in Germany in 1933 up to the end of the Second
World War."[12] This was what prompted American author Ray
Bradbury to write one of the greatest contributions to dystopian fiction in the twentieth century, *Fahrenheit 451*. In an
interview he gave in 2005, Bradbury explained how he came
up with the idea of a bleak future where fire departments burn
books:

> Well, Hitler, of course. When I was 15, he burned the books in
> the streets of Berlin. Then along the way I learned about the
> libraries in Alexandria burning 5000 years ago. . . . That grieved
> my soul. Since I'm self-educated, that means my educators – the
> libraries – are in danger. And if it could happen in Alexandria,
> if it could happen in Berlin, maybe it could happen somewhere
> up ahead, and my heroes would be killed.[13]

Unfortunately, heroes continued to be killed, for all sorts of reasons and by all sorts of regimes – as Bradbury himself was painfully aware. When asked about the burning of Harry Potter books in 2006, the 86-year-old author said he thought Reverend Doug Taylor and his ilk were deluded. "He [Reverend Taylor] doesn't know what witchcraft is," he continued. "It's about wits. There's nothing wrong with the Potter books, because they're not promoting witchcraft. They're promoting being wise."[14]

The New Evangelists

Bradbury did not live long enough to see that the ritual that inspired him to pen *Fahrenheit 451* is being taken up by the so-called progressive Left which has traditionally been a stalwart defender of freedom of thought and speech. On September 16, 2020, *Newsweek* ran an article titled "J.K. Rowling Book Burning Videos Are Spreading Like Wildfire Across TikTok." This time it was not evangelical pastors or far right Trump supporters who were burning Rowling's books, but former *Harry Potter* fans protesting the author's alleged transphobia.[15] The article referred to a video posted on the Chinese-owned social media platform TikTok by @elmcdo which featured a number of Harry Potter books placed on a burning pyre. "You have to stop using 'death of the author' as an excuse to have your cake and eat it too," the voice-over said according to the article. "While the reader's perspective is an important part of interpretation and meaning, it is impossible to completely divorce a work from its creator." The voice-over continued: "The positive impact J.K. Rowling's work had on millions of readers does not negate how her hateful lobbying has affected the trans community." The video ended with the following message: "Your love of 'Harry Potter' is not more important than the lives of trans women."[16]

The article also reported that a number of videos showing Harry Potter books being destroyed were circulating on the platform, though at the time of writing, none of these videos were available, and @elmcdo's account followed by 17.4K people was private. A similar discussion was circulating on Twitter at around the same time, triggered by a tweet posted by the Irish pop duo Jedward. "Does anyone need firewood this winter!," the tweet read. "JK's new book is perfect to burn next to a Romantic fire. Aww get all cozy and comfy can't wait."[17] The new book Jedward was referring to was *Troubled Blood*, the fifth of Rowling's Cormoran Strike detective series written under the pseudonym Robert Galbraith. An early review by Jake Kerridge published in *The Telegraph* talked about a plotline involving "a transvestite serial killer" which, Kerridge claimed, reflected Rowling's "stance on trans issues": "never trust a man in a dress."[18] It was later revealed by *The Guardian* that this character was "just one of many suspects"; he was neither the main villain, nor was he portrayed as trans or even called a "transvestite."[19]

But how could book burning, a ritual notoriously associated with the Nazis in contemporary times, and widely regarded as a hallmark of censorship and totalitarianism, be appropriated by progressive activists in the name of solidarity with one of the most marginalized groups in society? According to Ella Kipling writing for the Irish football, movies and gaming website *HITC*, it wasn't. Disputing *Newsweek*'s reporting, Kipling wrote that if we search "JK Rowling book burning" on TikTok, we will find only one video of a book being burned, and the video had only 49 likes as of September 18, 2020. While book burning was a "hot topic" on Twitter, she continued, very few people are actually practicing it, and Jedward themselves referred to their tweet as a "joke."[20]

Kipling seems to have a very magnanimous view of the symbolism of book burning, at least of the woke Left kind. It is unrealistic to expect droves of people to post videos of themselves burning J. K. Rowling books publicly, and still more so if they are self-described progressive activists (not to mention the many legal problems this might cause for both the user and the social media platform in question). In any case, does this really matter? Shouldn't we be worried about the fact that book burning is considered as a legitimate way of protesting by so many on the Left? Do we need to actually watch people shouting #RIPJKRowling – a viral hashtag at the time – in unison, and dancing around a pyre of burning Harry Potter or Cormoran Strike books to notice and be concerned about the unsettling similarity? What should we think of the fact that Jedward's tasteless "joke" had been retweeted 6,004 times and had 51.4K likes by March 12, 2022? Or that a simple Twitter search yields thousands of tweets calling for the burning of Rowling's books?

The woke Left tends to dismiss these reactions as the grumbles of a few frustrated readers or as typical social media drivel with little, if any, real-life consequences (conveniently forgetting that according to their own understanding of harm, it is only those who have been subject to an offense, in this case Rowling, who can decide what its consequences are). But it is not just tweets. The idea of rewriting the *Harry Potter* series by someone other than Rowling herself is a recurrent theme of woke Rowling-bashing in more serious publications as well. Hence Aja Romano, a culture staff writer for the left-leaning American news and opinion website *Vox*, muses that a new Harry Potter TV series could allow Warner Bros. to reject Rowling's "intolerance" with a different story that embraces inclusivity and diversity. It could have:

> a trans main character who receives their Hogwarts letter after they discover they can shape-shift into their true form. Desi Harry, Black Hermione, Remus/Sirius or Albus/Scorpius in a queer life partnership, queer and genderqueer wizards running amok. Asian characters whose identities aren't fetishized,

Jewish characters whose identities aren't trivialized, non-demonized fat characters, non-nuclear, non-heteronormative families everywhere![21]

Romano, writing in a magazine which has an average of 23 million visitors per month, is not a lone-wolf social media user venting their frustrations (they define themselves as non-binary – hence the grammatical quirks),[22] or boycotting a powerful figure whom they believe is promoting ideas that they find offensive. They are not talking from a position of powerlessness; quite the contrary, they are among the many who have the power to set the terms of the debate on these issues, and determine what is culturally acceptable and what is unacceptable, a key element of cancel culture as we have seen earlier. True, Romano who, in their own words, has "spent years critiquing the many problems embedded in J.K. Rowling's stories," do not go so far as to issue a call for a ban on or the burning of Rowling's books. But they talk about the need for separating the art from the artist, and erasing her name, even though it may be difficult to do so "when the artist is right there, reminding you that she intended for her art to reflect her prejudice all along."[23] For Romano and scores of like-minded woke activists, it is not the books that pose a threat but the author herself, her mere existence which is "presumed to" threaten the existence of others. So they imagine a *Harry Potter* without Rowling. "*Harry Potter* is ours now," they write; "J.K. Rowling lost custody over her kids and now we can spoil them, let them get tattoos, express themselves however they want, love whomever they want, transition if they want, practice as much radical empathy and anarchy as they want."[24]

Note the language and the tone here. First, Romano effortlessly slip from impact to intentions, and tell us, authoritatively, that Rowling aims for "her art to reflect her prejudice." But how do they know her true intentions? Rowling's widely vilified tweet of December 19, 2019 – the initial spark that ignited the wildfires of accusation and abuse – simply expresses her support for Maya Forstater, a consultant who lost her job at the Center for Global Development for holding gender-critical beliefs:[25] "Dress however you please. Call yourself whatever you like. Sleep with any consenting adult who'll have you. Live your best life in peace and security. But force women out of their jobs for stating that sex is real?"[26] Second, how could a writer (or, for that matter, a reader) decide that another writer should lose custody of her work? Let's be more direct: how dare they? This is not a question about Rowling's views on transgender rights; she may or may not be transphobic (Rowling herself vehemently denies these allegations, and many in the LGBTQ+ community believe she isn't; for what it's worth, I agree with the latter). That might prompt her readers not to buy her books or call for a boycott. But erase her authorship? Strike through her name?

And how different is this from the paranoid mindset that has motivated much of book burning by totalitarian regimes? After all, the circular containing the fire oaths to be read during the 1933 book burnings included the names of individual authors, not the books, considered to be polluting the spirit of the German youth. Who is polluting the youth today? And who decides whose books to burn?

Let me reiterate. None of the mainstream publications mentioned here urge readers to actually burn Rowling's books. Yet, not unlike evangelical pastors or far right Trump supporters, they present her ideas as an existential threat to true believers, one that needs to be symbolically smoldered so that the phoenix of a new, genderqueer, spirit can emerge from the ashes.[27] Analogies and metaphors aside, what matters here is that book burning is considered legitimate, in fact encouraged, by the dominant strand of so-called "progressive activism" today. But there is nothing progressive about this dogmatic and fanatical activism. Perhaps it is time to call a spade a spade and expose the proselytizing zeal of this new form of evangelism.

In *Fahrenheit 451*, book burning is not imposed from above by a totalitarian regime; it is the people who want them to be burned. "Remember, the firemen are rarely necessary," says Faber, a retired English professor who Montag, the protagonist of Bradbury's novel, meets on a regular basis. "The public itself stopped reading of its own accord. You firemen provide a circus now and then at which buildings are set off and crowds gather for the pretty blaze, but it's a small sideshow indeed, and hardly necessary to keep things in line." This is indeed the problem with woke activism – not the circus, but self-imposed censorship, voluntary intellectual impoverishment, always hailing from a position of perpetual victimhood.

Identity as Commodity

The transmutation of the once-progressive concept of identity politics into a reactionary activist mantra did not take place in a vacuum. The DiAngelos and Kendis of the "Diversity, Equity, Inclusion" industry were simply responding to the demands of an ever-growing market which treats identity as a commodity. And as befits the nature of neoliberal capitalism, the need for this commodity is insatiable. Once a particular identity is consumed, an upgraded version emerges, and becomes the new coveted object of the identity clientele. Yet the free-market analogy goes only so far. The inner logic of the identity economy dictates that the old is not only uncool, but also harmful. As customers, we do not have the freedom to stick to the earlier model, or to forego "coolness." The choices we make, we are told by the gatekeepers of the new identity economy, may have life-threatening consequences on others. Whether we have the means or the willingness to buy the new model is irrelevant; and showing respect for others' preferences is not enough. We need to keep up with the inexorable pace of change and adapt. We need to conform. Or risk excommunication.

But where does all this come from? What are the origins of the identity economy? How did the process of commodification of identity begin, and when did the identity economy and identity politics merge? The most popular answer to these questions is also the most disconcerting one: the birthplace of the identity economy is the university campus. The answer is disconcerting because this is also what lies at the heart of populist anti-intellectualism, often deployed by the Right to launch a frontal attack on higher education. Many on the Left fall into this trap and play into the Right's hands, denying or trivializing the existence of the problem – treating it as mere right-wing propaganda to capture the last bastion of progressive activism. But, as I showed in the previous chapter, it is not only the Right that pinpoints the universities as the source of a different model of identity politics. As early as the 1990s, it was the liberal Martha Nussbaum who anathematized the rise of a new type of academic feminism detached from the world of practical politics. Influenced by postmodernist thought, in particular "the extremely French idea that the intellectual does politics by speaking seditiously," Nussbaum wrote, many young feminists had lapsed into fatalism, and started to believe that any real-life reform will end up reinforcing the all-encompassing structures of power they set out to dismantle. As a result, the new feminism shunned material change, telling a new generation of talented activists that they can do politics in the safety of their campuses by engaging in subversive speech. But symbolic politics does not bring about real change, she said. "Hungry women are not fed by this, battered women are not sheltered by it, raped women do not find justice in it, gays and lesbians do not achieve legal protections through it."[28]

Writing at about the same time, Marxists like Adolph Reed Jr. or Todd Gitlin also pointed to universities as the breeding ground of a new type of identity politics which they believed moved into the vacuum created by the defeat of revolutionary universalism. This "dilettantish politics" is the result of a generation of marginalization, "of decades without any possibility of challenging power or influencing policy," Reed wrote. Today the term Left "signifies a cultural sensibility rather than a critique of the existing social order; [it] has no particular place it wants to go."[29] Cut off from ecumenical political goals, Gitlin pressed on, practitioners of campus identity politics spoke of "disruptions," "subversions," and "ruptures." "The more their political life was confined to the library, the more their language bristled with aggression." No wonder radical identity politics flourished in the university; it was only there that its demands could be met.[30]

Yet by far the starkest condemnation of the ways in which identity politics is transfigured by academics came from the women who coined the term "identity politics." This was what motivated academic Keeanga-Yamahtta Taylor to publish a collection of interviews with the founders of the Combahee River Collective in 2017 – "to reconnect the radical roots of Black feminist analysis and practice to contemporary organizing efforts."[31] Black feminism found a sanctuary in academic circles, Taylor wrote, as the political movements that gave birth to it receded from the streets. This was a welcome development, and it opened up spaces for a deeper investigation into the lives of oppressed groups but, at the end of the day, "Black feminism is a guide to political action and liberation." Bereft of a connection with political struggle, it becomes abstract and discourse driven.[32] Barbara Smith and Demita Frazier, co-authors (with Beverly Smith) of the Combahee River Collective Statement, also had issues with the hollowing out of their original model. It is true that the Right hijacked the term and used it as a punching bag to denounce progressive activism, Smith said, but left-wing academics who introduced identity politics into the younger generations were not entirely free from blame because they did not fully grasp its potential for political action. The reason the Combahee women used the term, Smith added, is that they were asserting the rights of Black women "at a time when Black women were being told to walk seven steps behind and have babies for the nation."[33] Today, it is used almost like an excuse for not engaging in the hard work of "crossing boundaries and working across differences." Demita Frazier, on the other hand, underscored the revolutionary potential of their activism. The main challenge for Black feminism today, she concluded, is how to confront late-stage capitalism, "its impact, and its continuing denigration of our life, our lives."[34]

What's remarkable in this context is not the Right's chronic obsession with identity politics. After all, as I argued in chapter 2, fanning the flames of culture wars is the Right's signature business model. The more intriguing question is why there is so little criticism of the excesses of identity politics on the contemporary Left. Why do the forebodings of earlier generations of liberal and Marxist thinkers, or indeed Black queer feminists, go unheeded? And, more importantly, why is even the slightest criticism of woke orthodoxies on questions of race, gender, and sexuality immediately dismissed as "enabling the far right," "cozying up to fascism," or being on "the wrong side of history"? When did the present-day Left lose its critical edge?

Given the deafening silence and almost pathological denialism of the mainstream Left, it is not surprising that these questions are taken up by the Right – and here, I am not necessarily talking about the far right, though admittedly the difference between the mainstream and the extreme has become harder to spot in recent years. Perhaps the most celebrated conservative critique of the new campus culture comes from Jonathan Haidt, the Thomas Cooley Professor of Ethical Leadership at New York University's Stern School of Business, and Greg Lukianoff, an attorney, and president and CEO of the Foundation for Individual Rights in Education (FIRE). First published in the September 2015 issue of *The Atlantic*, Haidt and Lukianoff's "The Coddling of the American Mind" was an instant hit (the article was viewed by six million people in two years), and propelled Haidt, the academic partner of the power duo, to the Professors' Walk of Fame, leading *The Chronicle of Higher Education* to label him as the "gadfly of the campus culture wars."[35] Haidt was also one of the founders of Heterodox Academy in 2015, a "nonpartisan collaborative of 5000+ professors, educators, administrators, staff, and students" committed to "open inquiry, viewpoint diversity, and constructive disagreement," according to its official website.[36]

For Haidt and Lukianoff, the root cause of the problem in higher education is the growth of a culture of safetyism and overprotectiveness. Safetyism, or the treatment of safety as a sacred value that trumps everything else, they write, leads to overregulation on the part of campus administrations to protect students from discomforting ideas, often for fear of bad publicity or threats of litigation. "Overregulation is less about policing actual offenses," Haidt and Lukianoff claim; "it is about preventing potential offense."[37] That includes speech, as increasing numbers of cases of deplatforming of guest speakers attest. Several universities have also adopted speech codes in order to eliminate language that might potentially be offensive to marginalized groups. The result, they argue, is an overcautious campus culture where fear and self-censorship reign supreme.

Predictably, *The Coddling of the American Mind* was not greeted with much enthusiasm by the Left. Some claimed that Jonathan Haidt, a social psychologist by training, is simply regurgitating commonplace conservative arguments, lending them a veneer of scientific respectability. Others raised concerns about Haidt's intentions and claimed that he was more interested in slagging off the Left than understanding campus polarization, and that he was either a closet conservative or at best a "useful idiot" for the Right.[38] "Haidt has led the campaign against political correctness, which became the mantra of the Trump movement," said Yale philosopher Jason

Stanley. His Heterodox Academy is a "scaremongering rage machine," Stanley continued, that targets "oppressed minorities who are vastly underrepresented in the academy."[39] In a September 2015 article published in *The New York Times* (the same month the Heterodox Academy was launched), Cornell philosopher Kate Manne slammed the idea that safetyism feeds into "a culture of victimhood" as "alarmist, if not completely implausible."[40] A more serious blow came on December 6, 2016, when Jarret Crawford, a Social Psychology Coordinator at the College of New Jersey and one of the co-founders of Heterodox Academy (HXA), resigned from the latter, accusing it of becoming "a tool for the political right to decry and smear the left." "My decision to leave HXA," wrote Crawford in his resignation letter, "was accelerated by the creation of the Professor Watchlist, a right-wing organization built to monitor and report on left-wing professors." Even though HXA and Haidt have publicly denounced it, "it is difficult not to see the Professor Watchlist as a logical extension of HXA's efforts, and its growing right-wing membership and following."[41]

Similar charges were brought against Greg Lukianoff's Foundation for Individual Rights in Education (FIRE), which received major grants, according to *The American Prospect*, from "the ultra-conservative Earhart, John Templeton, and Lynde and Harry Bradley Foundations; the Scaife family foundations; the Koch-linked Donors Trust."[42] The Right's crusade against progressive academics is not new, Moira Weigel wrote in *The Guardian*, but it was given a fresh lease of life in the final years of Obama's presidency, as movements like Black Lives Matter and #MeToo gathered strength. The conversation again focused on universities, Weigel said, only this time the buzzwords were different, and students received more attention than professors. Haidt and Lukianoff's 2015 article belonged to this decades-old conservative tradition (even the title of their article was a nod to conservative philosopher Allan Bloom's popular treatise against "political correctness," *The*

Closing of the American Mind), and suffered from the same problems as its predecessors. "They cherry-picked anecdotes and caricatured the subjects of their criticism," Weigel said. "They complained that other people were creating and enforcing speech codes, while at the same time attempting to enforce their own speech codes."[43]

These allegations have been consistently denied by Lukianoff and Haidt. Lukianoff insists that he is "a liberal democrat trying to identify and stop what's gone wrong in liberalism."[44] Similarly, Haidt declared that he has "never voted for a Republican, never given a penny to a Republican candidate, never worked for a Republican or conservative cause."[45] "By temperament and disposition and emotions, I'm a liberal," he told *The New York Times*; "but in my beliefs about what's best for the country, I'm a centrist. I'm now really just trying to step back and study things."[46]

Still, it is hard not to detect the anti-Left slant in their writings. Despite repeated pleas for viewpoint diversity and critical thinking, in their 2015 article there is no mention of structural power disparities between the Right and the Left, the billions of dollars funneled into conservative causes by a network of wealthy donors, or the Right's own attempts to stifle free speech. Their book, published three years after the original article and two years into Donald Trump's presidency, does not do any better. Yes, there is a passing reference to Trump's infamous there were "very nice people on both sides" remarks in the wake of the White supremacist showdown in Charlottesville, Virginia, which led to the killing of the 32-year-old paralegal Heather Heyer by a Neo-Nazi. And yet, even then Haidt and Lukianoff are at pains to point to conservatives' efforts to distance themselves from White supremacists, and how the tragic events of Charlottesville presented an opportunity for unity, which was eventually squandered by the campus Left. There is also a brief discussion of "outrage from off-campus Right," but here too, I would argue that the sequence of the polarization cycle they present is heavily biased toward the Right. Hence the cycle begins with a left-wing professor saying or writing something provocative and inflammatory, which is then picked up by the Right, and often distorted, to amplify outrage. The cycle ends with most partisans confirming their worst beliefs about the other side.[47] The authors display genuine concern about the right-wing conservative campus groups which created the above-mentioned Professor Watchlist, but devote only one paragraph to this blatant attack on freedom in their 338-page-long book.

In Harm's Way

But none of this should distract us from the changes that have been taking place in university campuses and, by derivation, in youth activism. Whilst we cannot be certain of the intentions of Haidt, Lukianoff, or other analysts on the Right who complain about "the coddling of the American mind," that does not change the fact that there are issues to be addressed here, though they are not about ridding the Right of ammunition – for they will always find a hot button to stoke a new moral panic – but refocusing identity politics on its original goals of freedom, equality, and justice. A major obstacle that the Left should confront in this context, one that will never be acknowledged by the free market Right, is the infiltration of neoliberal capitalism into today's campus culture, in particular the ways in which *individualism*, *narcissism*, and *consumerism* have been reshaping identity politics.

Perhaps the most glaring manifestation of this is the ongoing expansion of the definition of the concept of "harm," and the practical implications this has on political activism. A decisive moment in this process was the popularization of the term "microaggressions," originally coined by Harvard psychiatrist Chester M. Pierce in 1970 to describe the subtle forms of discrimination experienced by Black people. The term moved to the forefront of campus controversies in 2007, when Columbia psychologist Derald Wing Sue and his co-authors published a widely cited article titled "Racial Microaggressions in Everyday Life," defining it as "brief and commonplace daily verbal, behavioral, and environmental indignities, whether intentional or unintentional, that communicate hostile, derogatory, or negative racial, gender, sexual orientation, and religious slights and insults to the target person or group."[48] Mounting concern over microaggressions led to a whole new vocabulary and the introduction of a host of practices, notably "safe spaces" and "trigger warnings," designed to protect students from potential harm. Some of these concepts, such as "safe spaces," had a long pedigree, but acquired new meanings as more and more universities incorporated them into their official guidelines in the sense of "a place or environment in which people, esp. those belonging to a marginalized group, can feel confident that they will not be exposed to discrimination, criticism, harassment, or any other emotional or physical harm." Others, like "trigger warnings," were of more recent vintage, making it to the *Oxford English Dictionary* only in March 2022, which defined it as "a statement preceding a piece of writing, video, etc., alerting the reader, viewer, etc., to the fact that it contains material or content that may cause distress, esp. by reviving upsetting memories in people who have experienced trauma."[49]

There is of course nothing wrong with the concepts of microaggressions, safe spaces, or trigger warnings per se. In fact, as a well-balanced 2016 PEN America report notes, several studies show that even minor and inadvertent slurs can be a source of long-term harm.[50] The problem here is (i) the fuzziness and arbitrariness of definitions of harm, (ii) the blurring of boundaries and the subsequent creation of a hierarchy between various forms of harm, and (iii) the ways in which perceived or real harm is dealt with. To begin with, there is understandably no objective definition of "emotional harm"; what counts as harm depends almost entirely on the perceptions of particular individuals or groups, and not necessarily those from the most vulnerable ones. Few would disagree today that legally defined hate speech causes harm and needs to be prohibited, but things are much more complicated when it comes to defining what constitutes "offensive speech," which is not only subjective but also highly context-dependent. Hence most commentators shrugged their shoulders when far right provocateur Milo Yiannopoulos was permanently banned from Twitter in 2016, or faced a series of disinvitations following the violent clashes his presence caused at the University of California's Berkeley campus in February 2017. Reactions were mixed when, in 2015, Brown University students created a safe space to offer solace to those who would find a debate on campus sexual assault between feminists Jessica Valenti and Wendy McElroy upsetting. The safe space, *New York Times* journalist Judith Shulevitz reported, "was equipped with cookies, coloring books, bubbles, Play-Doh, calming music, pillows, blankets and a video of frolicking puppies, as well as students and staff members trained to deal with trauma."[51] Similar problems beset what constitutes content that may cause distress. Defenders of trigger warnings liken them to "Parental Advisory" notices affixed to material potentially unsuitable for children. "The costs to students who don't need trigger warnings is minimal," Kate Manne says. "It may even help sensitize them to the fact that some of their classmates will find the material hard going."[52] But scientific evidence points to the contrary. According to an article by Harvard law professor Jeannie Suk Gersen, the results of a dozen studies published between 2018 and 2021 show that trigger warnings do not reduce negative reactions to potentially upsetting content in trauma survivors, or those diagnosed with post-traumatic stress disorder (PTSD).[53] In fact, in some cases the opposite may be true. This was the conclusion of a recent randomized experiment conducted at Harvard University, which found substantial evidence that trigger warnings work in a counter-therapeutic fashion, reinforcing survivors' view of their trauma as central to their identity.[54] The analogy with "Parental Advisory" notices is also self-undermining inasmuch as it equates university students to children under a certain age, incapable of deciding what's good or what's bad for them without the guidance of an adult.

At any rate, the definition of distressing content is also arbitrary and expanding. The risk of a traumatic injury is considered to be similar to actual sexual violence, Suk Gersen wrote in 2014, making it difficult for her to teach about rape law. "Student organizations representing women's interests now routinely advise students that they should not feel pressured to attend or participate in class sessions that focus on the law of sexual violence," she said, as they might "trigger" traumatic memories. "Some students have even suggested that rape law should not be taught because of its potential to cause distress."[55] Somewhat ironically, even the term "trigger warning" could be distressing in this context. Hence an article on trigger warnings published in the *Everyday Feminism* blog on July 7, 2015, started with an Editor's Note which described the word "trigger" as triggering as it "relies on and evokes violent weaponry imagery."[56] The list of triggering material has grown exponentially since 2015. In 2018, a memo sent to Journalism lecturers at Leeds University told them to refrain from using capital letters as they "can generate anxiety and even discourage students from attempting the assessment at all."[57] In 2017, Evergreen State University told professors to take the "emotional commitment" of students who had been involved in recent protests into account when determining their final grades.[58] In 2019, students at Washington University in St. Louis erased the word "vagina" from the title of the popular play, *The Vagina Monologues* – calling it instead *The [Blank] Monologues* – in order to be inclusive of other genitals.[59] The list can be extended infinitely. On the other hand, no trigger warnings were issued when a student doing a Master's degree in Gender (Sexuality) at the London School of Economics (LSE) presented a paper at a conference held in April 2021 which concluded with the following words: "If TERFs think trans* is an endemic threat to feminism, let us be the threat to feminism . . . Picture this: I hold a knife to your throat and spit my transness into your ear. Does that turn you on? Are you scared? I sure fucking hope so."[60]

This last example exposes another problem – the systematic application of double standards. Current definitions of harm, and by extension microaggressions, are premised on a vertical, top-down power dynamic between victims and perpetrators, often associating each role with particular identities which are presumed to be fixed and homogeneous. This leaves no room for agency or change, and it turns both roles into a destiny one cannot escape. It is also deeply flawed, methodologically and politically. It is methodologically flawed because it goes against the grain of decades of critical thinking which rejects any form of essentialism, be it biological or cultural. Surprisingly enough, this move comes from purportedly the most progressive groups in society, notably students, faculty, and younger generations of activists. The essentialist turn is also politically flawed, indeed perilous, for it reduces political resistance to symbolic subversion on issues that are relevant to only a tiny and yes, "privileged," segment of the population. There is a reason why the concept of microaggressions did not catch on among the chronically unemployed and impoverished inhabitants of Mississippi, Louisiana, Kentucky or, on the other side of the Atlantic, of Blackpool, Coventry, Burnley (even though some of these people are among those subject to the worst forms of everyday abuse). Unlike the identity politics of Black queer feminists, which drew its strength from their lived reality, microaggressions were invented and became "a thing" among the relatively well-off and educated members of the middle and upper-middle classes, often with some link to elite Ivy League or Russell Group universities.

It is not only the arbitrariness of definitions of harm that makes these real-life issues so intractable. It is also the over-valuation of victimhood which is increasingly conceived of as a virtue-conferring moral status. As sociologists Bradley Campbell and Jason Manning observe in their book, *The Rise of Victimhood Culture: Microaggressions, Safe Spaces, and the New Culture Wars*, grievances are often aired publicly, not only – or at least, not always – to call attention to systemic injustice, but also to seek sympathy and attract the support of third parties.[61] And once victimhood becomes a moral status, then it could also be a resource for group formation and cohesion which might in turn lead, sometimes inadvertently, to a hierarchy of victimhood where certain forms of harm are considered to be more consequential than others.

On the face of it, this might not be an unreasonable position to hold. There is after all a difference between being subjected to online abuse or bullying and actual acts of violence as – to pick an off-campus, but highly pertinent example – the stabbing of award-winning writer Salman Rushdie before his lecture at the Chautauqua Institution in Buffalo, New York, on August 12, 2022 painfully reminded us. Here, it is important to remember that despite living in hiding for several years because of a fatwa issued by the Iranian Supreme Leader Ayatollah Ruhollah Khomeini calling for his assassination following the publica-tion of his novel *The Satanic Verses*, Rushdie himself never claimed to be a victim. "One thing I feel, well, proud of," he said in an interview he gave in 2021, "is if you knew nothing about my life, if all you had were my books, I don't think you would feel that something traumatic happened to me in 1989. I'm glad I had the brains to think in the middle of all that: I don't want to be the victim of this. I could write frightened or revenge books, and both would make me a creature of the event."[62] Obviously, we cannot expect the same defiant attitude from everybody – in the face of such a serious threat. But that is not the problem with most claims of victimhood today, on or off campus; rather, it is the manipulation and deliberate exploitation of victim status, often with the purpose of claiming the moral high ground in politically charged conflictive situations which may or may not involve real harm. In any case, what is real harm? How can we compare, say, the trauma of a female sexual assault survivor who is triggered by the presence of a naked pre-op trans woman in a single-sex dressing room with that of a trans woman who is rejected by her family, pushed out onto the streets or denied employment?[63] Both traumas are real, as long as they are felt as such, and both cause harm. Who decides which trauma is worse, or more important, than the other?

Going back to campus politics, this brings us to the third, and final, problem with the expansion of the definition of harm. More often than not, the victimhood hierarchy is established by the most radical members of a particular identity group – activists, various associations, and lobby groups – and enforced by university administrations in line with existing legislation. Haidt and Lukianoff miss a crucial point when they describe this as a matter of overregulation by zealous university bureaucracies, since the latter are simply responding to a demand, trying to keep up with the neoliberal logic of the identity economy. Universities need to work with, or are simply obliged to follow, the rules set by governments, as in the case of what is known as the "Dear Colleague" letters of the US Department of Education's Office for Civil Rights. And this is another reason why victimhood claims are made publicly. Once a complaint is made, universities are compelled to take action, deploying government-issued laws, such as the Title IX of the Education Amendments of 1972 by the Office for Civil Rights in the US or the Equality Act 2010 in the UK. Expanding definitions of harm and the subsequent proliferation of victimhood claims lead higher education institutions to take preventive measures, setting up safe spaces for designated vulnerable groups, or adopting detailed and regularly updated speech codes which determine what could be said or taught in campus. As sensitivities change, so does the definition of what constitutes offensive speech, or even "harassment," as demonstrated in the widely publicized case of Laura Kipnis, a cultural critic and professor emerita in the Department of Radio/TV/ Film at Northwestern University, who went through two Title IX investigations – one in 2015 for writing a polemical article titled "Sexual Paranoia Strikes Academe" in *The Chronicle of Higher Education*; another in 2017, this time for writing a book about her previous investigation.[64]

Needless to say, the Right is also heavily invested in victimhood and policing speech even if it uses different terms to describe the same phenomena. But this is only to be expected. As we saw in chapter 2, the Right lives *off* and *for* culture wars, and spends vast amounts of resources to keep the fire of moral panic burning. What is surprising is the Left's complicity in culture wars, and its willing or unthinking appropriation of the Right's ways – the censorship, the intolerance, the demonization of the "enemy within," and a growing tendency to appeal to outside authority to "discipline and punish" or to impose a particular version of truth.[65]

The disciplinary turn of the Left is the end result of a cycle that begins with an expansion of the meaning of harm and erosion of the boundaries between individual and collective, and physical and emotional suffering; it continues with overvaluation of victimhood as a moral status opposed to privilege and the creation of a hierarchy of victimhood; and it concludes by transforming identity, which was originally a tool for justice, into a sacred value in and of itself, a commodity that needs to be safeguarded at any cost. The anti-capitalist logic of identity politics is replaced by a neoliberal logic which turns *activists into entrepreneurs* (here I am using "neoliberalism" in the sense in which American political theorist Wendy Brown uses the term, not simply as an economic system, but a "rationality [which] involves extending and disseminating market values to all institutions and social action").[66] Paradoxical as it may seem, campus activists are "the model neoliberal citizen" that Brown talks about, "one who strategizes for her/himself among various social, political and economic options, not one who strives with others to alter or organize these options." Identity politics loses its revolutionary potential and becomes "the opposite of public-minded"; "the body politic ceases to be a body but is, rather, a group of individual entrepreneurs and consumers."[67]

But the Left cannot win the fight for justice by becoming a copy of its rival, and a cheap one at that for it lacks the immense resources the Right possesses. For every classical text dropped from the canon in the name of "decolonizing the curriculum," the Right moves hundreds, if not thousands, of books from libraries through lobbying or the force of law. Hence PEN America's "Index of School Book Bans" lists 2,532 instances of individual books being banned in 138 school districts in 32 states from July 2021 to June 2022. The report estimates that at least 40 percent of bans listed "are connected to either proposed or enacted legislation, or to political pressure exerted by state officials or elected lawmakers to restrict the teaching or presence of certain books or concepts." It probably will not surprise you to learn that the bans aim at pushing through a reactionary/conservative agenda: 41 percent of the titles explicitly address LGBTQ+ themes or have protagonists or prominent secondary characters who are LGBTQ+; 40 percent contain protagonists or prominent secondary characters of color; and 21 percent directly address issues of race and racism.[68] Other data show that 42 states in the US have introduced bills or other measures that would restrict the teaching of Critical Race Theory or limit how teachers can discuss racism and sexism.[69] While the Right rampages through schools and legislatures, the Left is stuck in endless navel-gazing and bickering over which pronouns to use for particular individuals, "recklessly flinging" the word fascist in every direction – to use George Orwell's ageless expression. Nothing illustrates the fusion of the Right and the Left into one humongous outrage machine better than what has come to be widely known as "cancel culture."

Cancel Culture

On July 7, 2020, *Harper's Magazine* published a fairly unexceptionable op-ed on threats to free speech, titled "A Letter on Justice and Open Debate." Coordinated by writer and *Harper's* columnist Thomas Chatterton Williams and penned by historian David Greenberg, writer Mark Lilla, and journalists Robert Worth and George Packer, the letter was signed by 153 well-known intellectuals and artists, including plain old liberals, Right or Left, such as Anne Applebaum, Michael Ignatieff, Garry Kasparov, Margaret Atwood, J. K. Rowling, Salman Rushdie, as well as figures with undeniably radical progressive credentials such as Noam Chomsky, Todd Gitlin, and Cornel West.[70] "Our cultural institutions are facing a moment of trial," declared the opening line of the letter, published at a time when the US was rocked by riots and protests over the killing of George Floyd. The need for police reform, greater equality, and inclusion was long overdue, the letter continued. But "this needed reckoning has also intensified a new set of moral attitudes and political commitments that tend to weaken our norms of open debate and toleration of differences in favor of ideological conformity":

> The free exchange of information and ideas, the lifeblood of a liberal society, is daily becoming more constricted. While we have come to expect this on the radical right, censoriousness is also spreading more widely in our culture: an intolerance of opposing views, a vogue for public shaming and ostracism, and

the tendency to dissolve complex policy issues in a blinding moral certainty.[71]

The response to the letter by the Left was swift. "The irony of several notable figures arguing that they have been 'silenced' in a prominent American magazine was not lost on many readers," wrote Sarah Manavis of the *New Statesman*. Cancel culture reflects "a collective desire for those in positions of power to be held responsible for their perceived wrongdoings," and "facing consequences for what you say and do is not a free speech violation."[72] "The letter is an example of how elites rush to occupy the moral high ground when their authority as arbiters of intellectual and political life is challenged from both the left and the right," said the Indian essayist and novelist Pankaj Mishra in *The Guardian*.[73] "Free speech has never been more widely available than it is today," he retorted on another occasion. "If those culpable for today's abysmal moral and political climate sense anger and frustration against them among younger people," he continued, "it is because they have never been held accountable."[74] None of the signatories attracted as much attention as J. K. Rowling whose name and picture featured in the headline of almost every piece of reporting on the letter, from *The Independent* and *The Guardian* to *The Washington Post*, *The Atlantic*, *The American Prospect*, CNBC, and BBC, among many others. For some, this was precisely why the letter was published. "J.K. Rowling and Other Assorted Rich Fools Want to Cancel 'Cancel Culture'," read the headline of *The Daily Beast*;[75] "Rich, Famous Transphobes Ask You to Stop Being So Mean to Them," said the feminist "geek culture" ezine, *The Mary Sue*.[76] *Pink News* was surprised to see Margaret Atwood, who "took a stand on trans rights," among the signatories alongside Rowling.[77]

The letter was also criticized for its timing and vagueness, and provoked a counter-letter by 150 other leading names of the culture industry. The *Harper's* Letter missed the point, wrote the authors of "A More Specific Letter on Justice and Open Debate." "Nowhere in it do the signatories mention how marginalized voices have been silenced for generations in journalism, academia, and publishing." The rest was a shopping list of trending buzzwords: elitism, bigotry, White, wealthy and privileged, with an honorary mention of Rowling for spouting "transphobic and transmisogynist rhetoric." The *Harper's* Letter "seeks to uphold a 'stifling atmosphere' and prioritizes signal-blasting their discomfort in the face of valid criticism," the critics concluded. "The intellectual freedom of cis white intellectuals has never been under threat en masse" and "they have never faced serious consequences – only momentary discomfort."[78]

Reactions to the *Harper's* Letter were a perfect example of woke Left denialism (of the neoliberal commodification and weaponization of identity), lack of insight (with regard to the myriad ways in which the contemporary Left appropriated the Right's tactics and "us versus them" mentality), projection and blame shifting (it's a dog whistle for the far right), narcissism (we have the moral high ground on account of possessing the right identity and victimhood credentials), and intellectual laziness (unwillingness to engage with arguments, and the frequent use of *ad hominem* attacks).

There is of course a lot to unpack here, but first a reminder. The *Oxford English Dictionary* defines cancel culture "as the action or practice of publicly boycotting, ostracizing, or withdrawing support from a person, institution, etc., thought to be promoting culturally unacceptable ideas." Though generally accurate, this definition is incomplete. Cancel culture, as practiced today, goes way beyond "boycotting, ostracizing, or withdrawing support." It covers a wide spectrum of sanctions from public naming and shaming and job loss to violation of basic rights such as due process, presumption of innocence, proportionality, and on occasion involves outright attacks in the form of verbal and physical abuse, even death threats

– often for an indefinite period of time. After all, as historian and journalist Anne Applebaum points out in an incisive essay, for cancellers, or what she calls the "New Puritans," "there is no statute of limitations."[79] Cancel culture is more than a boycott to draw attention to systemic injustice or abuse of power. It is a call for retribution and revenge. Perhaps the best way to understand these problems is to subject some of the arguments used to defend cancel culture to critical scrutiny.

Cancel culture does not exist. The most common argument in defense of cancel culture is also the flimsiest one: cancel culture is a myth, the proverbial monster under the bed.[80] You do not see it, yet you fear it. Woke Left denialism takes one of two forms: wholesale rejection or trivializing. For barrister Sam Fowles writing in Politics.co.uk, this is a "pseudo-crisis" invented by a small but highly influential group who claimed the mantle of free speech to expand coercive state power over what can be said in public. These people might normally be "dismissed as cranks," says Fowles, but they exercise considerable power over the government and laws.[81] Political correctness (in many ways, the antecedent to cancel culture) is "a useful invention for the Republican right because it helped the movement to drive a wedge between working-class people and the Democrats who claimed to speak for them," writes Moira Weigel of *The Guardian*.[82] Others, like Pankaj Mishra, choose to play down the impact of cancel culture. "Institutions and businesses have long been able to fire employees at will," he says. "A few may have acted even more hastily in recent months out of fear of being publicly shamed, or the desire to appear in tune with the anti-racist zeitgeist," but that should not be overstated.[83]

As a "crank" who believes that cancel culture does exist, I cannot help but notice the similarities between the Left and the Right's denialism. Censorship and silencing have been a hallmark of reactionary thinking throughout history. Overlooking this centuries-old tradition, the contemporary

Right is all too happy to cast the blame on the Left, avoiding any discussion of progressives who are cancelled for their pro-Palestine, pro-Antifa, or pro-Black Lives Matter views, not to mention the hysterical anti-Critical Race Theory campaign currently sweeping across the US. An almost identical rhetorical move has been embraced by the woke Left which rushes to dismiss cancel culture as the latest example of a right-wing moral panic or, in Stanley Cohen's words, a condition, episode, person, or group of persons that is perceived as a threat to societal values and interests.[84] The problem here, of course, is that most targets of woke cancel culture are liberals or fellow progressives, who are considered to be posing a greater challenge to established orthodoxies. When *The Observer*, the sister paper of *The Guardian*, published an editorial on the right to free expression on June 27, 2021, *Guardian* writer Owen Jones was the first to tweet: "The Observer newspaper has written another editorial legitimising the obsessive media onslaught against trans people, during Pride month and on the weekend of Trans Pride. The same newspaper backed the Iraq war. They were on the wrong side of history then, and they are again."[85] How did *The Observer* end up being on the wrong side of history? By simply arguing that "there is growing evidence that women who have expressed a set of feminist beliefs that have come to be known as 'gender-critical' have, in some cases, faced significant professional penalties as a result," and that this should be of concern to anyone who claims to be a democrat.[86] Jones's tweet was not a stand-alone. Speaking of what she calls "white feminism," Alison Phipps, a professor of Sociology at the University of Glasgow, says: "These feminist groups are using the trope of gender ideology in their attacks on trans people. And they know – they must know, it's been pointed out to them so many times – that this is a far-right dogwhistle."[87] This move allows woke denialists to deprive their interlocutors of their status as legitimate conversational partners. "Why should trans people have to treat anti-trans voices as legitimate argumentative partners," *Vox*'s Zack Beauchamp asks, "when no one would, for instance, expect a Jewish writer (like me) to debate a neo-Nazi?"[88]

The delegitimization of critical voices is intrinsically related to the expansion of the definition of harm. Once harm is redefined to include perceived emotional suffering, which is sometimes equated with existential threat, then any questioning of received wisdom becomes out of bounds, and free speech is restricted. Some believe that this is to conflate speech with platform, and censorship with criticism. The second point here is plainly false; cancelling is not criticism (if it were, there would be no point in discussing it), and champions of cancel culture know that. It can, and often does, involve real sanctions such as loss of one's job, income, permanent reputational damage, and social ostracism. The first point, on the other hand, is correct, at least in theory; "Speech is a right, platform is a privilege," Sam Fowles tells us. "Universities and students unions are independent organisations and are entitled to offer their platform to whoever they choose."[89] But cancel culture does not only target particular individuals; it involves widespread and systematic deplatforming of an entire set of views; it establishes, as the *OED* definition shows, the boundaries of acceptable speech. It is important to remember here that institutions, in particular universities, are not ideological monoliths. Certain viewpoints may be deemed offensive by some groups of students, but welcome by others – not to mention the obvious fact that progressive views are held by a minority within the population as a whole. As we have seen earlier, the original model of identity politics did not consider diversity of opinion as an obstacle to community-based activism; it sought ways to work with or around it, and even to learn from it. Cancel culture denialists would do well to listen to activists who have to deal with difference on a day-to-day basis rather than counterposing freedom of speech to freedom to life (so far as marginalized groups are concerned)[90] which is, at the end of the day, a form of "moral blackmail."[91] As Alicia Garza, one of the co-founders of the Black Lives Matter movement, put it:

> Our movements also have to be composed of people from across the class spectrum and people who also have power. Right? If we want to compete for power, then part of what it means is we have to amass our power as a unit. And it also means we have to take some of theirs . . . our vision for what a new society can look like has to appeal to more than just the intellectual class of activists and organizers.[92]

Cancel culture is about accountability and agency. According to its protagonists, cancel culture is about dismantling existing power relations. "Our new wave of social justice activism contends that arguments from minority groups deserve a special kind of deference," writes Zack Beauchamp; "that white people should 'listen to Black voices' on racism and grant authority to their lived experiences in conversations about oppression."[93] "These are not 'attacks on free speech' but, rather, examples of traditionally privileged individuals being treated like everyone else," says Sam Fowles.[94] As such, it is an example of agency, and a form of activism. Writing in *The Chronicle of Higher Education*, philosophers Kate Manne and Jason Stanley agree: "Oppressed people are often met with the political analogue of stonewalling. In order to be heard, they need to shout; and when they shout, they are told to lower their voices." Their freedom of speech is often curtailed by this "tone policing."[95] In this respect, cancel culture is liberating; it brings the perspectives of marginalized groups into the public sphere.

There are several problems with these arguments. First, they are all based on a static understanding of power relations, a problem that I discussed at some length earlier. This presumption is still true on a systemic level – People of Color, women, LGBTQ+ people, the poor are indeed chronically oppressed and discriminated against – but that does not explain individual cases. Not all attempts at cancelling can be read as a last-ditch appeal for justice by the powerless. On the contrary, in some cases, it is not until "the powerful" take up the cause that these attempts gain momentum. Take #MeToo. The original, unhashtagged Me Too was founded by Tarana Burke, a Black civil rights activist in the Bronx, who was herself sexually abused and raped as a child and teenager. In 1997, after a young girl told her that she'd been abused by her mother's boyfriend, she didn't know what to say, and afterwards wished she'd said "me too." This led her to found first the non-profit organization, Just Be Inc., for girls from minority groups aged between 12 and 18, which is, as its website states, "focused on the health, well-being and wholeness of brown girls everywhere" and then, in 2006, the Me Too movement, using the Myspace page. Yet the movement became viral only on October 15, 2017, after the "White" American actress Alyssa Milano created the hashtag #MeToo to draw attention to endemic sexual assault and harassment of women. Her message was retweeted nearly a million times in 48 hours, and spread to other social media platforms like Facebook where it was shared more than 12 million times in 24 hours.[96] Was this a case of punching up? It was, but nobody heard about it until a White woman with privilege and large platform took over the movement. Was it a victory for the powerless? Certainly, as it brought down several powerful abusers like Harvey Weinstein and Bill Cosby. But it was not all black-and-white, as its original founder Tarana Burke commented in an interview she gave in 2018. #MeToo has also brought ". . . this extreme backlash and this narrative that's not useful with this work we're doing around it being a witch hunt – basically, just watching the idea of Me Too become weaponized has been a challenge."[97]

Second, power dynamics change, even at the systemic level. Transgender people are still a disadvantaged group, especially if they are also non-White and poor, but there is also an influential trans rights movement today, involving charities like Stonewall (with over 900 organizations across the UK registered in its Diversity Champions Program) and Mermaids, NGOs such as GLAAD (Gay & Lesbian Alliance Against Defamation) in the US, in addition to friendly governments and politicians, media organizations, lobby groups, and multinational corporations. It is telling that most woke commentators who purportedly reject cancel culture are also its foremost practitioners on this particular issue, leading cancel campaigns against women, lesbians and, yes, transgender people – students, academics, and activists alike – for raising concerns about certain aspects of trans rights activism, or even the definition of the term "woman." One need only browse through the regularly updated Academics for Academic Freedom's (AFAF) list of "individuals who were banned from speaking at universities in the UK and Ireland, or faced campaigns to silence them, or sack them for their views" (both by the woke Left and the Right), to grasp the magnitude of these crusades.[98] In fact, the findings of a recent survey on "Academia's Gender Wars" show that what protagonists call "trans-inclusive feminism" is now the dominant position in Gender Studies departments of universities in the UK. Out of 51 academics "who self-define as feminist and research and/or teach on topics related to gender studies" interviewed by City, University of London's Laura Favaro from October 2020 to December 2021, 11 held senior editorship positions at feminist, gender, and sexuality studies journals. "All confirmed that genderist perspectives dominate these publications," Favaro says, "in the sense that 'on the editorial board, none of us would describe ourselves as in the gender critical camp'." The 11 interviewees also hinted at the preferred perspective of authors, readers, and publishing houses. "For some, it was a matter of scholarly values, with gender-critical feminism described as 'wrong-headed', 'outdated' or 'completely delegitimised'." Others, however, acknowledged that "the objection is a political one."[99]

Third, and at the risk of reiterating, it is not only celebrities or the powerful who become the target of cyber avengers. Ordinary people are cancelled too, for posting an off-the-cuff comment, inadvertently using a politically incorrect term, or being on "the wrong side of history" without even knowing what the right and the wrong sides are. Few had heard of Justine Sacco, the Senior Director of Corporate Communications at a private company (IAC), until she shared a tacky tweet with her 170 followers during a layover at Heathrow on her way to South Africa on December 20, 2013: "Going to Africa. Hope I don't get AIDS. Just kidding. I'm white!" She then boarded her plane and slept through an 11-hour flight. She turned on her phone again when the plane landed in Cape Town, only to realize that her tweet had gone viral. Among the thousands of comments, there was one by a co-worker who said, "I'm an IAC employee and I don't want @JustineSacco doing any communications on our behalf ever again. Ever," followed by a tweet from the employer itself, IAC, the corporate owner of *The Daily Beast*, OKCupid, and Vimeo: "This is an outrageous, offensive comment. Employee in question currently unreachable on an intl flight." The anger soon turned into excitement, writes journalist Jon Ronson who interviewed Sacco for his book *So You've Been Publicly Shamed*, and a hashtag began trending worldwide: #hasjustinelandedyet. Some people even found out which flight she was on and linked the hashtag to a flight tracker website so that everyone could watch its progress in real time. During the 11 days between December 20 and the end of December, Sacco's name was googled 1,220,000 times (up from 30 the previous month).[100] It took more than a year for Sacco to find a job. But the internet never forgets. At the time of writing, the infamous tweet is still the first thing we encounter when we type her name in Google. Indeed, there is no statute of limitations for either the cancellers, or indeed the cancelled!

Finally, the narrow focus on power relations also conceals the protagonists' own privileged positions. Almost all outspoken critics of the *Harper's* Letter in particular, and cancel culture in general, are themselves prominent intellectuals, not random bloggers or hapless victims of systemic oppression with no other platform than an anonymous Twitter account. If they can claim to be "speaking for" the powerless, then why not use the same argument for the writers of the *Harper's* Letter? How do we know that the signatories are "a bunch of wealthy blowhards" or "assorted rich fools" trying to protect their privileged positions, as *The Daily Beast* tells us – and note the populist anti-intellectualism of this argument?[101] What if the reverse is true? What if cancel culture denialists themselves are the new elites who live off woke sensibilities, much like right-wing culture warriors? And it is not just activists in university campuses; it is also the legacy media, culture industry, and a significant part of the corporate world, as I have noted above. Yes, we have several reactionary outlets with desks devoted to digging out every cancellation attempt in the US and the UK. But we also have an equal number of so-called progressive platforms with counter-insurgency units ready to be activated the moment a cancel attempt makes right-wing headlines. We do not know the extent to which the latter are concerned with the well-being of marginalized groups, but we can safely assume that they care for profit, the main driver of identity politics of all hues. In that sense, cancel culture is not immune to commodification; it *is* commodification – and *commodification with an attitude*.

Does this mean that the powerful and the privileged should be beyond criticism? Are we supposed to refrain from calling out systemic injustice and inequality, say, ongoing police brutality, income disparities, suppression of voting rights, judicial bias against People of Color, endemic harassment and sexual abuse against women or LGBTQ+ people? Of course not! But, to hammer the point home, cancel culture is *not* criticism. The differences can be sometimes difficult to observe in practice, but as American author and journalist Jonathan Rauch summarizes in his 2021 book *The Constitution of Knowledge: A Defense of Truth*:

> Criticism seeks to engage in conversations and identify error; canceling seeks to stigmatize conversations and punish the errant. Criticism cares whether statements are true; canceling cares about their social effects . . . Criticism is a substitute for social punishment (we kill our hypotheses rather than each other); canceling is a form of social punishment (we kill your hypothesis by killing you socially).[102]

Perhaps more importantly, cancel culture does not seek redemption or redress. One may try to apologize, of course, but apologies are parsed, examined for sincerity, and then rejected, writes Anne Applebaum. As apologies have become ritualized, "they invariably seem insincere. Websites now offer 'sample templates' for people who need to apologize; some universities offer advice on how to apologize to students and employees, and even include lists of good words to use (*mistake, misunderstand, misinterpret*)." In any case, not many are interested in an apology. Cancel campaigns call for instant, often disproportionate, retribution without due process. They do not want to forgive; "they want to punish and purify."[103]

Cancel culture does not have real-life consequences. Even if all the above were true, it does not matter, supporters tell us, since cancel culture rarely has any real-life consequences. "The majority of those 'cancelled', like J.K. Rowling, Dave Chappelle, or Aziz Ansari," Sarah Manavis tells us, "go on to experience continuing commercial success. Even those rare cases where a job is lost, it's often that they never needed that job in the first place."[104] In fact, in many cases, the opposite is true. In the wake of Rowling's "transphobic manifesto," Aja Romano writes, the sales of her books actually "increased tremendously" in her home country.[105] Comedian Aziz Ansari was back to Netflix with a special directed by Spike Jonze a year after a sexual misconduct allegation surfaced against him on Babe.net.[106] And despite a huge backlash to his comments on transgender people, comedian Dave Chappelle's Netflix special "The Closer" was nominated for two Emmy Awards in 2022.

Once again, these arguments are deeply flawed on several levels. First, the fact that someone survives cancellation does not mean that we should not take those campaigns seriously. Some, like J. K. Rowling or Dave Chappelle, are simply too big to cancel. Often, however, this makes the attacks more vicious, and all the more dangerous. On May 3, 2022, Dave Chappelle was tackled onstage by a member of the audience who, carrying a replica gun equipped with a knife blade, said "I identify as bisexual . . . and I wanted him to know what he said was triggering."[107] On June 14, 2022, a trans rights activist shared J. K. Rowling's family address on Twitter, alongside the picture of a bomb-making manual (the tweet in question remained online for hours despite violating Twitter's terms of services).[108] Another, and more serious, threat to Rowling's life followed the savage stabbing of Salman Rushdie on August 12, 2022. Hours after the attack, J. K. Rowling took to Twitter to express her shock with the words, "Horrifying news," only to be threatened with death herself by a religious extremist Twitter account. "Don't worry you are next," said the user of the account who had earlier called Rushdie's attacker a "revolutionary." Even though Police Scotland took the threat seriously and immediately started an investigation, Twitter itself did not find the threat in violation of its terms of services (the tweet was deleted one day later, after a huge public backlash).[109] In the meantime, author Joanne Harris, the chair of the Society of Authors (SoA) – the UK's largest trade union for writers – launched a Twitter poll, asking her followers whether they had ever received a death threat, with the following answer options: "Yes," "Hell, yes," "No, never," and "Show me, dammit." The poll was considered by some to be "a sideswipe at J.K. Rowling" and led to an open letter penned by feminist author and activist Julie Bindel, signed by more than 100 writers and industry professionals, calling for Harris's resignation as "Chair of the Management Committee" of SoA.[110] Harris did not resign from her position, dismissing the row as an instance of a "fabricated culture war."[111]

But the row between Rowling, Bindel, and Harris is not the heart of the matter here. The key question is whether the death threat itself was fabricated. Should we ignore such threats? More generally, how should progressives broach attacks on freedom of speech? The answer is easy when the attack comes from the reactionary Right. What about speech that is deemed to be offensive by woke identity activists? Should we just dismiss it as "fabricated" as Joanne Harris does? Should we stick to the mantra "cancel culture doesn't exist" as Pankaj Mishra does in a hastily written op-ed in the wake of Rushdie's stabbing? Unlike "bonesaw-wielding Saudi goons," virtual lynch mobs "have not managed to silence" any of the Western signatories of the *Harper's* Letter, he writes, without much reflection on alternative, and less benevolent, readings of his rather peculiar choice of words (i.e., "silence"). We should not link the attack on Rushdie to cancel culture – an "unproven and unprovable notion," he concludes. "Lacking concrete evidence for widespread stifling of free speech, culture warriors have become purveyors of fearful speculation."[112] But why does Mishra not tell us that Salman Rushdie himself was one of the "purveyors of fearful speculation" as a signatory of the *Harper's* Letter? Might he have forgotten about it?

And how do we define real-life consequences? Having a successful career or resuming it after a hiatus does not offset the mental, social, or indeed financial toll of cancellation attempts. Rowling – herself a domestic abuse and sexual assault survivor – may continue to sell books, but this does not mean she is unaffected by the death or rape threats she has been receiving on a daily basis since she publicly expressed her views on what she perceives as a threat to women's rights (and lest we forget, subjective perceptions have objective value in woke world-view). In the case of Benny Fredriksson, the artistic director of Stockholm's Kulturhuset Stadsteatern, the city's leading arts and culture center, who was accused by the country's leading tabloid *Aftonbladet* for allegedly abusing employees, real-life consequences were harsher. Six months after he resigned from his job in 2018, he committed suicide while accompanying his wife, the Swedish opera star Anne Sofie von Otter, in Australia. The investigation following his death revealed that the allegations were presented in a misleading way, and the newspaper did not publish the testimonies of several actresses who supported him by refuting the accusations.[113]

What about the price paid by ordinary people with no platform or resources to share their stories, or the passive victims of particular cancel campaigns? One of the most damaging aspects of the cancel culture, and again one that distinguishes it from traditional boycotts and commonplace criticism, is its performative character. Those who join online mobs are more interested in "virtue-signaling" and moral grandstanding than in bringing about structural change since, in the free market of woke activism, the possession of the "right virtues" is itself a value and a means to status attainment. Often, this has a chilling effect on those who deviate from the norm, discouraging them from speaking out or showing support for fear of being a *target by association*. The feeling is well summarized by freelance journalist Marie Le Conte who has become the target of a Twitter pile-on for calling Alexandria Ocasio-Cortez's "scruffy" partner a "bin racoon" in a self-described "mean tweet" (both Ocasio-Cortez and her partner laughed at the joke on Instagram):

> It's hard to describe what it feels like, being the main charac-ter on Twitter. People tweet at you, at first to criticize what you said, then insulting you for what you said, then trying to find other things you said to criticize and insult you for, then

moving on to discussing your appearance, what you may be like in bed, and anything else they can think of. They also tweet about you, which is more disconcerting if you aren't a celebrity, which I am not. They are no longer talking to you but about you to each other; it's a book club and you're the book.[114]

When confronted with these examples, champions of cancel culture resort to various logical fallacies, in particular "whataboutism" – the practice of responding to an accusation by making a counter-accusation or raising a different issue – or invoking unverified statistics. This is precisely why the expansion of the concept of harm and the subsequent creation of a hierarchy of victimhood are, well, harmful. We do not know the exact number of people who find Rowling's comments transphobic and those who do not, and why the former find these comments transphobic; is it the message or the medium, the online hysteria which surrounds every 280 words she posts? Then there are others who find American philosopher and gender theorist Judith Butler's views on gender-critical feminists as well as their use of the term "TERF" problematic, if not outright offensive. "I am not aware that terf is used as a slur," they say in an extended interview they gave to *The New Statesman*. "If they do favour exclusion, why not call them exclusionary? If they understand themselves as belonging to that strain of radical feminism that opposes gender reassignment, why not call them radical feminists?" It is painful to see, they conclude, "that Trump's position that gender should be defined by biological sex, and that the evangelical and right-wing Catholic effort to purge 'gender' from education and public policy accords with the trans-exclusionary radical feminists' return to biological essentialism."[115] Whose harm counts more? That of Rowling who is subject to constant online abuse for her alleged views on trans rights, of Butler who laments the far right backlash against feminist and LGBTQ+ rights, of LGBTQ+ people who are offended by Rowling's alleged views, radical feminists who resent their association with the far right and the use of the term TERF to refer to them, or of far right Christians who are unhappy with progressive legislation which they perceive to be contrary to the conservative values they hold dear?

The answer, obviously, depends on who you are asking. This should be a no-brainer for today's activists, who proudly trace the origins of their politics to the moral relativism of French postmodernist thought. Yet, bizarrely enough, when it comes to promoting "its truth," the woke Left is no less absolutist than the Right. The inevitable corollary of this rigid stance, which reduces all differences of opinion to an existential threat to this or that marginalized group, is the (in)famous "no debate" position popularized by the pro-LGBTQ+ charity Stonewall, encapsulated in the following statement: "We will always debate issues that enable us to further equality but what we will not do is debate trans people's rights to exist."[116] On the face of it, this position is reasonable, and no one who calls oneself a progressive should have qualms with it. The problem begins when the woke Left presents itself, in American journalist Chris Hedges's words, as "self-appointed moral arbiters of speech," deciding who or what views challenge a particular group's right to exist.[117] Once that line is crossed, power relations become bamboozling and we move into the realm of outrage, the *great political neutralizer.*

In Outrage We Trust

When academics Jeffrey M. Berry and Sarah Sobieraj wrote their book *The Outrage Industry: Political Opinion Media and the New Incivility* in 2014, their aim was to explore the new genre of political opinion media they called "outrage," which is defined by the rhetoric it uses, "its hallmark venom, vilification of opponents, and hyperbolic reinterpretations of current events."[118] Controversial and provocative content has always been part of the US media landscape, they conceded, but the sheer volume and popularity of outrage-based commentary, particularly on the Right, made it a new ball game. In the early 2010s, at the time of the publication of the book, influential right-wing media personalities like Rush Limbaugh or Sean Hannity attracted 15 and 14 million weekly listeners to their respective radio shows. Berry and Sobieraj's overall estimate for talk radio, using data for the top 12 hosts, was roughly 35 million listeners daily. Even though the book was focused on the development of the genre in the right-wing media landscape, the authors did not shy away from pointing to the commonalities between the Right and the Left:

> the way conservative and progressive commentators use outrage unites them . . . Consider practices such as using ideologically extremizing language (e.g., describing someone as "far-right wing" or "far-left wing"), "proving" an opponent is a hypocrite (often with decontextualized quotes offered as evidence), presenting their version of current affairs as the "real story" and other accounts as biased. Taken together, we find remarkable mirroring between conservatives and progressives. There are scripts that could easily be rewritten for the other side by simply replacing the nouns.[119]

I cannot help but wonder whether Berry and Sobieraj would be able to write this in 2022 without attracting the ire of online outrage mobs from both sides of the political divide. For the Right, what we are witnessing today is a "free speech" crisis generated by woke takeover of institutions of higher education, a process which can only be reversed by "external government intervention."[120] For the woke Left, this is simply right-wing propaganda. Regurgitating the argument from accountability and agency, Jason Stanley and Kate Manne claim that free speech is being co-opted by privileged groups and "distorted to serve their interests, and used to silence those who are oppressed and marginalized."[121] Nesrine Malik doubles down in *The Guardian* and argues that "The purpose [of the myth of the free speech crisis] is to secure the licence to speak with impunity; not freedom of expression, but rather freedom from the consequences of that expression."[122]

But the outrage industry is not the outcome of a free speech crisis, for the issue is not whether speech is restricted or not. It is about *what counts as free speech* and *who makes that decision*. Conflict over the definition of free speech, or to recall the expression used in official definitions of cancel culture, the boundaries of what is culturally acceptable and what is unacceptable, is the oil that greases the wheels of the outrage machine. And it is here that the reactionaries and the woke Left team up. The Right is completely blind to reactionary cancel campaigns or, more generally, the all-out assault on fundamental rights and freedoms by conservative (at times openly and proudly illiberal) legislatures and executives all around the world. One need only mention the recent Supreme Court decision to overturn the constitutional right to abortion which was established by the landmark 1973 ruling in *Roe v Wade*, or the slew of anti-Critical Race Theory bills and educational gag orders that target speech about LGBTQ+ groups (and this is only the US).[123] The woke Left, on the other hand, is more concerned with policing speech and identifying microaggressions among fellow progressives than building a common front against the Right's transgressions. Much like the Right, it is oblivious to egregious breaches of fundamental freedoms when they are committed by what they perceive as disadvantaged groups, claiming the authority to determine who the victims and the perpetrators are. This move allows them to create a false moral binary between freedom of speech on the one hand, and the sanctity of life on the other – a tripwire blocking the road to progress.[124] But why do new activists retreat into performative outrage instead of fighting for real change? Is it because they lack the courage or the organizational skills to take on actual centers of power, as Chris Hedges claims?[125] Or is this an inevitable outcome of the commodification of identity I discussed in the previous chapter which, with the encouragement of legacy media and big corporations, also leads to the *domestication of progressive politics*? Outrage provokes emotional responses from the audience, Berry and Sobieraj inform us, through the use of "overgeneralizations, sensationalism, misleading or patently inaccurate information, *ad hominem* attacks, and belittling ridicule of opponents." More importantly, it "sidesteps the messy nuances of complex political issues in favor of melodrama, misrepresentative exaggeration, mockery, and hyperbolic forecasts of impending doom."[126] It creates a safe space for those who think alike, not only reducing potential risks for the participants, but also producing a sense of community and belonging, by isolating them in echo chambers. At the end of the day, however, outrage kills politics. Or, in Hedges's snappy formulation, "it turns antipolitics into politics."[127]

What the Left needs is a new vision that would break the outrage cycle, a socially and economically progressive agenda that would include all those who are negatively affected by rampant neoliberalism. The aim of the final chapter is to give an account of how such an agenda can be achieved.

5

Toward a New Progressive Left

Black Lives Matter

On February 26, 2012, Trayvon Benjamin Martin, a 17-year-old African American high-school junior from Miami Gardens, Florida, was fatally shot by George Zimmerman, while visiting his father's fiancée in Sanford, Florida. Wearing a hoodie to protect himself from the pouring rain, Martin rushed to the local 7-Eleven store during the halftime of the 61st NBA All-Star Game to buy a bag of Skittles candy and an iced tea. On his way back, he caught the eye of Zimmerman, a 28-year-old German-Peruvian neighborhood watch volunteer, who suspected he could be related to a string of burglaries that had taken place in the area a few days earlier. Phone records and witness testimonies showed that Martin noticed Zimmerman, and tried to run away. The ensuing confrontation ended up with Zimmerman firing his semi-automatic handgun at close range, killing Martin. When the police came, Zimmerman claimed that he'd been attacked by Martin, and that he fired his weapon in self-defense. Five hours later, he was released.

Amidst intense media coverage and public pressure, George Zimmerman was charged with second-degree murder by the State of Florida in April 2012. The trial lasted a little over 15 months. On July 13, 2013, after 16 hours and 20 minutes of deliberations over the course of two days, the six-person jury found Zimmerman "not guilty."

That day, Alicia Garza, a 32-year-old civil rights activist, was sitting with a friend at a bar, waiting for the verdict. "As much as I'd seen in the years I'd been organizing – the disappointments as mothers of slain children were forced to watch their children's character be questioned and denigrated," she later recalled, "for some reason, unbeknownst to me then or now, I truly believed that Zimmerman would not walk free."[1] When the news broke, she couldn't breathe. "At first I felt nothing. I stared at the television blankly, and the words and images became a blur. I remember turning around and walking outside, to get away from people, to try to find my breath again." Then she rushed to Facebook to unleash her rage:

> Where those folks at saying we are in post-racial America? Where those folks at saying we have moved past race and that black folks in particular need to get over it? The sad part is, there's a section of America who is cheering and celebrating right now.
>
> And that makes me sick to my stomach. We GOTTA get it together y'all. Our lives are hanging in the balance. Young black boys in this country are not safe. Black men in this country are not safe. This verdict will create many more George Zimmermans. #blacklivesmatter

Garza had no idea that the hashtag she affixed to her post would become the rallying call of a movement that would generate the largest wave of protests since the Civil Rights era. In its first year, Black Lives Matter (BLM) remained mostly online, with Garza and her fellow activist friends Patrisse Cullors and Opal

Tometi using various social media platforms to post information about other cases of racist violence across the country and do activist work.

Things took a dramatic turn on August 9, 2014, when 18-year-old Michael Brown was killed by police officer Darren Wilson in Ferguson, Missouri. According to official records, a total of 12 bullets were fired by Wilson's gun, at least six of them hitting Brown's body, which was left lying in the street under the scorching sun for four-and-a-half hours before it was cleared to be taken to the morgue. "You could just see all the blood. Every time you looked at the sheet, it was more and more blood," the father of Michael Brown said. "We was treated like we wasn't parents, you know? That's what I didn't understand. They sicced dogs on us. They wouldn't let us identify his body. They pulled guns on us."[2] Several police units were dispatched to the crime scene to deal with the growing unrest, but the protestors remained undeterred despite heavy-handed intervention with military-grade equipment. In a few hours, Ferguson became the flashpoint of a nationwide uprising against police brutality.

One of the activists working on the ground was none other than Alicia Garza. "It was a guttural response to be with our people, our family – in support of the brave and courageous community of Ferguson and St. Louis as they were being brutalized by law enforcement, criticized by media, tear gassed, and pepper sprayed night after night," she reminisced.[3] The biggest need was the media to come, BLM organizers were told, and tell the story from the perspective of the local community. Within a matter of two weeks, Patrisse Cullors and Darnell Moore organized a national Black Lives Matter Freedom Ride to Ferguson, inspired by the anti-segregation Freedom Rides of the 1950s and 1960s. More than 500 people from 13 states joined the effort, converging on Ferguson during the Labor Day weekend, three weeks after the killing of Michael Brown. The group spent four days in Ferguson, attending marches and protests, establishing connections between locals and the wider activist community. Tensions existed, Garza said; "but there was also a deep love and sense of community building from being in some shit together."[4]

Garza returned to Ferguson in October to help coordinate a national Weekend of Resistance under the auspices of a coalition of local organizations. "All in all, I spent nearly five weeks in St. Louis. I worked with a team of seventeen people, all from the St. Louis area, including some from Ferguson," she said.[5] Garza and her team started to knock on doors, asking people whether they would be willing to join a movement, not just attend an event. They managed to talk to more than 1,500 people in 10 days and convinced almost a thousand to join the movement. The Weekend itself was a success, with over a thousand protestors from across the US marching in downtown St. Louis. The unrest continued in the following weeks, reaching a breaking point on November 24, 2014, when a grand jury decided not to indict Darren Wilson on any criminal charges. That night, several buildings were torched; police cars were burned; and windows of local businesses were smashed. Missouri Governor Jay Nixon, who had already declared a state of emergency and deployed the National Guard a week before the decision was announced, called up additional members of the National Guard to protect the Ferguson Police Department.[6] The local riot was soon brought under control, but at this point the protests had already spread to other parts of the country.

Ferguson was a turning point for Black Lives Matter. The Freedom Ride and the Weekend of Resistance "were moments of resistance that showed us how far we've come and how far we still have to travel, who we are and who we can be," Alicia Garza said. It was time to turn these moments into a movement, or to "unite to fight."[7] Organizers from 18 different cities who had gathered in Ferguson went back and set up Black Lives Matter chapters in their own communities. In the meantime, Garza, Cullors, and Tometi created the Black Lives

Matter Global Network infrastructure, a loose network which had 26 chapters as of 2015.[8] "We decided to take control of our own narrative and place ourselves more prominently in our own story," Garza wrote in her 2020 memoir, *The Purpose of Power: How We Come Together When We Fall Apart*, a decision they knew would have consequences, both individually and collectively.[9] Being the public face of one of the most successful – and to some, equally contentious – movements in the history of the Black freedom struggle was indeed exacting. Patrisse Cullors resigned as the executive director of the network in May 2021 amidst criticisms regarding her allegedly lavish lifestyle (Cullors denied the allegations, claiming that her decision to step down had nothing to do with "right-wing attacks to discredit [her] character").[10] Opal Tometi distanced herself from the movement gradually, declaring in a statement to *BuzzFeed* that she has not been involved in "the day-to-day organizational and fiscal management of [BLM] since December 2015."[11] Alicia Garza went on to found the Black Futures Lab dedicated to increase the visibility and power of the Black community in politics. She also partnered up with Cecile Richards and Ai-jen Poo to launch Supermajority, a voting advocacy hub to bring women together. Nevertheless, the original trio continued to represent Black Lives Matter on media – for example, posing together for the *Time 100: Most Influential People of 2020* photoshoot in Los Angeles.[12]

The movement itself has come under heavy criticism from all sides of the political spectrum for its decentralized organizational structure, and for placing too much attention on individuals, which appears to contradict the movement's aim to dismantle systemic injustice; lack of accountability and mismanagement of its finances; its decision not to support any candidate in the 2016 and 2020 US presidential elections; the "radicalism" of some of its policy proposals such as defunding the police, which has little support from the wider populace; its tactical choices, in particular its reluctance to condemn violence during protests, among others. Some of these criticisms – voiced not only by the Right but also the Left, including organizations affiliated with or operating under the umbrella of the network – have merit, as the founders of the movement also admit. But this does not change the fact that Black Lives Matter has been, and still is, one of the most successful social movements in modern history, in terms of both the number of people it has been able to mobilize and of achieving some of its goals, in particular raising public awareness about police brutality. At its peak, following the murder of George Floyd by a police officer in Minneapolis, Minnesota on May 25, 2020, the movement enjoyed the support of 67 percent of the US population.[13] About 15–26 million people participated in the demonstrations over the death of Floyd in the US alone, and there were 7,750 demonstrations in all 50 states and Washington, D.C. between May and August 2020. Support for Black Lives Matter declined between June and September 2020, according to a survey by Pew Research Center, but remained stable throughout 2021, with 55 percent of US adults expressing at least some support for the movement (this ratio increased to 83 percent among Black adults and to 68 percent among Asian adults).[14]

Community Activism

What accounts for the success of Black Lives Matter, despite its shortcomings and the constant vitriol heaped on it by the influential figures of the reactionary Right? Does it have a centrist, catch-all message which appeals to both conservative and progressive constituencies? Hardly. "Defund the police," the signature slogan of the movement, is supported by only a minority of the US population, decreasing from 42 percent in June 2020 to 37 percent in September 2021.[15] Is the movement against identity politics, which would have certainly increased its allure to centrists and the Right? Far from it. It was headed by three Black women – two of them queer and one with immigrant parents – who meticulously differentiated themselves from traditional Black leadership represented by more embraceable figures like the Reverend Jesse Jackson and Reverend Al Sharpton. "Black liberation movements in this country have created room, space, and leadership mostly for Black heterosexual, cisgender men," Garza wrote on one occasion. "As a network, we have always recognized the need to center the leadership of women and queer and trans people."[16]

Rather, the Black Lives Matter organizers took the lessons of Black queer feminist activism to heart. In practical terms, this meant three things. First, they understood the importance of power to achieve their goals. Most contemporary social movements confuse power with empowerment, says Alicia Garza, but these two concepts are not one and the same. "Power is the ability to impact and affect the conditions of your own life and the lives of others"; empowerment, on the other hand, "is feeling good about yourself, akin to having high self-esteem." "Unless empowerment is transformed into power," she adds, "not much will change about our environments. It's power that determines whether or not a community will be gentrified, a school district funded, a family provided with quality healthcare that is affordable on any budget."[17] The purpose of organizing, Garza concludes, should be to build power.

The distinction Garza draws between power and empowerment is key to understanding the failure of the woke Left to mount a successful challenge to the far right's growing influence. The personal may well be political as second-wave feminism has taught us, but politics is not personal, or at least not exclusively so. And if it is only personal, it is not politics. Too much focus on microaggressions, trigger warnings, and safe spaces, often at the expense of bread-and-butter issues which matter more to average voters, leads to alienation and frustration, pushing people either to reactionary populism or to apathy as decreasing rates of turnout across many Western democracies show. This does not mean that empowerment has no place in conventional politics, or the broader struggle for social justice. We know that identity matters, and that, at the end of the day, all politics is identity politics. The problem progressive movements face today is rather the opposite – the colonization of power by individual empowerment, or the reduction of politics into subversive performance and symbolic resistance. This is probably what led activist Loretta J. Ross to write the *New York Times* article cited in the Prologue. "We need to stop seeing feminism as our personal therapy spaces," Ross said on another occasion. "The purpose of feminism is to end the oppression of women. Full stop. Not to create safe spaces where your feelings won't get hurt."[18] What is true for feminism, I would argue, is also true for the fight against racism, sexism, or economic inequalities – in fact, for politics as a whole.

This leads to the second lesson Black Lives Matter organizers incorporated into their activism. Power itself cannot be achieved without nurturing relationships and forming alliances. "In many movement-building efforts," says Garza, "there is a tendency to build alliances with only those we are the most comfortable with, those who already speak our language and share our views on the world." Once again, this is related to the quest for empowerment which is "what happens when people come together and don't feel alone anymore and don't feel like they're the only ones who experience what they do."[19] But when it comes to politics, and "when it comes to building power, being small is something we cannot afford," Garza adds. "The longer I'm in the practice of building a movement, the more I realize that movement building isn't about finding your tribe – it's about growing your tribe across difference to focus on a common set of goals."[20]

This does not require activists to abandon their ideals or water down their politics. Black Lives Matter enjoyed such a broad base of support and achieved some of its goals by reaching out to organizations that are not necessarily radical, or even progressive. This did not mean that "we had to be less radical," Garza says. "It meant that being radical and having radical politics were not a litmus test for whether or not one could join our movement."[21] As we have seen in chapter 1, this important lesson was not lost on the organizers of the 2017 Women's March on Washington either. The original protest included women from all walks of life and political persuasions – White and People of Color, pro-choice and pro-life, heterosexual and gender-nonconforming, young and old. The movement started to fizzle out once certain women were or felt excluded on the basis of their beliefs, identities, or other characteristics that others found threatening. The fifth Women's March, held on October 2, 2021, was attended by a mere 5,000 people in Washington, D.C., down from an estimated 4,157,894 in 2017.[22]

This is the third lesson learned by Black Lives Matter organizers. There has been much discussion about the role of social media in spurring movements, but as Garza says, "You cannot start a movement from a hashtag. Only organizing sustains movements."[23] The actual work of community organizing involves much more than launching or liking a hashtag on social media. It requires knocking on doors, engaging in difficult conversations, listening and putting oneself in other people's shoes. The reason we feel so comfortable with those who think like us, Garza claims, is that "we fear being challenged. It's natural to seek safety and comfort, and yet, if we have a long-term vision for our communities and the people we care about, we owe it to ourselves to get a little uncomfortable."[24]

Regrettably, much of woke activism is not prepared to go the extra mile and experience discomfort. For all the talk of diversity and inclusion, differences of opinion are shunned – if not categorically rejected – and solidarity is reduced to "proximity and empty slogans, without the work it takes for us to really have each other's back in the face of oppression."[25] This often comes with a sense of entitlement which allows move-ment leaders to believe that they, and only they, can determine the criteria of inclusion and exclusion. But as law professor Kimberlé W. Crenshaw reminds us, this process of categoriza-tion is itself an exercise of power.[26] By claiming to speak for, or on behalf of, disadvantaged groups, radical identity politics confers legitimacy on certain forms of oppression over others. This is problematic not only from a strategic point of view, precluding the possibility of working across differences, but also politically, as it ignores intragroup differences. Ironically enough, since few woke activists have actually read Crenshaw's seminal 1991 article "Mapping the Margins: Intersectionality, Identity Politics, and Violence against Women of Color," they are not aware that the whole concept of intersectionality is based on a critique of identity politics. "In the context of violence against women, this elision of difference in identity politics is problematic," Crenshaw says, "because the violence that many women experience is often shaped by other dimen-sions of their identities, such as race and class. Moreover, ignoring difference within groups contributes to tension among groups."[27] And as Garza points out, "intersectionality does not say that the experiences of Black women are more important or more valid than those of white women." Instead, it "asks why white women's experiences are the standard that we use when addressing inequality based on gender."[28] Black-only organizing (we might of course extend this to any identity category) will not be effective if it replicates the systems of oppression it sets out to eradicate by refusing to cooperate with other marginalized communities.

These three lessons account not only for the success of Black Lives Matter or the 2017 Women's March on Washington, D.C. They also offer a roadmap for building movements in the twenty-first century. "Movements require people to come together, across difference, united in pursuit of a common goal," says Alicia Garza.[29] Woke activism does the exact opposite and preaches to the already converted. And it prioritizes individual empowerment over systemic change; symbolic resistance over collective struggle; and online activism over offline organizing. These strategic choices push away large swathes of the population – not only conservatives, but also centrists and dissenting progressives – who stand at the crossroads of one or several interlocking systems of oppression. What needs to be done, then, is to follow the advice offered by generations of Black feminist activists and reach out to those who do not think like us, try to convince as many of them as possible to make common cause to achieve change that will benefit the most. For that, we need to offer a vision, a story, and "the more people you can get to invest in that story, to make your story their own, the more powerful you become."[30] Such a story should begin with what we share, and not with what divides us; then we need to add layers to it to better address the myriad (interrelated) threats and injustices we face today.

Making Social Justice Social Again

When conservatives hear the phrase "social justice," they reach for their guns, to paraphrase the well-known expression by the German poet and Nazi ideologue Hanns Johst. But the term "social justice" has a long pedigree and did not initially carry the negative connotation the Right attaches to it today. The nineteenth-century Irish philosopher William Thompson is credited to be the first to use it in his 1824 book, *An Inquiry into the Principles of the Distribution of Wealth Most Conducive to Human Being*, in a sense akin to distributive justice, as a principle which promotes "the happiness of the whole of the community." Subsequent references to the term have also been quite complimentary. In fact, even the more ideologically loaded "social justice warrior" was used in a neutral or laudatory way, as in a 1991 piece in the *Montreal*

Gazette which referred to union activist Michel Chartrand as a "Québec nationalist and social-justice warrior."[31]

Things went sour in 2011, when the expression made its appearance on Twitter. There were no authoritative definitions of social justice warrior at the time, other than an Urban Dictionary entry in April 2011 which egregiously transformed its meaning into:

> A pejorative term for an individual who repeatedly and vehemently engages in arguments on social justice on the Internet, often in a shallow or not well-thought-out way, for the purpose of raising their own personal reputation. A social justice warrior, or SJW, does not necessarily strongly believe all that they say, or even care about the groups they are fighting on behalf of. They typically repeat points from whoever is the most popular blogger or commenter of the moment, hoping that they will "get SJ points" and become popular in return.[32]

The term became popular in 2014, due to its association with what is commonly known as "Gamergate," a year-long misogynistic online harassment campaign prompted by a right-wing backlash against feminism and diversity in the online gaming community, and finally making its way into Oxford Dictionaries in 2015 – but not the *Oxford English Dictionary* itself – as an informal term which refers to "A person who expresses or promotes socially progressive views."[33]

Since then, social justice warriors (SJWs) have become the whipping boy of the Right and, as we have seen in chapter 2, were routinely blamed for the retreat from liberalism. The irony here is, of course, that the Right has never really cared about illiberalism as long as it was politically expedient. Just remember the praises showered upon prohibitive immigration policies adopted in a number of authoritarian countries, the emphatic support for the normalization of anti-Muslim feelings, increasing calls for law and order, and a more active surveillance state. Nor is the Right much concerned about illiberalism within its own ranks, in particular the swelling number of culture warriors "bravely" battling social justice warriors in their fantasy world. For the more dedicated, what we are witnessing is indeed "a war on the West," pure and simple. Hence in his latest book to date, Douglas Murray claims that the greatest threat to Western civilization comes from the "people inside the West intent on pulling apart the fabric of our societies, piece by piece . . . By assaulting the majority populations in these countries. By saying that our histories are entirely reprehensible and have nothing good to be said about them."[34] But, of course, the woke Left is not the absolute evil of this fantasy world as Murray and others on the reactionary Right might have us believe. There are far too many competitors for the pole position, from far right extremist groups and followers of the conspiracist QAnon, which alleges that the world is run by a cabal of Satan-worshiping pedophiles to their mainstream enablers and religious fundamentalists, though it is certainly true that the woke Left is much more than a passive observer of raging culture wars.

Yet actually existing social justice activism is not the only form of progressive politics possible. On the contrary, it is a historical aberration, a radical departure from the ideals of *rights-based universalism* and *equality across differences*. I believe that these goals are still worth pursuing, and should be part of any struggle for social justice which I define as "justice at the level of a society or state as regards the possession of wealth, commodities, opportunities, and privileges."[35]

My choice of this standard, dictionary definition is deliberate. Despite, or perhaps because of, its simplicity, the definition encapsulates two essential questions that any progressive movement needs to grapple with: the "who" of justice (who are the subjects of justice?) and the "what" of justice (what does justice entail?). The answers to these questions bring the differences between the Right and the Left (as well as the great schism within the Left) into sharp relief. For the faith-family-flag Right, justice is confined to the boundaries of the territorial state, and its subjects are the "authentic" members of the nation, i.e., those who were born in or somehow ethnically connected to that nation. The authenticity test is a complicated one, and involves more than ancestry, kinship, or geographical happenstance. To be a subject of justice, one has to possess the right kind of ideological and cultural credentials, preferably those of the majority. For the diversity-equity-inclusion Left, justice transcends territorial boundaries, for what matters is membership of a particular identity group, or those who share the same subjective experience of oppression. Radical identity politics does not give much shrift to either the society or the state, which it considers (often rightly) as major sources of oppression. Commitment to transnational solidarity does not make the authenticity test easier, since the criteria for being a subject of justice are subjective and ever-shifting, though belonging to some sort of minority always helps. Territorial boundaries are irrelevant for the traditional, Marxist Left too. Justice requires membership of a particular group, this time defined on the basis of socioeconomic status, not cultural or political disadvantage, which are seen to be the outcome of exploitative relations of production. On the face of it, the authenticity requirements for the traditional Left are fewer than those of their woke successors since they are based, at least in theory, on objective economic criteria, or class membership. There are two problems here. First, economic class is not defined in the same way it was half a century ago, when neoliberal economics first began taking over our lives. Second, class has never been the only identity that matters for a great majority of people. This expectation mismatch between the intellectual or activist vanguard and its target audience regarding who is entitled to justice and what justice entails is the only thing that unites the traditional and the woke Left, and continues to be a problem that plagues progressive politics.

An Ecumenical Understanding of Justice

But there is a way out, and one that has already been subject to much discussion. I am referring here to the debate on the concept of recognition that was rekindled in the 1990s, following the publication of an influential essay by Canadian philosopher Charles Taylor titled "The Politics of Recognition."[36] The essay itself was an attempt to respond to the various demands for recognition raised by political movements organized around race, ethnicity, gender, and sexuality at the time and, as such, it went to the heart of the broader discussion on multiculturalism and identity politics. For Taylor, these demands were given a new urgency because of the supposed link between recognition and identity. "Our identity is partly shaped by recognition or its absence," Taylor wrote. We therefore suffer real damage if the society around us mirrors back a demeaning or contemptible picture of ourselves. "Nonrecognition or misrecognition can inflict harm, can be a form of oppression." In such a context, "due recognition is not just a courtesy we owe people," he concluded: "It is a vital human need."[37] This view led to a heated exchange between philosophers Axel Honneth and Nancy Fraser, which is published in book form in 2003 with the title *Redistribution or Recognition? A Political-Philosophical Exchange.*[38] Honneth, like Taylor, conceived of recognition as "a fundamental, overarching moral category," treating other issues, including redistribution, as derivative. Fraser, on the other hand, objected to both Taylor and Honneth, pointing to the dangers of giving primacy to recognition over redistribution – a position she continued to defend and elaborate on in her later work.

According to Fraser, recognition and redistribution ultimately correspond to two different kinds of justice claims. The problem with Taylor and Honneth's position, and more generally with identity politics, is twofold. First, it simplifies and essentializes group identities, "pressuring individual members to conform, denying the complexity of their lives, the multiplicity of their identifications." Thus, instead of promoting interaction across differences, "it reifies group identities and neglects shared humanity, promoting separatism and repressive communitarianism." Second, by treating lack of recognition as a free-standing cultural harm, it abstracts injustice from its institutional underpinnings and obscures its links to neoliberal globalization, thereby undermining the struggle against economic inequality.[39]

Fraser's critique of identity politics is also helpful for understanding the great schism within the Left. The traditional Left often roots for a politics of redistribution that aims for economic equality, dismissing other types of injustices on the basis of race, gender, and sexuality as either irrelevant or secondary. The woke Left, on the other hand, supports a politics of recognition which aspires to identity-based equality, reducing injustice to cultural and symbolic oppression. This leads to a decoupling of class politics from identity politics, and presents us with an either/or choice between the economic and the cultural. Fraser's response to this dilemma is fairly simple: justice requires both redistribution and recognition. In practical terms, this means a broad-based program that would seek to remedy different forms of injustice, without reducing them into one another. In her later work, Fraser adds a third dimension to her conceptualization of justice – "representation" – which serves to account for political injustices that arise when some members of society are deprived of their voice or their right to participate in the political process (though not specifically mentioned by Fraser, gerrymandering and voter suppression are good examples of this form of injustice).

The philosophy behind the progressive politics I propose draws heavily on this three-dimensional account of justice, with the ultimate aim of achieving social justice for all. This emphasis on "all," and the repudiation of distinctions and inequalities in terms of wealth, commodities, opportunities, and privileges encapsulated in the standard definition of social justice, requires an *ecumenical* understanding of justice based on our common humanity and the basic rights that derive from it as opposed to the *denominational* justice of the woke Left which compartmentalizes and ranks rights on the basis of essentialized group identities.

The idea of common humanity is often rebuffed by both the Right and the Left, for being too thin to generate a sense of belonging and for failing to cater to the needs of disadvantaged groups given existing power imbalances. Both criticisms would be valid if our conception of justice were limited to those that are attached to our common humanity, for example, those codified in the Declaration of the Rights of Man and the Citizen of 1789, the American Declaration of the Rights and Duties of Man, and the more recent Universal Declaration of Human Rights of 1948. But it is not. Common humanity, above all "the recognition of the inherent dignity and of the equal and inalienable rights" of all human beings (the right to life, liberty and security, equality before the law, freedom from discrimination),[40] is just the first building block, or the fundament of a more comprehensive political program. Its relatively abstract and thin nature makes it ideal as a common denominator that could bring everybody together, from centrists and conservatives to justice- and equality-driven progressives.

The progressive vision I propose includes three additional, closely intertwined and mutually reinforcing, building blocks, namely *redistribution, recognition,* and *participation,* which are derived from the above-mentioned three dimensions of justice. I would like to stress at the outset that the way I understand these dimensions does not overlap neatly with Fraser's definitions. Hence, for her, the political dimension sets the frame within which struggles over redistribution and recognition take place; in that sense, it is mainly about representation, determining who counts as a subject of justice, who is entitled to and who is excluded from making justice claims. I argue that participation is a more appropriate term to denote the political dimension of justice since representation has other, more specific, connotations in democratic theory (which are well beyond the scope of this book). In any case, boundary-setting, both physical and symbolic, is merely one aspect of the political dimension; participation involves not only being or forming part of something, but also "the sharing of something," an attribute that is reflected even in dictionary definitions of the term. According to the *OED*, for example, participation comprises "The process or fact of sharing in an action, sentiment, etc.; (now *esp.*) active involvement in a matter or event, esp. one in which the outcome directly affects those taking part."[41] Debates around the fairness and inclusiveness of elections, forms of participation that are not part of regular democratic processes such as protests, acts of civil disobedience, indeed boycotts and call outs, or feelings of alienation and apathy, are better captured by the term participation, which implies emotional bonding and sharing.

Participation is part and parcel of the modern construct of citizenship, but goes beyond that since, as history has shown us time and again, (i) citizenship itself is a contested category – a culturally and historically specific status that is not automatically extended to all inhabitants of a particular territory, in particular latecomers and newcomers (e.g., refugees and immigrants); (ii) legal membership of the state is no guarantee of political equality, for not all citizens are considered to be authentic members of the nation. Even in nation-states which, in theory, subscribe to civic/liberal forms of nationalism, nationhood is defined on the basis of a number of ethnic and cultural markers which historical minorities and immigrants often lack. To give but one example, most Arabs living in Israel are granted citizenship and are allowed to vote for the Knesset, but the state denies citizenship to Palestinians from the occupied territories of Gaza and the West Bank even if married to Israeli citizens; and those Palestinians who became legal citizens of the State of Israel following the 1980 amendment to Israel's Nationality Law are still excluded from several aspects of the Jewish welfare state.

The political dimension also helps to settle procedural questions concerning, for example, "who can make claims for redistribution and recognition" and "how such claims are to be mooted and adjudicated."[42] In other words, it establishes the ground rules of dialogue which is central to any decision-making or deliberation process, including the definition of key values and objectives which cannot be dictated by either the state or the self-appointed vanguards of any group or movement.

The universalist bent of the progressive politics I am advancing does not deny the dialogical nature of identity formation, and the heuristic and political utility of a distinction between "us" and "them." It thus explicitly promotes recognition and accommodation of identity-based differences, unlike various right-wing formulations which call either for their eradication or their assimilation into the majority identity. But this acknowledgment of difference needs to be qualified in two important ways. In most discussions of cultural diversity, justice and equality require not only the recognition of individual differences, but also of group-based differences. This follows from a critique of difference-blind liberalism which regards the state as a neutral arbiter responsible for an equitable distribution of our common needs such as a reasonable income, jobs, healthcare, education, and basic freedoms. Yet, as several commentators have noted, hands-off neutrality is a pipedream. "Liberalism is not a possible meeting ground for all cultures," Charles Taylor reminds us, "but is the political expression of one range of cultures, and quite incompatible with other ranges" – as many Muslim refugees and immigrants to Europe have probably learned the hard way. Liberalism cannot claim complete cultural neutrality because it is itself a fighting creed.[43] And that explains why the right-wing defense of majority values is couched in the language of liberalism which is often presented as the hallmark of Western civilization threatened by "illiberal" newcomers. On the other hand, the remedy to this is not recognition of group-based differences, as defenders of multiculturalism argue. It is true that human rights do not provide a solution to all the conflicts that may arise between majorities and minorities, or different identity groups. It does not tell us which languages should be officially recognized by the state or whether Muslim women should have the right to wear hijab in all public spaces including schools. It does not specify what form police reform should take or what adjustments are required in the job market in order to eliminate the gender pay gap. The examples are endless. The point is, the answers to these questions do not necessarily or always require us to "officially" recognize the groups in whose name these claims are made because, as I have noted above, this carries the risk of leading to the hardening of the boundaries separating different groups (reification), the erasure of intragroup differences (homogenization), and the ruining of any chances of interaction or dialogue across differences (separatism) – the discrimination/oppression women face as a "sex class," or qua women, is a huge exception to this rule. The answer, I argue, is to stick to the individual as a unit of analysis, and redefine common humanity in a way that would include membership in various identity- or value-based groups.

This process of redefinition of common humanity could be facilitated through a structuralist approach which treats problems related to recognition, or the lack thereof, as an institutional violation of justice, which can only be remedied by systemic change.[44] Hence Diversity, Equality and Inclusion training does not work because, for one thing, it does not address the root causes of racism. It is not possible to change the way an individual thinks or acts without dismantling the structural conditions that allowed that particular way of thinking or acting in the first place. This stress on the institutional

sources of injustice helps us to distance ourselves from subjective and ever-shifting definitions of harm, and situates us
firmly in the realm of the structural, or the systemic. Racism,
patriarchy, and transphobia are institutional forms of injustice
that can only be tackled with a collective effort which involves
all parties to a particular conflict as well as the state.

It's Still the Economy, Stupid

The final dimension of the ecumenical understanding of justice
I am suggesting is (economic) redistribution which is closely
related to the political and the cultural dimensions. This might
be a good time to recall the Combahee women's objection
to contemporary forms of identity activism, in particular the
extent to which the term was detached from its anti-capitalist
origins. This is not a nostalgic call for a return to old-style
class-first politics. The Combahee women themselves knew
that economic deprivation and inequality were only one
source of oppression among many – hence the emphasis on
"interlocking systems of oppression." Equally importantly, the
dominant form of capitalism today, or neoliberalism, is not
the capitalism the Combahee River Collective was fighting
against almost half a century ago. Neoliberalism is much more
than an economic project that favors market liberalization,
privatization, deregulation, monetarism, and austerity. It is
also a moral logic that seeks to reduce the role of the welfare
state, reshaping the social and the political through the extension and dissemination of market values to all institutions and
spheres of life.[45] Nothing is left untouched by neoliberal logic,
political theorist Wendy Brown tells us, pointing to the extent
to which "neoliberalism's attack on democracy has everywhere
inflected law, political culture, and political subjectivity."[46]

What is missing in Brown's account is the impact this logic
has had on the political subjectivity of the Left. We are offered

glimpses of an "anti-democratic culture" emerging from below, parallel to the authoritarian turn of the state but, overall, we are left with the impression that this is a virus that affects only the Right, or those with a conservative-reactionary mindset. However, as I have tried to show throughout this book, the Left is not immune to the enticements of neoliberalism either, understood both as an economic system and a broader moral logic. In that sense, the problem is not only the privileging of recognition over redistribution, or the cultural over the economic – though this is part of the problem too – but the cooptation of the Left by neoliberalism, or what I referred to earlier as the commodification of identity. Fraser's solution to this dilemma is what she calls "progressive populism": "Only by joining a robustly egalitarian politics of distribution to a substantively inclusive, class-sensitive politics of recognition can we build a counterhegemonic bloc capable of leading us beyond the current crisis to a better world."[47]

Despite disagreements regarding the specifics, from a purely economic point of view, the formula is sound and compelling. Practically speaking, this translates into a revamped version of social democracy (or democratic socialism in the US context), welfare policies designed not only to provide a safety net, but also to reduce economic inequalities, including perhaps the much-debated idea of "universal basic income" (UBI) – "a term used to describe a number of different proposals where the state would provide income for all citizens, without any conditions attached, and regardless of their other resources."[48] I should add in passing that UBI would be a non-starter in some contexts, for example Nordic countries which already have a highly developed welfare system based on a specific "alliance between state and citizens, whereby citizens work, pay taxes and earn their fundamental social rights . . . a combination of a national solidarity project, an egalitarian social investment scheme, and a giant insurance company," in the words of Swedish historian Lars Trägårdh.[49] In contexts that lack a comprehensive social security system, this program might include loans, income tax credits, healthcare insurance, educational reform, child support, and other childcare policies in addition to UBI and a number of affirmative action policies designed to address the needs of particularly disadvantaged groups.[50]

And it is precisely here that we bump into the elephant in the room, namely immigration. How do we convince the majority to make sacrifices for the greater collective good when the collective almost invariably includes a substantial number of latecomers and newcomers who are not considered to be deserving of a share of "our" common wealth? The problem is well captured by Lars Trägårdh in the case of Sweden which has always presented itself as the model social democratic welfare state and a "global moral superpower." According to Trägårdh, it was the refugee crisis of 2015 that laid bare the already existing tensions between the national and the global, between the rights of citizens and human rights.[51] Even though the two are historically related, the gradual incorporation of human rights into the concept of democratic citizenship meant that the latter developed within territorially bounded, sovereign states where they achieved a legal status – becoming, as political philosopher Hannah Arendt famously observed, "a right to achieve rights." As such, citizenship is by definition exclusionary since it offers full rights only to those who have the requisite legal status. But there will always be a substantial number of residents who do not have citizenship (yet) and, as I argued earlier, being a citizen does not guarantee membership of the inevitably culturally defined nation. Just remember Douglas Murray's derisive description of "Streets in the cold and rainy northern towns of Europe filled with people dressed for the foothills of Pakistan or the sandstorms of Arabia." How do we solve this dilemma, then – one that involves not only the tension between the national and the global, but also between the citizen and the non-citizen, or the national and the non-national?

Fraser and Trägårdh have different answers to this question. For Fraser, given increasing levels of global interdependence, there is no going back to distinct national economies. Decisions taken in one state affect the lives of those who live outside it, as do the actions of transnational corporations and supranational organizations. Hence, she concludes, the territorial state is no longer the appropriate frame to determine the "who" and the "what" of justice.[52] The most promising alternative, Fraser says, is the "all-affected principle," which holds "that all those affected by a given social structure or institution have moral standing as subjects of justice in relation to it. In this view, what turns a collection of people into fellow subjects of justice is not geographical proximity, but their co-imbrication in a common structural or institutional framework."[53]

For Trägårdh, the connection between rights and duties underlying the idea of citizenship requires a bounded political community, as rights and duties are reciprocal and conditional. In other words, a democratic welfare state is conditional on the idea of tax-paying citizens and a trustworthy state that supplies social insurance benefits in return. Rights that go beyond the logic of insurance, such as healthcare, education, care for the elderly, and the protection of the disabled, are part of a social contract that assumes a link across generations within the national community.[54] This does not amount to a wholesale rejection of universal human rights. Trägårdh argues that solidarity at the global level follows a different logic, namely compassion and unconditional altruism. Short of a global state which has the power to enforce rights, the best we can do is to bring citizenship and human rights into closer harmony, and work toward a division of labor between the state and civil society, with the former ensuring reciprocal and conditional rights for its citizens and the latter providing assistance on a global scale in the spirit of common humanity.

My own answer to the citizenship versus human rights dilemma is closer to Trägårdh's formula. Even though I am sympathetic to the ongoing quest for post-national solutions that would enable us to better address justice claims on a global scale – not to mention the challenges posed by unprecedented planetary emergencies such as climate change, environmental degradation, species extinction, and raging pandemics – I do not believe that this is feasible in the short to medium term. And the threats posed by the inexorable rise of illiberal identity politics (on both Right and Left) are too pressing for any dawdling about finding the ideal political recipe, assuming that there is one. The model of progressive politics that I propose does not repudiate or underestimate the importance of social cohesion, trust and solidarity for the survival and flourishing of a democratic socialist welfare state. But it modifies the foundations upon which these are based. It preserves, even cherishes, the idea of citizenship, but liberates it from both populist understandings of culture which invariably reflect the values and traditions of national majorities, and identitarian projects, which conceive of society as an archipelago of isolated cultures with no sense of obligation toward one another. It promotes the idea of a new social contract which establishes equal rights and duties for all citizens; it replaces assimilation into the dominant culture with respect for the social contract which will be negotiated, agreed upon and fine-tuned dialogically, with the equal participation of all those who will be affected by the outcome; and it fosters a belief in common destiny rather than adherence to myths of common ancestry or an obsessive preoccupation with the past.

Obviously, this vision is predicated upon the existence of a strong, interventionist state and high levels of social trust. There is a reason why Trägårdh's formula is derived from, and works best in, Nordic societies, which are characterized by high levels of generalized trust based on the rule of law as opposed to particularized trust, that is, trust in "known" or "similar" others, such as family, relatives, friends, and neighbors. And this is not only based on anecdotal evidence.

Various studies, including Our World in Data and the World Values Survey, show that generalized trust levels in Denmark, Norway, Sweden, Iceland, and Finland are among the highest in the world (60% or above), compared to other democracies such as the UK, the US, Germany, and France, where trust levels vary between 20 and 40 percent.[55]

This is all good – though perhaps a little too abstract and jargon-laden – on paper, I hear you say, but how does it work in practice? How could we make this "our" story and present it in an intelligible form? How do we overcome existing racial and socioeconomic tensions, the crippling political polarization, the toxic value wars and convince the greatest number of people to invest in this story? How do we create an effective progressive force capable of achieving power, even winning elections? In short, as Lenin famously put it, what is to be done?

The Race-Class Narrative

"I'm from Berkeley, California, a sociologist, and I am trying to understand the deepening divide in our country. So I'm trying to get out of my political bubble and get to know people in yours," said Arlie Russell Hochschild when she met Tea Party voter Mike Schaff, one of her respondents in Lake Charles, Louisiana. This was the beginning of a long journey into the heartland of the American Right, one of the poorest of so-called red states, to understand how those who were "not like us," those who held different views than our own, felt. In Hochschild's terms, this was a journey to the other side of the "empathy wall." "Is it possible, without changing our beliefs," she asked, "to know others from the inside, to see reality through their eyes, to understand the links between life, feeling, and politics; that is, to cross the empathy wall?"[56]

The answer she came up with – after spending five years immersed in the community around Lake Charles, talking with

60 people and accumulating over 4,000 pages of transcribed interviews – was "yes." Her National Book Award finalist book, *Strangers in Their Own Land: Anger and Mourning on the American Right*, was hailed by *The New York Times* as one of the six books that helped people to understand Trump's win in November 2016.[57] The book does not provide all the answers, of course (who could anyway?), but it does manage to build an "empathy bridge" in Hochschild's terms – and one, I argue, that is compatible with the experiences and lessons of Black feminist activists, from Combahee River Collective to Black Lives Matter.

It is not possible to convince others to hear, let alone invest in, our story without first acquainting ourselves with their concerns and fears, and the language in which they are couched. The results of the 2016 presidential elections, Berkeley public law professor Ian Haney López informs us, show that one of the strongest indicators of support for Trump was how Republican voters felt about Blacks, immigrants, and Muslims, and how much discrimination they believed Whites themselves faced. The issue here is not objective hardship, of course, but subjective feelings, "the sense of losing ground compared to others, especially groups perceived as undeserving."[58] In fact, according to a 2017 study by Public Religion Research Institute (PRRI), almost half of White working-class Americans agreed with the statement "things have changed so much that I often feel like a stranger in my own country."[59] The first step for crossing over the empathy bridge, then, is simply *to listen*. Effective activism requires us to step out of our comfort zones and echo chambers, and to lend an ear to what others have to say. This is easier said than done. "Community organizing is often romanticized, but the actual work is about tenacity, perseverance, and commitment," says Alicia Garza. It is "the messy work of bringing people together, from different backgrounds and experiences . . . It is the work of building relationships among people who may believe they have nothing in common so that together they can achieve a common goal."[60] As a sociologist specialized in the role of emotions in politics, Hochschild also knew the importance of understanding how her respondents felt, or what she called their "deep story," the "feels-as-if" story that moved them into action. And that was precisely what most mainstream commentators missed in their accounts of Trump's success. They did not know how people felt, but thought they knew how they "should feel" – about abortion, same-sex marriages, immigration, affirmative action policies. Trump, however, knew; he was the "emotions candidate," not only evoking emotion, but also making "an object of it, presenting them back to his fans as a sign of collective success."[61]

After four years of Trump presidency, a neck-and-neck presidential race and an insurrection to overturn the results of a democratic election, the mainstreaming of anti-immigrant feelings even by social democratic parties, the woke Left is not doing any better. We are still told by some Diversity, Equity and Inclusion trainers and anti-racist activists that simply by dint of being born White, we are racists contributing to the reproduction of White supremacy. We are still instructed by some trans rights activists that asking questions about the legal, political, and social implications of the blurring of the distinction between biological sex and the social construct gender makes us transphobic at best, fascist at worst.[62] And we are the "good ones" so to speak, White progressives or "nice racists" to use Robin DiAngelo's terminology. Others, actual conservatives, are beyond salvation. There is no point in trying to reach out to them. In fact, that is the mistake some people on the Left, "including some of the most intelligent and sensitive commentators, such as Arlie Russell Hochschild, seem to me to be making at the moment," says Cornell philosopher Kate Manne. Listening and offering sympathy feeds "the very need and sense of entitlement that drives [these misogynistic mobs] in the first place." If you are frustrated

– like me, she hastens to add – by "the apathy, indifference, and pernicious ignorance of most people . . . maybe the thing to say, somewhat reluctantly, is – fuck 'em, in the limited sense of ceasing to even try to catch the moderate with mild honey."[63]

Quite a statement, coming from an academic with a large social media following – in fact one that is hailed as "The Philosopher of #MeToo."[64] But how are we supposed to bring about change if we dismiss the conservative and the reactionary (not to mention a substantial chunk of fellow progressives)? After all, they are the majority, and an active one at that. As Ian Haney López documents in his 2019 book *Merge Left: Fusing Race and Class, Winning Elections, and Saving America*, White evangelical Christians constituted one out of every five voters in 2016, and accounted for one-third of all Trump's votes, thus outdoing the margin that Blacks and Latino voters provided to Hillary Clinton.[65] If we turn our attention to White non-college voters, the situation is not any better. First, this group is huge, making up 44 percent of all voters in 2016. Second, Trump won this group by a very large margin, 64 percent compared to 28 percent for Clinton.[66]

One ambitious, empirically tested, answer to this question is the Race-Class Narrative, developed by an international group of academics including Ian Haney López, author and policy advocate Heather McGee, strategic communications consultant Anat Shenker-Osorio, and progressive think tanks and policy firms such as Lake Research Partners, Brilliant Corners, Service Employees International Union (SEIU) and Demos in 2017. Created with the aim of neutralizing "dog whistle politics" – i.e., "an expression or statement that has a secondary meaning intended to be understood only by a particular group of people" – which uses racism to pit Whites against People of Color, the race-class narrative seeks to come up with an alternative framing of racism, one that portrays "racism as a weapon of the rich."[67]

The origins of the race-class narrative can be traced to the concept of "interest convergence" coined by the late Derrick Bell, law professor and the founder of Critical Race Theory, who believed that racial equality could only be achieved when the interests of Blacks converge with the interests of Whites. Even though people do sometimes act altruistically, López says, it is not realistic to expect Whites, or any other group for that matter, to relinquish their privileges simply because it is the right thing to do. Rather, we should convince them that what hurts Blacks or People of Color will eventually hurt them too. This requires shifting the "us" versus "them" dynamic of racism, and presenting it as a divide-and-conquer strategy on the part of the rich.[68] López is careful to distinguish between the race-class narrative and two alternative, well-discussed, approaches. The first, or the "race before class" approach, sees race as more important than class, and seeks to replace the latter in political organizing. The "race and class" approach, on the other hand, treats race and class as separate categories that should both be addressed (this is akin to Nancy Fraser's redistribution *and* recognition strategy). This approach does not work because it leaves people unclear about the links between racial and class-based oppression, and in turn uncertain about which one to prioritize. The race-class narrative, or race-hyphen-class, starts from the premise that "race and class . . . blend together like welded steel." We believed, López says, "the Left could prevail by turning this fusion to progressive advantage. Our theory was that the Left must simultaneously fight for racial justice and for economic fairness because they are inseparably connected."[69]

The next step for López and his colleagues was to test this theory. With the help of several organizations, they conducted a large survey interviewing activists, drafting potential messages, and trying them out with focus groups involving different racial communities across the US. The results were encouraging, and showed, against conventional wisdom, that most Whites hold progressive views on race, that majorities of Blacks and Latinos find large parts of the Right's "racial fear" story convincing and, most importantly, that a message urging the construction of a multiracial coalition to demand that the government should promote both racial and economic justice was more convincing to all groups than both the Right's racial fear story and other progressive narratives.[70]

And this is not an exclusively American story. In the UK, the Centre for Labour and Social Studies (CLASS) conducted research based on the methodology of the Race-Class Narrative project, with the aim of exposing "the way dog-whistle racism is used by the hard right (but also some parts of the left and centre) to create a divisive, 'anti-woke' narrative of the 'white working-class' being 'left behind' while people of colour and migrants are showered with unfair advantages." The results of the one-year survey, published online on May 17, 2022, showed that:

(i) Despite being truly diverse, working-class people have a lot in common, above all everyday experiences of precarity, prejudice, and a lack of power and place. They share hopes and desires for their families and futures.

(ii) A number of politicians, their wealthy friends, and the media use racism, xenophobia, and classism to divide working-class people. "The race-baiting that we frequently see (i.e., 'the white working class are left behind' and 'the woke brigade shout down ordinary people and label us racist')," the report says, "appeals to white people while alienating working-class people of colour."

(iii) The standard way progressives talk about race and class does not resonate with the ethnically diverse working class. The progressives often fall into the trap set by the Right and repeat their talking points, counterposing race and class and siloing issues. Hence, the report concludes, the Left is losing the battle.

(iv) The race-class messaging is effective, and acts as an anti-
dote by creating an inclusive "us" emphasizing the things
we have in common, what we want and value.[71]

The lesson to be drawn from these findings, and the race-
class narrative in general, is clear. If all politics is identity
politics, and identity formation is dialogical, in the sense that
we cannot define ourselves without establishing who we are
not, then the best strategy is to first look for the perfect Other
against which the greatest possible number of people define
themselves. This requires an active process of seeking allies,
people who may not necessarily be or think like us, but who
share our predicament – precarity, discrimination, marginalization, and so on. Being human is only the starting point
of this process (and in any case, it is not only humans who
suffer from the devastating effects of climate change or other
environmental hazards). Equally important is an awareness
that our "survival depends not on dominance over, but interdependence with others."[72] And that is precisely where the
woke Left fails. "Too much precious social justice space gets
sucked down into the black holes of performance rituals," says
activist Loretta J. Ross. "Rituals have their place in politics and
organizing, but they are no substitute for action, no more than
prayer at church substitutes for taking responsibility for one's
choices."[73]

It is time that the Left takes responsibility for its choices.
Because tomorrow will be too late.

Epilogue

An Early Reply to Critics

"I think that your argument is mostly going to be used against the Left, not the Right. And the Left is not the main problem at the moment," said a colleague when I told her about my book some months ago. We were not that close, but I counted her as a friend, and I knew that she had my best interests in mind. Her cautionary words reminded me of George Orwell's struggle to get *Animal Farm*, an allegory of the Russian Revolution and the early stages of the Soviet Union, published. The book was rejected by four publishers until it finally saw the light of day in 1945. "Both publicly and privately you were warned that it was 'not done'," Orwell wrote in a proposed preface to the book. "What you said might possibly be true, but it was 'inopportune' and played into the hands of this or that reactionary interest."[1] The intellectual atmosphere is no better today, so my friend certainly had a point. As I was making my way out of the woke rabbit hole, I decided I would address her concerns in the Epilogue of the book – rather than in person – since they raise a number of important issues that are worth breaking down one by one.

First, is my argument going to be used by the Right? I doubt it, at least not by anyone acting in good faith. My argument is against identity politics on both the Right and the Left, not only against woke activism. I make it clear from the get-go that I consider right-wing populism, nativism, and White nationalism (not to mention far right extremism) as variations on one form of identity politics, namely White identity politics. And I am hardly the only one who suggests that. Quite a few writers, moderates and progressives alike, make the same point. It was, after all, Arlie Russell Hochschild who said that "Trump was the identity politics candidate for white men."[2] I devote several pages to debunking the myths propagated by the reactionary Right both in the UK and the US, and expose their duplicitous approach to cancel culture. Where were free speech warriors when American philosopher and activist Cornel West shared his official resignation letter from Harvard University online, where he insinuated that the denial of his tenure was linked to his support for the Palestinian cause?[3] How much time was allotted to conservative activist Christopher F. Rufo and his government-supported all-out-war against Critical Race Theory compared to the time devoted to the renaming of buildings to allegedly rid campuses of the last vestiges of the colonial past?[4] I could go on forever, but I think I've made my point.

So no, the Right will not "use" my arguments. More likely, they will dislike my characterization of their work, or White identity politics in general, and resort to the same tactics they claim the woke Left is deploying, i.e., *ad hominem* attacks, straw man arguments, decontextualizing or misrepresenting my position, and so on. Possibly, I will be dismissed as yet another globalist dilettante or a hopeless Bernie Sanders wannabe who is detached from the realities of the left behind. This, of course, would mean that these critics have not bothered to read the book to the end since (i) I take working-class grievances, White or Black, very seriously, (ii) I blame the woke

Left for pouring scorn on them, and (iii) I support active state intervention to address these grievances.

What they will do, then, is to ignore the book altogether so as not to amplify its message and boost its circulation. They will possibly be joined by the moderates who will keep their distance for fear of guilt by association or, God forbid, *cancel by association*. After all, we live in times where simply retweeting the hashtag #IStandWithJKRowling could get you banned from Twitter or even cost you your job.[5] You think I'm exaggerating? Just ask Gillian Philip, a Glasgow-born bestselling children's author. Or Amy Hamm, a nurse in Vancouver who founded the Canadian Women's Sex-Based Rights.[6]

Second question. Is my argument going to be used against the Left? Well, the answer depends on which Left. If we are talking about the universalist Left, that is inconceivable because, despite some disagreements, this is where I am speaking from. The book owes a lot to class-based analyses, the left liberal tradition, and internationalism, among others. And it issues a call for a human rights-based universalism which should be complemented with a progressive program, a new social contract if you will, based on an ecumenical understanding of social justice within the framework of a democratic socialist welfare state firmly committed to economic redistribution, cultural recognition, and political participation.

Probably the most important difference of this model from Marxism and other universalist visions is its stress on taking the individual as the basic unit of analysis. It is important to note here that this heuristic choice, i.e., considering the individual as the ultimate subject of justice claims, is not the same thing as defending "individualism," understood as a political doctrine or theory. The classical liberal theory of individualism upholds the principle that individuals should be allowed to act independently, free from the interference of the state or any other collectivity. It also champions a vaguely defined notion of self-reliance. My model is the exact opposite of this, and equidistant to both classical liberalism, which prescribes a minimal state, and communitarianism, which conceives of individuals as social beings shaped by the communities to which they belong. As a matter of fact, both these visions are riddled with obvious tensions. The classical liberal is individualist when it comes to the exercise of various freedoms, but immediately turns to the state (especially its policing and punitive capacity) when any of these freedoms are perceived to be under threat. It is no coincidence that the most ardent supporters of The Higher Education (Freedom of Speech) Bill in the UK are those who position themselves on the right of the political spectrum, even though the Bill creates a statutory tort enabling individuals to sue for compensation for losses suffered as a result of an academic institution's failure to protect freedom of speech as well as a new position, the office of Director for Freedom of Speech and Academic Freedom, known as the "free speech champion," which would monitor potential infringements. It is also amusing to watch how quickly right-wing culture warriors forget their disdain for group-based differences when the latter derive from membership of the nation or the dominant religious faith. It is not difference per se that ruffles the feathers of the Right; rather, it is difference of a particular type – that of the ethnic minority who resists voluntary assimilation, of gender non-conforming people who reject traditional family values, of the atheist who refuses to abide by the rules set out in religious texts, and so on.

Communitarians are a different breed. They are liberals, in that they value individual rights and freedoms, but consider group membership as part of these rights, and a fundamental one at that, without which it is not possible for the individual to flourish and enjoy her full potential. I have already discussed the problems associated with such a valorization of group-based rights, so I will not dwell too much on them here. Suffice to say that the communitarian view reifies groups, hardening the boundaries that separate them from each other, and ignores intragroup differences, often ending up empowering self-appointed leaders to speak on behalf of the whole group and impose ideological conformity.

I have taken pains to differentiate myself from different strains of individualism, not only to show that my choice of the individual as a heuristic device is not individualist as such – philosophically speaking – but also to highlight another reason why the Right will not attempt to hijack my argument. My model explicitly recognizes identity-based differences without rooting them in predetermined, tightly knit, and self-reproducing groups. It is intersectionalist, for it admits that each individual is subject to various interlocking forms of oppression. This in itself is enough to keep the Right away, since so far as right-wing pundits are concerned, intersectionalism is what garlic is to vampires. On the other hand, my intersectionalism does not reduce oppression to membership of a particular group, and only that. To give a concrete example: as some feminists rightly note, women are a sex class who are subject to forms of oppression that biological men and certain categories of gender non-conforming people do not experience. That should be recognized and accommodated via appropriate policies. But, in its original formulation, intersectionality tells us that various forms of oppression women face qua women are not the same for each member of this group. Some, say, Black women are doubly oppressed by Black nationalist men and White feminist women. Others, like the authors of the Combahee statement, face a third oppression for being queer. This means that no woman will be subject to the same kind or level of oppression, or experience oppression in the same way. But, as the example of the 2017 Women's March on Washington has shown us, these differences do not constitute an impediment to working together to achieve a common goal or build a better future.

The Privileged and the Entitled

There is, of course, another way of interpreting the second question. Is my argument going to be used to challenge or undermine the woke Left? I hope so! That's the whole point of the book – to show that woke identity politics is a radical departure from, in fact contradicts, the beliefs of Black queer feminist activists who coined the term in the first place. I won't waste your time rehashing the arguments put forward in previous chapters, and turn to the real question we should be asking here: how will the woke Left treat this book? It is interesting that my friend was only concerned by the Right's reaction, and did not raise any questions with regard to the identitarian Left, the main target of my argument. I can only speculate of course, but I guess it's because she already knew what's going to happen. If you're on social media, or interested in politics, you'll know it too.

The woke Left's reaction to this book will be identical to that of the populist-nationalist Right.

Instead of being accused of shutting my ears to the disgruntled voices of White majorities, I will be accused of being one, a White middle-class man reeking of privilege and entitlement. Once branded as such, the question is no longer whether to argue or not; rather it is whether "to tar and feather" or "to tie on a stake and burn." Whatever the final decision, the menu is set. Mansplaining for starters, transphobia as the main dish, and some misogyny with a topping of White racism as dessert – not to mention the trendy "useful idiot" and "far right enabler" as compliments of the chef.

Fine, I accept. I walked into the restaurant myself, knowing full well what's on the menu, including the specialty of the day, the succulent "proto-fascist." I won't complain about the food, dispute the bill, and try to reason with the manager. I confess to my privilege and my entitlement. I have a job that I like, and I can pay for my bills. I hold one of the strongest passports in the world, so I can travel anywhere I like as long as I have the means. I am not suffering from discrimination on the basis of my skin color or my sexual orientation, at least not in the country that I live in. I have access to free healthcare and other basic needs. Most importantly, I am surrounded with people who love me, and I love them back. My life hasn't been a bed of roses, but whose is? And yes, I feel entitled to write this book and question dominant orthodoxies.

How about the woke Left's privilege and entitlement? What gives them the right to wield these two words to decimate anyone who puts a spoke in their wheel? I don't know about you, but I am fed up with this disingenuity and this sense of, yes, entitlement. My concerned friend is ultimately right; the woke is not indeed the main problem at the moment. But does the woke know about this? And the silent majority? What are they afraid of? Being cancelled? But how can you be afraid of something you believe doesn't exist?

Let me tell you what my problems are then. My problem is Giorgia Meloni, the winner of the 2022 elections in Italy who once said "each of us has a unique genetic code that is unrepeatable. And, like it or not, that is sacred. We will defend it. We will defend God, country and family."[7] My problem is the 500 bombings that have taken place since 2018 in Sweden[8] and the 5,996 people killed in the Russia–Ukraine war (as of September 26, 2022 –quite possibly an underestimate).[9] I am more worried about accelerating climate change which made 2021 officially the sixth warmest year on record than I am about Canada's first Federal 2LSLGBTQI+ Action Plan, proudly presented as the first document to use the term "gendercide."[10] I believe it is more urgent to address the problem of legal deforestation which destroys about 5 million hectares of forest a year (a third of global tropical deforestation occurs in Brazil's Amazon forest egged on by far right leader Bolsonaro) than the recognition of "eunuch" as a new gender identity.[11] And I am more troubled by the 1,700 environmental activists murdered in the past decade or the 85 percent of the world population who live on less than $30 per day than finding the most inclusive pronouns to address each other.[12] I am also aware that the "lesser" concerns are, in many ways, symptoms of the major concerns. It is not an either/or matter.

So, does all this mean the issues that the woke Left is pre-occupied with are not important? Of course not. Should we postpone dealing with them until other, more urgent, issues are resolved? Not necessarily. Do I think that radical identity politics is distracting us from non-culture-war-related issues? Yes, I do. Do I believe that woke activism is an individual empowerment-driven, narcissistic middle- and upper middle-class pastime? Absolutely. And I wonder: why are there so few progressive leftists who shout "the emperor has no clothes"?

Orwell was right when he said, "The enemy is the gramo-phone mind, whether or not one agrees with the record that is being played at the moment." Last I checked, I wasn't a gramophone. And I'm certainly not scared of the tarring and feathering. I want to be in the trenches, and fight against the real enemy, the reactionary Right, shoulder-to-shoulder with whoever feels threatened by the global illiberal onslaught against our freedoms.

Notes

* Almost all books cited below are eBooks. As the eReader used or the size of font and screen orientation change the numbering of the pages, I will cite relevant chapters when a direct quote is used. In all other cases, page numbers will be provided in line with APA rules.

Prologue
1 This book is not about the state-supported attempt to cancel me. For details, see umutozkirimli.com/thetrial.
2 Lewis Carroll, *Alice's Adventures in Wonderland*, Collector's Library, New Edition, 2009.
3 See, for example, Umut Özkırımlı, *Theories of Nationalism: A Critical Introduction*, Palgrave Macmillan, 2017 and Umut Özkırımlı, "I was a natural cosmopolitan. Sweden, and the far right, changed all that," *The Guardian*, January 23, 2019, https://www.theguardian.com/commentisfree/2019/jan/23/cosmopolitan-sweden-far-right-refuge-europe.
4 "woke, adj.2." *OED Online*, Oxford University Press, September 2022, www.oed.com/view/Entry/58068747.
5 "FULL TEXT: Donald Trump's 2020 Republican National Convention speech," ABC News, https://abcnews.go.com/Polit

ics/full-text-donald-trumps-2020-republican-national-conventi
on/story?id=72659782.

6 "cancel, v." *OED Online*, Oxford University Press, September
   2022, www.oed.com/view/Entry/26916.

7 See, for example, "Transgender Studies and Feminism: Theory,
   Politics, and Gendered Realities" (Special Issue), *Hypatia*, 24 (3),
   2009 and Ruth Pearce, Sonia Erikainen, and Ben Vincent, "TERF
   Wars: An Introduction," *The Sociological Review*, 68 (4), 2020,
   https://doi.org/10.1177/0038026120934713.

8 Jessica Parker and Eleanor Lawrie, "Stonewall boss defends new
   strategy amid criticism," BBC News, May 29, 2021, https://www
   .bbc.co.uk/news/uk-57281448.

9 J. K. Rowling, Twitter, @jk_rowling, July 2, 2022, https://twitter
   .com/jk_rowling/status/1543001990942318594.

10 Aja Romano, "Can more Harry Potter ever be okay?," *Vox*,
    February 1, 2021, https://www.vox.com/culture/22254435/harry
    -potter-tv-series-hbo-jk-rowling-transphobic.

11 Ibid.

12 Kevin Rawlinson, "'Abolish whiteness' academic calls for
    Cambridge support," *The Guardian*, June 25, 2020, https://www
    .theguardian.com/education/2020/jun/25/abolish-whiteness-
    academic-calls-for-cambridge-support.

13 Robin DiAngelo, *White Fragility: Why It's So Hard for White
    People to Speak About Racism*, Beacon Press, 2018, chapter 7
    ("Racial Triggers for White People").

14 Robin DiAngelo, *Nice Racism: How Progressive White People
    Perpetuate Racial Harm*, Allen Lane, 2021, chapter 1 ("What is a
    Nice Racist?").

15 Robin DiAngelo, *White Fragility*, chapter 12 ("Where Do We Go
    From Here?").

16 Ibid.

17 "Accountability Statement," https://www.robindiangelo.com/ac
    countability-statement/.

18 Loretta J. Ross, "I'm a Black Feminist. I Think Call-Out Culture
    Is Toxic," *The New York Times*, August 17, 2019, https://www.ny

times.com/2019/08/17/opinion/sunday/cancel-culture-call-out
.html.

19 Loretta J. Ross, interview by Joyce Follet, transcript of video recording, Voices of Feminism Oral History Project, Sophia Smith Collection, November 3, 2004, p. 3.

20 Loretta J. Ross, Erika Derkas, Whitney Peoples, Lynn Roberts, and Pamela Bridgewater Toure (eds.), *Radical Reproductive Justice: Foundations, Theory, Practice, Critique*, The Feminist Press, 2017, "Introduction."

21 Al Kamen and Benjamin Weiser, "3 SE Men Plead Guilty to Murder of Housing Activist," *Washington Post*, November 17, 1981, https://www.washingtonpost.com/archive/local/1981/11/17/3-se-men-plead-guilty-to-murder-of-housing-activist/530f8f37-4bc2-4b9b-98d6-23be95d312be/.

22 Loretta J. Ross, interview by Joyce Follet, transcript of video recording, Voices of Feminism Oral History Project, p. 122.

23 Loretta J. Ross, "I'm a Black Feminist."

24 Loretta J. Ross, "Ritualizing Social Justice – Dred Feminist Rant #9," December 16, 2017, https://lorettajross.com/dred-feminist-blog/ritualizing-social-justice-dred-feminist-rant-9.

Chapter 1: A Rude Awakening

1 Amanda Hess, "How a Fractious Women's Movement Came to Lead the Left," *The New York Times*, February 7, 2017, https://www.nytimes.com/2017/02/07/magazine/how-a-fractious-womens-movement-came-to-lead-the-left.html.

2 Erica Chenoweth and Jeremy Pressman, "This is what we learned by counting the women's marches," *Washington Post*, February 7, 2017, https://www.washingtonpost.com/news/monkey-cage/wp/2017/02/07/this-is-what-we-learned-by-counting-the-womens-marches/.

3 Anna North, "The Women's March changed the American left. Now anti-Semitism allegations threaten the group's future," *Vox*, December 21, 2018, https://www.vox.com/identities/2018/12

/21/18145176/feminism-womens-march-2018-2019-farrakhan
-intersectionality.

4 Ibid.

5 "Transcript: Donald Trump's Taped Comments About Women,"
   The New York Times, October 8, 2016, https://www.nytimes.com
   /2016/10/08/us/donald-trump-tape-transcript.html.

6 Kristen Jordan Shamus, "Pink pussyhats: The reason feminists
   are ditching them," *Detroit Free Press*, January 10, 2018, https://
   eu.freep.com/story/news/2018/01/10/pink-pussyhats-feminists
   -hats-womens-march/1013630001/.

7 Julie Compton, "At 2nd annual Women's March, some protesters
   left 'pussy hats' behind," NBC News, January 23, 2018, https://
   www.nbcnews.com/feature/nbc-out/2nd-annual-women-s-mar
   ch-some-protesters-left-pussy-hats-n839901.

8 C. Mandler, "Please Stop Wearing Those Pussy Hats To Women's
   Marches," *Seventeen*, January 8, 2019, https://www.seventeen
   .com/life/a15854506/stop-wearing-pussy-hats-womens-mar
   ches/.

9 Jamie E. Shenton, "The Pussyhat's Identity Crisis," *Sapiens*,
   January 17, 2019, https://www.sapiens.org/biology/pussyhat
   -identity-crisis/.

10 Ibid.

11 Farah Stockman, "Women's March on Washington Opens
    Contentious Dialogues About Race," *The New York Times*,
    January 9, 2017, https://www.nytimes.com/2017/01/09/us/wom
    ens-march-on-washington-opens-contentious-dialogues-abo
    ut-race.html.

12 Emily Crockett, "Can you be a 'pro-life feminist'? The Women's
    March on Washington offered some insights," *Vox*, January 22,
    2017, https://www.vox.com/identities/2017/1/22/14335292/wo
    mens-march-washington-abortion-pro-life-feminists.

13 "Louis Farrakhan," SPLC (Southern Poverty Law Center), https://
    www.splcenter.org/fighting-hate/extremist-files/individual/lou
    is-farrakhan.

14 Tamika Mallory, "Tamika Mallory Speaks: 'Wherever My People Are Is Where I Must Be'," *NewsOne*, March 7, 2018, https://news one.com/3779389/tamika-mallory-saviours-day/.

15 Leah McSweeney and Jacob Siegel, "Is the Women's March Melting Down?," *Tablet*, December 11, 2018, https://www.table tmag.com/sections/news/articles/is-the-womens-march-mel ting-down.

16 Ibid.

17 Anna North, "The Women's March changed the American left. Now anti-Semitism allegations threaten the group's future," *Vox*, December 21, 2018, https://www.vox.com/identities/2018/12 /21/18145176/feminism-womens-march-2018-2019-farrakhan -intersectionality.

18 Erica Chenoweth and Jeremy Pressman, "January's Women's March brought out more than a million people – and many more also protested during the month," *Washington Post*, February 26, 2018, https://www.washingtonpost.com/news/monkey-cage/wp /2018/02/26/januarys-womens-march-brought-out-more-than -a-million-people-and-many-more-also-protested-during-the -month/.

19 Erica Chenoweth and Jeremy Pressman, "The 2019 Women's March was bigger than you think," *Washington Post*, February 1, 2019, https://www.washingtonpost.com/news/monkey-cage/wp /2019/02/01/the-2019-womens-march-was-bigger-than-you-th ink/.

20 "Women's Rights are Human Rights," White Ribbon Alliance, https://whiteribbonalliance.org/campaigns/womens-march-glo bal/.

21 Ella Nilsen, "The women, people of color, and LGBTQ candi-dates who made history in the 2017 election," *Vox*, November 8, 2017, https://www.vox.com/policy-and-politics/2017/11/8/1662 2884/women-minorities-lgbtq-candidates-made-history.

22 Kristen Jordan Shamus, "Pink pussyhats: The reason feminists are ditching them."

23 Tamika Mallory, "Tamika Mallory Speaks: 'Wherever My People Are Is Where I Must Be'."

24 Loretta J. Ross, "Enough with Intersectionality – Dred Feminist Rant #4," February 18, 2018, https://lorettajross.com/dred-feminist-blog/enough-with-intersectionality.

25 "Freedom in the World 2021: Democracy Under Siege," Freedom House, https://freedomhouse.org/sites/default/files/2021-02/FI W2021_World_02252021_FINAL-web-upload.pdf.

26 "Global democracy has a very bad year," *The Economist*, February 2, 2021, https://www.economist.com/graphic-detail/2021/02/02 /global-democracy-has-a-very-bad-year.

27 "Autocratization Turns Viral: Democracy Report 2021," V-Dem Institute, March 2021, https://www.v-dem.net/static/website/ files/dr/dr_2021.pdf.

28 Michael Powell, "A Black Marxist Scholar Wanted to Talk About Race. It Ignited a Fury," *The New York Times*, August 14, 2020, https://www.nytimescom/2020/08/14/us/adolph-reed-cont roversy.html. See also Benjamin Wallace-Wells, "The Marxist Who Antagonizes Liberals and the Left," *The New Yorker*, January 31, 2022, https://www.newyorker.com/news/annals-of -inquiry/the-marxist-who-antagonizes-liberals-and-the-left.

29 Michael Powell, "A Black Marxist Scholar Wanted to Talk About Race. It Ignited a Fury."

30 "Tensions arise between 'Standing for Women' and balaclava-clad trans activists in Manchester," https://www.youtube.com /watch?v=XINVuhNa8GY.

31 Caroline Lowbridge, "The lesbians who feel pressured to have sex and relationships with trans women," BBC News, October 26, 2021, https://www.bbc.co.uk/news/uk-england-57853385.

32 Noah Sheidlower, "J.K. Rowling responds to Twitter pipe bomb death threat," *New York Post*, July 20, 2021, https://nypost.com /2021/07/20/j-k-rowling-responds-to-twitter-pipe-bomb-death -threat/; "J.K. Rowling and Joanne Harris in death threat row," *The Week*, August 16, 2022, https://www.theweek.co.uk/news

/uk-news/957665/jk-rowling-accuses-joanne-harris-in-death-th
reat-row.

33 Tauriq Moosa, "The 'punch a Nazi' meme: what are the ethics of punching Nazis?," *The Guardian*, January 31, 2017, https://www .theguardian.com/science/brain-flapping/2017/jan/31/the-pun ch-a-nazi-meme-what-are-the-ethics-of-punching-nazis.

34 These and other examples can be found at https://terfisaslur .com/.

35 Stanley Cohen, *Folk Devils and Moral Panics: The Creation of the Mods and Rockers*, 3rd edition, Routledge, 2002, p. viii.

36 Arianne Shahvisi, "What's the difference?," *London Review of Books*, 44 (17), September 8, 2022, https://www.lrb.co.uk/the-pa per/v44/n17/arianne-shahvisi/what-s-the-difference.

37 Stanley Cohen, *Folk Devils and Moral Panics*, p. xxxiii.

38 Ibid.

39 Ian Haney López, *Merge Left: Fusing Race and Class, Winning Elections, and Saving America*, The New Press, 2019, pp. 14–15.

40 Ibid., p. 15.

41 Franklin D. Roosevelt, "Franklin D. Roosevelt, 1941 State of the Union Address 'The Four Freedoms'," January 6, 1941, https://vo icesofdemocracy.umd.edu/fdr-the-four-freedoms-speech-text/.

42 John Stuart Mill, *On Liberty* (edited by David Bromwich and George Kateb), Yale University Press, 2003, p. 87.

Chapter 2: Identity Politics on the Right

1 Dan Barry, Mike McIntire, and Matthew Rosenberg, "'Our President Wants Us Here': The Mob That Stormed the Capitol," *The New York Times*, November 10, 2021, https://www.nytimes .com/2021/01/09/us/capitol-rioters.html.

2 Devlin Barrett and Matt Zapotosky, "FBI report warned of 'war' at Capitol, contradicting claims there was no indication of loom- ing violence," *Washington Post*, January 12, 2021, https://www .washingtonpost.com/national-security/capitol-riot-fbi-intelli gence/2021/01/12/30d12748-546b-11eb-a817-e5e7f8a406d6_ story.html.

3 Julia Jacobo, "This is what Trump told supporters before many stormed Capitol Hill," ABC News, January 7, 2021, https://abc news.go.com/Politics/trump-told-supporters-stormed-capi tol-hill/story?id=75110558.

4 Bob Woodward and Robert Costa, *Peril*, Simon and Schuster, 2021.

5 Cameron Joseph, "Meet the Obscure Think Tank Powering Trump's Biggest Lies," *Vice*, November 4, 2021, https://www .vice.com/en/article/qjb4y3/john-eastman-claremont-institute -supporting-jan-6-trumpism.

6 See, for example, Jaclyn Diaz and Rachel Treisman, "Members Of Right-Wing Militias, Extremist Groups Are Latest Charged In Capitol Siege," NPR, January 19, 2021, https://www.npr.org/sec tions/insurrection-at-the-capitol/2021/01/19/958240531/mem bers-of-right-wing-militias-extremist-groups-are-latest-charged -in-capitol-si; "Identifying far-right symbols that appeared at the U.S. Capitol riot," *Washington Post*, January 15, 2021, https:// www.washingtonpost.com/nation/interactive/2021/far-right-sy mbols-capitol-riot/; Sam Levin, "US Capitol riot: police have long history of aiding neo-Nazis and extremists," *The Guardian*, January 16, 2021, https://www.theguardian.com/us-news/2021 /jan/16/us-capitol-riot-police-neo-nazis-far-right.

7 Cas Mudde, *The Far Right Today*, Polity, 2019.

8 "American Face of Insurrection: Analysis of Individuals Charged for Storming the US Capitol on January 6, 2021," Chicago Project on Security & Threats, January 5, 2022.

9 "'Patriotic Counter-Revolution': The Political Mindset that Stormed the Capitol," Chicago Project on Security & Threats, April 11, 2022.

10 Ibid.

11 Ashley Jardina, *White Identity Politics*, Cambridge University Press, 2019, p. 16.

12 Ibid., p. 262.

13 Roger Eatwell and Matthew Goodwin, *National Populism: The Revolt Against Liberal Democracy*, Penguin, 2018, p. xvi.

14 Ibid., p. xxix.

15 Ibid.

16 Eric Kaufmann, "'Racial Self-Interest' Is Not Racism: Ethno-demographic Interests and the Immigration Debate," Policy Exchange, March 3, 2017, https://policyexchange.org.uk/wp-con tent/uploads/2017/03/Racial-Self-Interest-is-not-Racism-FIN AL.pdf.

17 Ibid.

18 "'Racial Self-Interest' Is Not Racism," Policy Exchange, March 3, 2017, https://policyexchange.org.uk/publication/racial-self -interest-is-not-racism/.

19 Ibid.

20 David Goodhart, Twitter, @David_Goodhart, January 11, 2021, https://twitter.com/David_Goodhart/status/13486489711709 63457; Eric Kaufmann, Twitter, @epkaufm, January 18, 2021, https://twitter.com/epkaufm/status/1351131863184773123; Matt Goodwin, Twitter, @goodwinmj, January 7, 2021, https:// twitter.com/goodwinmj/status/1347110031234379778?lang=en -GB.

21 Roger Eatwell and Matthew Goodwin, *National Populism*, pp. xxx–xxxi.

22 Matthew Goodwin, "Can Britain survive the woke wave?," *UnHerd*, July 12, 2021, https://unherd.com/2021/07/can-britain -survive-the-woke-wave/.

23 Ibid.

24 David Goodhart, "Too Diverse?," *Prospect*, February 20, 2004, https://www.prospectmagazine.co.uk/magazine/too-diverse-david-goodhart-multiculturalism-britain-immigration-globalisa tion.

25 Trevor Phillips, "Genteel xenophobia is as bad as any other kind," *The Guardian*, February 16, 2004, https://www.theguardian.com /world/2004/feb/16/race.equality.

26 David Goodhart, *The Road to Somewhere: The Populist Revolt and the Future of Politics*, Hurst & Co., 2017.

27 Ibid., pp. 2–3.

28 Ibid., pp. 5, 9, 23–4, 58, 68.

29 Ibid., p. 220.

30 "Author eats book after incorrect general election prediction – video," *The Guardian*, June 10, 2017, https://www.theguardian .com/politics/video/2017/jun/10/author-eats-book-after-incor rect-general-election-prediction-video.

31 Roger Eatwell and Matthew Goodwin, *National Populism*, p. xii.

32 Ibid., p. xxxii.

33 Stephen Moss, "Lord Glasman: 'I'm a radical traditionalist'," *The Guardian*, July 19, 2011, https://www.theguardian.com/politics /2011/jul/19/lord-glasman-radical-traditionalist.

34 Paul Embery, *Despised: Why the Modern Left Loathes the Working Classes*, Polity, 2021.

35 Ibid., p. 18.

36 Ibid., p. 176.

37 Roger Eatwell and Matthew Goodwin, *National Populism*, pp. 74–6.

38 Paul Embery, *Despised*, pp. 195 and 196.

39 David Goodhart, *The Road to Somewhere*, p. 22; Roger Eatwell and Matthew Goodwin, *National Populism*, p. 74; Paul Embery, *Despised*, p. 193.

40 David Goodhart, *The Road to Somewhere*, p. 106; Matthew Goodwin, "Can Britain survive the woke wave?"; Paul Embery, *Despised*, p. 11.

41 Roger Eatwell and Matthew Goodwin, *National Populism*, p. 72.

42 John Lichfield, "The racist myth of France's 'descent into savagery'," *Politico*, September 7, 2020, https://www.politico.eu/arti cle/marine-le-pen-racist-myth-france-descent-into-savagery/.

43 David Goodhart, *The Road to Somewhere*, p. 210.

44 Paul Embery, *Despised*, pp. 188–9.

45 Academics For, "Framing ethnic diversity as a 'threat' will normalise far-right hate, say academics," *openDemocracy*, October 23, 2018, https://www.opendemocracy.net/en/opendemocracy uk/framing-ethnic-diversity-debate-as-about-threat-legitimises -hat-0/.

46 Lisa Tilley, "On resigning from Birkbeck Politics . . .," August 31, 2021, https://litilley.medium.com/on-resigning-from-birk beck-politics-3681c0f65a91.

47 Eric Kaufmann, *Whiteshift: Populism, Immigration and the Future of White Majorities*, Allen Lane, 2018, p. 1.

48 Ibid., p. 21.

49 Ibid., p. 7.

50 Ibid., p. 22.

51 Ibid., pp. 4 and 11.

52 Matt McManus and Nathan J. Robinson, "Taking White Supremacist Talking Points Mainstream," *Current Affairs*, September 2, 2022, https://www.currentaffairs.org/2022/09/taking-white-supremacist-talking-points-mainstream; Peter Oborne, "Douglas Murray and the mainstreaming of the 'Great Replacement' theory," *Middle East Eye*, May 20, 2022, https://www.middleeasteye.net/opinion/douglas-murray-mainstrea ming-great-replacement-theory.

53 "Prime Minister Viktor Orbán met with several speakers of the conference 'The Future of Europe'," May 24, 2018, https://minis zterelnok.hu/prime-minister-viktor-orban-met-with-several-speakers-of-the-conference-the-future-of-europe/.

54 Renaud Camus, *You Will Not Replace Us!*, Chez l'Auteur, 2018.

55 Douglas Murray, *The Strange Death of Europe: Immigration, Identity, Islam*, Bloomsbury, 2017, "Introduction."

56 Ibid., chapter 1 ("The Beginning").

57 Ibid.

58 "white, adj. (and adv.) and n." *OED Online*, Oxford University Press, September 2022, www.oed.com/view/Entry/228566.

59 Eric Kaufmann, *Whiteshift*, p. 480.

60 Ibid., p. 478.

61 Ibid., p. 2.

62 Ibid., p. 14.

63 Ibid., pp. 27–8.

64 Ibid., p. 533.

65 Eric Kaufmann, "'Racial Self-Interest' Is Not Racism," p. 9.

66 Douglas Murray, "Introduction," in *The Madness of Crowds: Gender, Race and Identity*, Bloomsbury, 2019.

67 Eric Kaufmann, "Only government can break the spell of woke activists over our universities," *The Telegraph*, February 16, 2021, https://www.telegraph.co.uk/news/2021/02/16/government-can-break-spell-woke-activists-universities/.

68 Ibid.

69 Eric Kaufmann, Twitter, @epkaufm, August 15, 2021, https://twitter.com/epkaufm/status/1427010507106660357.

70 Matthew Goodwin, "Can Britain survive the woke wave?"

71 Matthew Goodwin, "Academics like me live in fear of the woke hate mob, writes MATTHEW GOODWIN, Professor of Politics at the University of Kent," *Daily Mail*, February 16, 2021, https://www.dailymail.co.uk/debate/article-9263781/Academics-like-live-fear-woke-hate-mob-writes-politics-professor-MATTHEW-GOODWIN.html.

72 James Davison Hunter, *Culture Wars: The Struggle to Define America*, Basic Books, 1991.

73 James Davison Hunter, "The Enduring Culture War," in James Davison Hunter and Alan Wolfe (eds.), *Is There a Culture War? A Dialogue on Values and American Public Life*, Pew Research Center and Brookings Institution Press, 2006, p. 21.

74 James Davison Hunter, *Culture Wars*, pp. 39 and 47.

75 Zack Stanton, "How the 'Culture War' Could Break Democracy," *Politico*, October 20, 2021, https://www.politico.com/news/magazine/2021/05/20/culture-war-politics-2021-democracy-analysis-489900.

Chapter 3: Identity Politics on the Left

1 Barbara Smith, in Keeanga-Yamahtta Taylor (ed.), *How We Get Free: Black Feminism and the Combahee River Collective*, Haymarket Books, 2017.

2 Duchess Harris, *Black Feminist Politics from Kennedy to Obama*, Palgrave Macmillan, 2011, p. 10.

3 Barbara Smith, in Keeanga-Yamahtta Taylor (ed.), *How We Get Free*.

4 The Combahee River Collective Statement, in Keeanga-Yamahtta Taylor (ed.), *How We Get Free: Black Feminism and the Combahee River Collective*, Haymarket Books, 2017.

5 Ibid.

6 Beverly Smith, in Keeanga-Yamahtta Taylor (ed.), *How We Get Free: Black Feminism and the Combahee River Collective*, Haymarket Books, 2017.

7 Demita Frazier, in Keeanga-Yamahtta Taylor (ed.), *How We Get Free: Black Feminism and the Combahee River Collective*, Haymarket Books, 2017.

8 Barbara Smith, in Keeanga-Yamahtta Taylor (ed.), *How We Get Free*.

9 Ibid.

10 Ibid.

11 Demita Frazier, in Keeanga-Yamahtta Taylor (ed.), *How We Get Free*.

12 Barbara Smith, in Keeanga-Yamahtta Taylor (ed.), *How We Get Free*.

13 Ibid.

14 William Julius Wilson, "'The Declining Significance of Race': Revisited & Revised," *Daedalus*, 140 (2), 2011, p. 57.

15 Adolph Reed, Jr., *Class Notes: Posing as Politics and Other Notes on the American Scene*, The New Press, 2000, p. xiv.

16 Todd Gitlin, *The Twilight of Common Dreams: Why America is Wracked by Culture Wars*, Metropolitan Books, 1995, p. 16.

17 Ibid., p. 32.

18 Ibid., p. 87.

19 Ibid., p. 148.

20 Martha Nussbaum, "The Professor of Parody: The Hip Defeatism of Judith Butler," *The New Republic*, February 22, 1999, https://newrepublic.com/article/150687/professor-parody.

21 Martha Nussbaum, "The Professor of Parody"; Adolph Reed, Jr., "Nothing Left: The long, slow surrender of American liberals,"

Harper's Magazine, March 2014, https://harpers.org/archive/20 14/03/nothing-left-2/.

22 Loretta J. Ross, "Enough with Intersectionality."

23 Thomas Kochan, Katerina Bezrukova, Robin Ely, et al., "The Effects of Diversity on Business Performance: Report of the Diversity Research Network," *Human Resource Management*, 42 (1), 2003, pp. 3–21.

24 "Workplace Diversity: Does It Work? Explaining 'Myth Vs. Reality'," http://www.braunconsulting.com/bcg/newsletters /winter2004/winter20042.html.

25 "Focusing on what works for workplace diversity," McKinsey & Company, April 7, 2017, https://www.mckinsey.com/featured -insights/gender-equality/focusing-on-what-works-for-workpla ce-diversity.

26 Pamela Newkirk, *Diversity, Inc. The Failed Promise of a Billion-Dollar Business*, Bold Type Books, 2019.

27 Frank Dobbin and Alexandra Kalev, "Why Doesn't Diversity Training Work? The Challenge for Industry and Academia," *Anthropology Now*, 10, 2018, https://scholar.harvard.edu/files /dobbin/files/an2018.pdf.

28 Pamela Newkirk, "Diversity Has Become a Booming Business. So Where Are the Results?," *Time*, October 10, 2019, https://time .com/5696943/diversity-business/.

29 Frank Dobbin and Alexandra Kalev, "Why Doesn't Diversity Training Work?"

30 Robin DiAngelo, https://www.robindiangelo.com/about-me/.

31 Daniel Bergner, "'White Fragility' Is Everywhere. But Does Antiracism Training Work?," *The New York Times*, July 15, 2020, https://www.nytimes.com/2020/07/15/magazine/white-fragility -robin-diangelo.html.

32 Robin DiAngelo, *White Fragility: Why It's So Hard for White People to Talk About Racism*, Beacon Press, 2018, "Author's Note."

33 Ibid., "Introduction: We Can't Get There From Here."

34 Ibid., chapter 6 ("Anti-Blackness").

35 Robin DiAngelo, *Nice Racism: How Progressive White People Perpetuate Racial Harm*, Penguin, 2021, chapter 1 ("What Is a Nice Racist?").

36 Ibid., chapter 3 ("There Is No Choir").

37 Ibid.

38 Robin DiAngelo, *Nice Racism*, chapter 1 ("Introduction").

39 "Are You a 'Nice Racist'? Robin DiAngelo on Her New Book | Amanpour and Company," https://www.youtube.com/watch?v=ANdiTJIKm-g.

40 Alicia Garza, in Keeanga-Yamahtta Taylor (ed.), *How We Get Free: Black Feminism and the Combahee River Collective*, Haymarket Books, 2017.

41 Robin DiAngelo, *Nice Racism*, chapter 7 ("Let's Talk About Shame").

42 Ibram X. Kendi, *Antiracist Baby* (Illustrations by Ashley Lukashevsky), Kokila, 2020.

43 Eric Levitz, "How Anti-Racist Is Anti-Racism?," *New York Magazine*, July 23, 2021, https://nymag.com/intelligencer/2021/07/how-anti-racist-is-ibram-x-kendis-anti-racism.html.

44 Ibram X. Kendi, https://www.ibramxkendi.com/.

45 Ibram X. Kendi, *How to Be an Antiracist*, One World, 2019, chapter 1 ("Definitions").

46 Ibid.

47 Ibid., chapter 1 ("Definitions"), chapter 12 ("Class"), and chapter 14 ("Gender").

48 Ibid., chapter 1 ("Definitions").

49 Alison Flood, "Reni Eddo-Lodge becomes first black British author to top UK book charts," *The Guardian*, June 16, 2020, https://www.theguardian.com/books/2020/jun/16/reni-eddo-lodge-first-black-british-author-top-uk-book-charts-why-i-m-no-longer-talking-to-white-people-about-race.

50 Reni Eddo-Lodge, *Why I'm No Longer Talking to White People About Race*, Bloomsbury, 2017, chapter 2 ("The System").

51 Martin Luther King, Jr., "Letter from Birmingham Jail," August

1963, https://www.csuchico.edu/iege/_assets/documents/susi -letter-from-birmingham-jail.pdf.

52 Reni Eddo-Lodge, *Why I'm No Longer Talking to White People About Race*, chapter 7 ("There's No Justice, There's Just Us").

53 Ibid., chapter 3 ("What is White Privilege?").

54 Gretchen Livingstone and Anna Brown, "Intermarriage in the U.S. 50 Years After Loving v. Virginia," Pew Research Center, May 18, 2017, https://www.pewresearch.org/social-trends/2017 /05/18/1-trends-and-patterns-in-intermarriage/#fn-22847-4.

55 Eric Levitz, "How Anti-Racist Is Anti-Racism?"

56 Neil Bhutta, Andrew C. Chang, Lisa J. Dettling, and Joanne W. Hsu with assistance from Julia Hewit, "Disparities in Wealth by Race and Ethnicity in the 2019 Survey of Consumer Finances," FEDS Notes, September 28, 2020, https://www.federalreserve .gov/econres/notes/feds-notes/disparities-in-wealth-by-race-a nd-ethnicity-in-the-2019-survey-of-consumer-finances-2020 0928.htm.

57 David Collier and James E. Mahon, Jr., "Conceptual 'Stretching' Revisited: Adapting Categories in Comparative Analysis," *The American Political Science Review*, 87 (4), 1993, pp. 845–55, https://doi:10.2307/2938818.

58 Robin DiAngelo, *Nice Racism*, chapter 1 ("Introduction").

59 Barbara Applebaum, "Critical Whiteness Studies," *Education*, June 9, 2016, https://doi.org/10.1093/acrefore/9780190264093 .013.5.

60 Peggy McIntosh, "White Privilege: Unpacking the Invisible Knapsack," *Peace and Freedom*, July/August 1989, https://psych ology.umbc.edu/files/2016/10/White-Privilege_McIntosh-1989 .pdf.

61 Barbara Applebaum, "Critical Whiteness Studies," p. 4.

62 Ibid., p. 6.

63 I am grateful to the anonymous reviewer of Polity for bringing this to my attention.

64 Cited in Jeffrey B. Perry, "The Developing Conjuncture and

Some Insights from Hubert Harrison and Theodore W. Allen on the Centrality of the Fight against White Supremacy," *Cultural Logic: A Journal of Marxist Theory and Practice*, 10, 2017, p. 78, https://doi.org/10.14288/clogic.v17i0.191523.

65 Theodore W. Allen, "Summary of the Argument of The Invention of the White Race by its author Theodore W. Allen: Part 1," *Cultural Logic*, 1998, https://credo.library.umass.edu/cgi-bin /pdf.cgi?id=scua:mums1021-s02-i002.

66 Daniel Bergner, "'White Fragility' Is Everywhere. But Does Antiracism Training Work?"

67 Mckenna Dallmeyer '22 and Adam Sabes, "EXCLUSIVE: UMich paid Kendi $20k for a one-hour virtual event," October 14, 2021, https://www.campusreform.org/article?id=18308; Asra Q. Nomani, "The 'Receipt' on Fairfax County Paying Ibram Kendi $20,000 for 1-Hour," September 25, 2020, https://asrainvestiga tes.substack.com/p/heres-the-receipt-on-fairfax-county; "CMS emails and contract with Ibram X. Kendi over $25,000 speaking fee," *The Charlotte Ledger*, July 15, 2021, https://cltledger.com /cms-emails-and-contract-with-ibram-x-kendi-over-25000-spe aking-fee/.

68 Nate Hochman, "Ibram X. Kendi Made About $541 a Minute for a Speech at the University of Virginia," *National Review*, February 9, 2022, https://www.nationalreview.com/corner/ibram-x-kendi -made-about-541-a-minute-for-a-speech-at-the-university-of -virginia/.

69 Andrew Barry, "The Anti-Political Economy," *Economy and Society*, 31 (2), 2002, pp. 268–84, http://dx.doi.org/10.1080/0308 5140220123162.

70 Ibid., p. 271.

71 Barbara Smith, in Keeanga-Yamahtta Taylor (ed.), *How We Get Free*.

Chapter 4: The Left Meets the Right

1 "Jack Brock Obituary," *Alamogordo Daily News*, published from April 3 to 5, 2020, https://www.legacy.com/us/obituaries/alam ogordonews/name/jack-brock-obituary?id=8905098.

2 "N.M. pastor leads flock in 'Potter' book burning," *Deseret News*, December 31, 2001, https://www.deseret.com/2001/12/31/19 629030/n-m-pastor-leads-flock-in-potter-book-burning. For a picture, see Anorak, "Biblioclasts: They Who Burn Books," *Flashbak*, April 4, 2015, https://flashbak.com/biblioclasts-they -who-burn-books-33438/harry-potter-book-burning/.

3 William H. Taylor and Kristi R. Humphreys, "Satan's Most Popular Pawn? Harry Potter and Modern Evangelical Cosmology," in Sharon Packer and Jody Pennington (eds.), *A History of Evil in Popular Culture: What Hannibal Lecter, Stephen King, and Vampires Reveal about America*, Praeger, 2014, p. 345.

4 "Pro-Potter Protesters Picket as Minister Destroys Book," BookWeb.org, November 20, 2002, https://www.bookweb.org /news/pro-potter-protesters-picket-minister-destroys-book.

5 Julia Alexander, "A history of Harry Potter books being burned – and J.K. Rowling's perfect responses," *Polygon*, February 1, 2017, https://www.polygon.com/2017/2/1/14474054/harry-potter-books-burning-jk-rowling-twitter.

6 Megan McCluskey, "J.K. Rowling Is Shutting Down Readers Who Burned All Their *Harry Potter* Books," *Time*, February 1, 2017, https://time.com/4657055/j-k-rowling-twitter-harry-pot ter-book-burning/.

7 Matthew Fishburn, *Burning Books*, Palgrave Macmillan, 2008.

8 United States Holocaust Memorial Museum, "Book Burning," *Holocaust Encyclopedia*, https://encyclopedia.ushmm.org/con tent/en/article/book-burning.

9 Richard Ovenden, *Burning the Books: A History of the Deliberate Destruction of Knowledge*, Harvard University Press, 2020, pp. 3–4.

10 Ibid., p. 3.

11 John Henley, "Book-burning: fanning the flames of hatred," *The Guardian*, September 10, 2010, https://www.theguardian.com /books/2010/sep/10/book-burning-quran-history-nazis.

12 Richard Ovenden, *Burning the Books*, p. 119.

13 Dana Gioia, "An Interview with Ray Bradbury," National Endowment for the Arts Reader Resources, January 5, 2005, https://www.arts.gov/sites/default/files/Reader-Resources-Fah renheit451.pdf.

14 "Harry Potter and the Ministry of Fire," *Forbes*, December 1, 2006, https://www.forbes.com/2006/11/30/book-burnings-pot ter-tech-media_cz_ds_books06_1201burn.html?sh=74bb29c6 318b.

15 Emma Nolan, "J.K. Rowling Book Burning Videos Are Spreading Like Wildfire Across TikTok," *Newsweek*, September 16, 2020, https://www.newsweek.com/jk-rowling-books-burned-tiktok -transgender-issues-1532330.

16 "Harry Potter books getting burned and banned to own JK Rowling!," https://www.youtube.com/watch?v=-dhdEqtIld0.

17 Jedward, Twitter, @planetjedward, September 15, 2020, https:// twitter.com/planetjedward/status/1305834661281697792.

18 Jake Kerridge, "Troubled Blood by Robert Galbraith, review: JK Rowling fails to Strike again," *The Telegraph*, September 13, 2020, https://www.telegraph.co.uk/books/what-to-read/troub led-blood-robert-galbraith-review-jk-rowling-fails-strike/.

19 Alison Flood, "JK Rowling's Troubled Blood: don't judge a book by a single review," *The Guardian*, September 15, 2020, https:// www.theguardian.com/books/booksblog/2020/sep/15/rowling -troubled-blood-thriller-robert-galbraith-review.

20 Ella Kipling, "JK Rowling book burning parties don't actually exist – Twitter and TikTok debate explained!," *HITC*, September 18, 2020, https://www.hitc.com/en-gb/2020/09/18 /jk-rowling-book-burning/.

21 Aja Romano, "Can more Harry Potter ever be okay?," *Vox*, February 1, 2021, https://www.vox.com/culture/22254435/har ry-potter-tv-series-hbo-jk-rowling-transphobic.

22 "Singular Nonbinary 'They': Is it 'they are' or 'they is'," *Merriam Webster*, https://www.merriam-webster.com/words-at-play/singular-nonbinary-they-is-or-they-are.

23 Aja Romano, "Harry Potter and the Author Who Failed Us," *Vox*, June 11, 2020, https://www.vox.com/culture/21285396/jk-rowling-transphobic-backlash-harry-potter.

24 Ibid.

25 For the full judgment, see "Maya Forstater v CGD Europe and Others: UKEAT/0105/20/JOJ," June 10, 2021, https://www.judiciary.uk/wp-content/uploads/2022/07/Forstater-JR-AG.pdf.

26 J. K. Rowling, Twitter, @jk_rowling, December 19, 2019, https://twitter.com/jk_rowling/status/1207646162813100033?lang=en.

27 "The Book Burning: Report by Louis P. Lochner, Head of the Berlin Bureau of the Associated Press," German History in Document and Images (GHDI), May 10, 1933, https://ghdi.ghi-dc.org/sub_document.cfm?document_id=1575.

28 Martha Nussbaum, "The Professor of Parody."

29 Adolph Reed, Jr., "Nothing Left: The long, slow surrender of American liberals."

30 Todd Gitlin, *The Twilight of Common Dreams*, pp. 147–8.

31 Keeanga-Yamahtta Taylor, "Introduction," in Keeanga-Yamahtta Taylor (ed.), *How We Get Free: Black Feminism and the Combahee River Collective*, Haymarket Books, 2017.

32 Ibid.

33 Barbara Smith, in Keeanga-Yamahtta Taylor (ed.), *How We Get Free*.

34 Demita Frazier, in Keeanga-Yamahtta Taylor (ed.), *How We Get Free*.

35 Ewan Goldstein, "Can Jonathan Haidt Calm the Culture Wars?," *The Chronicle of Higher Education*, June 11, 2017, https://www.chronicle.com/article/can-jonathan-haidt-calm-the-culture-wars/.

36 "Our Mission," Heterodox Academy, https://heterodoxacademy.org/our-mission/.

37 Greg Lukianoff and Jonathan Haidt, *The Coddling of the American Mind: How Good Intentions and Bad Ideas Are Setting Up a Generation For Failure*, Penguin, 2018, chapter 10 ("The Bureaucracy of Safetyism").

38 Ewan Goldstein, "Can Jonathan Haidt Calm the Culture Wars?"

39 Ibid.

40 Kate Manne, "Why I Use Trigger Warnings," *The New York Times*, September 19, 2015, https://www.nytimes.com/2015/09/20/opinion/sunday/why-i-use-trigger-warnings.html.

41 Jarret Crawford, "Why I Left Heterodox Academy," December 6, 2016, https://docs.google.com/document/d/1OSf9OBr-ch3rG2xjyD779LKrcwlfqHBHaOgWDG6GOyE/mobilebasic.

42 Jim Sleeper, "The Conservatives Behind the Campus 'Free Speech' Crusade," *The American Prospect*, October 19, 2016, https://prospect.org/education/conservatives-behind-campus-free-speech-crusade/. See also Jim Sleeper, "Political Correctness and Its Real Enemies," *The New York Times*, September 4, 2016, https://www.nytimes.com/2016/09/04/opinion/sunday/political-correctness-and-its-real-enemies.html.

43 Moira Weigel, "Political correctness: how the right invented a phantom enemy," *The Guardian*, November 30, 2016, https://www.theguardian.com/us-news/2016/nov/30/political-correctness-how-the-right-invented-phantom-enemy-donald-trump.

44 Jim Sleeper, "The Conservatives Behind the Campus 'Free Speech' Crusade."

45 Ewan Goldstein, "Can Jonathan Haidt Calm the Culture Wars?"

46 Andrew Goldman, "A Liberal Learns To Compete," *The New York Times*, July 17, 2012, https://www.nytimes.com/2012/07/29/magazine/a-liberal-learns-to-compete.html.

47 Greg Lukianoff and Jonathan Haidt, *The Coddling of the American Mind.*

48 Derald Wing Sue, Christina M. Capodilupo, Gina C. Torino, Jennifer M. Bucceri, Aisha M. B. Holder, Kevin L. Nadal, and

Marta Esquilin, "Racial Microaggressions in Everyday Life: Implications for Clinical Practice," *American Psychologist*, 62 (4), 2007, pp. 271–86.

49 "trigger, n.1." *OED Online*, Oxford University Press, September 2022, www.oed.com/view/Entry/206003.

50 Pen America, "And Campus for All: Diversity, Inclusion, and Freedom of Speech at U.S. Universities," Pew Research Center, October 17, 2016, https://pen.org/and-campus-for-all-diversity-inclusion-and-free-speech-at-u-s-universities/.

51 Judith Shulevitz, "In College and Hiding from Scary Ideas," *The New York Times*, March 21, 2015, https://www.nytimes.com/2015/03/22/opinion/sunday/judith-shulevitz-hiding-from-scary-ideas.html.

52 Kate Manne, "Why I Use Trigger Warnings."

53 Jeannie Suk Gersen, "What if Trigger Warnings don't Work?," *The New Yorker*, September 28, 2021, https://www.newyorker.com/news/our-columnists/what-if-trigger-warnings-dont-work.

54 "The Following News Release Contains Potentially Disturbing Content: Trigger Warnings Fail to Help and May Even Harm," Association for Political Science, June 9, 2020, https://www.psychologicalscience.org/news/releases/trigger-warnings-fail-to-help.html; Payton J. Jones, Benjamin W. Bellet, and Richard J. McNally, "Helping or Harming? The Effect of Trigger Warnings on Individuals with Trauma Histories," *Clinical Psychological Science*, 8 (5), 2020, pp. 905–17, https://doi.org/10.1177/2167702620921341.

55 Jeannie Suk Gersen, "The Trouble with Teaching Rape Law," *The New Yorker*, https://www.newyorker.com/news/news-desk/trouble-teaching-rape-law.

56 Gillian Brown, "Not Sure What People Mean By 'Triggering?' This Article Is Your One-Stop 101," *Everyday Feminism*, June 7, 2015, https://everydayfeminism.com/2015/06/guide-to-triggering/.

57 Katherine Timpf, "Lecturers Warned Not to Use Capital Letters to Avoid Scaring Students," *National Review*, November 21, 2018, https://www.nationalreview.com/2018/11/lecturers-warned-not-to-use-capital-letters-to-avoid-scaring-students/.

58 Katherine Timpf, "Evergreen State Asks Profs to Take Protestors' Feelings into Account When Grading Them," *National Review*, July 7, 2017, https://www.nationalreview.com/2017/07/evergreen-state-professors-grading-student-protesters-feelings/.

59 Katherine Timpf, "Students Drop 'Vagina' from The Vagina Monologues to Be More 'Inclusive'," *National Review*, February 20, 2019, https://www.nationalreview.com/2019/02/students-drop-vagina-from-the-vagina-monologues-to-be-more-inclusive/.

60 "Gender studies and sexualised threats," Sex Matters, July 26, 2021, https://sex-matters.org/posts/the-workplace/gender-studies-and-sexualised-threats/.

61 Bradley Campbell and Jason Manning, *The Rise of Victimhood Culture: Microaggressions, Safe Spaces, and the New Culture Wars*, Palgrave Macmillan, 2018.

62 Hadley Freeman, "Salman Rushdie: 'I am stupidly optimistic – it got me through those bad years'," *The Guardian*, May 15, 2021, https://www.theguardian.com/books/2021/may/15/salman-rushdie-i-am-stupidly-optimistic-it-got-me-through-those-bad-years.

63 "The struggle of trans and gender-diverse persons," United Nations Human Rights Office of the High Commissioner, https://www.ohchr.org/en/special-procedures/ie-sexual-orientation-and-gender-identity/struggle-trans-and-gender-diverse-persons.

64 Laura Kipnis, *Unwanted Advances: Sexual Paranoia Comes to Campus*, HarperCollins, 2017.

65 Laura Kipnis, "Why Are Scholars Such Snitches?," *The Chronicle of Higher Education*, March 17, 2022, https://www.chronicle.com/article/academe-is-a-hotbed-of-craven-snitches.

66 Wendy Brown, "Neo-liberalism and the End of Liberal

Democracy," *Theory & Event*, 7 (1), 2003, https://doi:10.1353 /tae.2003.0020. No page numbers.

67 Ibid.

68 Jonathan Friedman and Nadine Farid Johnson, "Banned in the USA: The Growing Movement to Censor Books in Schools," Pew Research Center, September 12, 2022, https://pen.org/ report/banned-usa-growing-movement-to-censor-books-in-schools/.

69 Sarah Schwartz, "Map: Where Critical Race Theory Is Under Attack," *Education Week*, June 11, 2021 (updated September 28, 2022), https://www.edweek.org/policy-politics/map-where -critical-race-theory-is-under-attack/2021/06.

70 Jennifer Schuessler and Elisabeth A. Harris, "Artists and Writers Warn of an 'Intolerant Climate.' Reaction Is Swift," *The New York Times*, June 7, 2020, https://www.nytimes.com/2020/07 /07/arts/harpers-letter.html.

71 "A Letter on Justice and Open Debate," *Harper's Magazine*, July 7, 2020, https://harpers.org/a-letter-on-justice-and-open -debate/.

72 Sarah Manavis, "'Cancel culture' does not exist," *The New Statesman*, July 16, 2020, https://www.newstatesman.com/ science-tech/2020/07/cancel-culture-does-not-exist.

73 Pankaj Mishra and Viet Thanh Nguyen, "'Free speech has never been freer': Pankaj Mishra and Viet Thanh Nguyen in conversation," *The Guardian*, July 24, 2020, https://www.theguard ian.com/books/2020/jul/24/free-speech-has-never-been-freer -pankaj-mishra-and-viet-thanh-nguyen-in-conversation.

74 Pankaj Mishra, "Cancel culture is not a threat to civilisation," *Gulf News*, July 15, 2020, https://gulfnews.com/opinion/op-eds /cancel-culture-is-not-a-threat-to-civilisation-1.72601156.

75 Laura Bradley, "J.K. Rowling and Other Assorted Rich Fools Want to Cancel 'Cancel Culture'," *Daily Beast*, July 7, 2020, https://www.thedailybeast.com/jk-rowling-and-other-assorted -rich-fools-want-to-cancel-cancel-culture.

76 Vivian Kane, "Rich, Famous Transphobes Ask You to Stop Being So Mean to Them in Terrible *Harper's Magazine* Open Letter," *The Mary Sue*, July 8, 2020, https://www.themarysue .com/harpers-mag-open-letter-dog-whistles/.

77 Emma Powys Maurice, "JK Rowling joins 150 writers, academics and activists calling for end to cancel culture – with an open letter in a major magazine," *Pink News*, July 8, 2020, https:// www.pinknews.co.uk/2020/07/08/harpers-magazine-letter-jk -rowling-margaret-atwood-cancel-culture/.

78 "A More Specific Letter on Justice and Open Debate," *The Objective*, July 10, 2020, https://objectivejournalism.org/2020 /07/a-more-specific-letter-on-justice-and-open-debate/.

79 Anne Applebaum, "The New Puritans," *The Atlantic*, August 31, 2021, https://www.theatlantic.com/magazine/archive/2021 /10/new-puritans-mob-justice-canceled/619818/.

80 Sarah Manavis, "'Cancel culture' does not exist."

81 Sam Fowles, "The 'invented' free speech crisis," Politics.co.uk, January 25, 2021, https://www.politics.co.uk/comment/2021 /01/25/the-invented-free-speech-crisis/.

82 Moira Weigel, "Political correctness: how the right invented a phantom enemy."

83 Pankaj Mishra, "Cancel culture is not a threat to civilisation."

84 Stanley Cohen, *Folk Devils and Moral Panics*.

85 Owen Jones, Twitter, @owenjones84, June 27, 2021, https://tw itter.com/owenjones84/status/1409205349786193922.

86 "The Observer view on the right to free expression," *The Observer*, June 27, 2021, https://www.theguardian.com/com mentisfree/2021/jun/27/the-observer-view-on-the-right-to-free -expression.

87 Vic Parsons, "13 troubling problems with white feminism, according to a white feminist who's seen them firsthand," *Pink News*, May 22, 2021, https://www.pinknews.co.uk/2020/05/22 /white-feminism-karen-alison-phipps-me-too-sex-work-trans -rights-middle-class/.

88 Zack Beauchamp, "The 'free speech debate' isn't really about free speech," *Vox*, July 22, 2020, https://www.vox.com/policy -and-politics/2020/7/22/21325942/free-speech-harpers-letter -bari-weiss-andrew-sullivan.

89 Sam Fowles, "The 'invented' free speech crisis."

90 Nesrine Malik, "The myth of the free speech crisis," *The Guardian*, September 3, 2019, https://www.theguardian.com /world/2019/sep/03/the-myth-of-the-free-speech-crisis.

91 Frank Furedi, "The free-speech crisis is not a right-wing myth," *Spiked*, March 12, 2021, https://www.spiked-online.com/2021 /03/12/the-free-speech-crisis-is-not-a-right-wing-myth/.

92 Alicia Garza, in Keeanga-Yamahtta Taylor (ed.), *How We Get Free: Black Feminism and the Combahee River Collective*, Haymarket Books, 2017.

93 Zack Beauchamp, "The 'free speech debate' isn't really about free speech."

94 Sam Fowles, "The 'invented' free speech crisis."

95 Kate Manne and Jason Stanley, "When Free Speech Becomes a Political Weapon," *The Chronicle of Higher Education*, November 13, 2015, https://www.chronicle.com/article/when -free-speech-becomes-a-political-weapon/.

96 Michael Love Michael, "Tarana Burke On the One-Year Anniversary of #MeToo Going Viral," *Paper*, October 15, 2018, https://www.papermag.com/tarana-burke-me-too-26114173 81.html.

97 Ibid.

98 "The 'Banned' List," Academics for Academic Freedom (AFAF), https://www.afaf.org.uk/the-banned-list/.

99 Laura Favaro, "Researchers are wounded in academia's gender wars," *Times Higher Education*, September 15, 2022, https:// www.timeshighereducation.com/depth/researchers-are-woun ded-academias-gender-wars. I am grateful to Laura Favaro for sharing the methodology section of her research with me.

100 Jon Ronson, *So You've Been Publicly Shamed*, Picador, 2015, chapter 4 ("God That Was Awesome").

101 Laura Bradley, "J.K. Rowling and Other Assorted Rich Fools Want to Cancel 'Cancel Culture'."

102 Jonathan Rauch, *The Constitution of Knowledge: A Defense of Truth*, Brookings Institution Press, 2021, chapter 7 ("Canceling: Despotism of the Few. Coercive conformity is corrupting the reality-based community").

103 Anne Applebaum, "The New Puritans."

104 Sarah Manavis, "'Cancel culture' does not exist."

105 Aja Romano, "Why we can't stop fighting about cancel culture," *Vox*, August 25, 2020, https://www.vox.com/culture/2019/12/30/20879720/what-is-cancel-culture-explained-history-debate.

106 Anna North, "Aziz Ansari has addressed his sexual misconduct allegation. But he hasn't publicly apologized," *Vox*, July 12, 2019, https://www.vox.com/identities/2019/7/12/20690303/aziz-ansari-sexual-misconduct-accusation-right-now; https://www.theguardian.com/tv-and-radio/2019/jul/20/aziz-ansari-netflix-special.

107 Elisha Fieldstadt, "Man suspected of attacking Dave Chappelle onstage says show was 'triggering'," NBC News, May 23, 2022, https://www.nbcnews.com/news/us-news/man-suspected-attacking-dave-chappelle-stage-says-show-was-triggering-rcna30057.

108 Natasha Livingstone, "Police investigating JK Rowling death threat after trans activist urged Twitter users to send bomb to author's home," *Daily Mail*, July 3, 2022, https://www.dailymail.co.uk/news/article-10976955/Police-investigating-JK-Rowling-death-threat-trans-activist-urged-Twitter-users-send-bomb.html.

109 Jacob Farr, "Edinburgh's JK Rowling shocked by Twitter response after receiving death threat," *Edinburgh Live*, August 16, 2022, https://www.edinburghlive.co.uk/news/edinburgh-news/edinburghs-jk-rowling-shocked-twitter-24766350.

110 Sarah Shaffi and Lucy Knight, "Society of Authors responds

to calls for Joanne Harris to step down as committee chair,"
The Guardian, August 17, 2022, https://www.theguardian.
com/books/2022/aug/17/society-of-authors-responds-joanne-harris
-step-down-committee-chair-jk-rowling; Julie Bindel, "An
Open Letter to the Society of Authors re Joanne Harris,"
Julie Bindel's Podcasts and Writing, August 16, 2022, https://
juliebindel.substack.com/p/an-open-letter-to-the-society-of?r
=7vxvx&s=r&utm_campaign=post&utm_medium=web.

111 Emma Powell, "Chocolat author Joanne Harris takes ANOTHER
swipe at JK Rowling on Twitter just hours after dismissing their
row as 'fabricated'," *Daily Mail*, August 18, 2022, https://www
.dailymail.co.uk/news/article-11121973/Joanne-Harris-takes-
swipe-JK-Rowling-Twitter-just-hours-dismissing-row-fabrica
ted.html.

112 Pankaj Mishra, "Stop Linking Rushdie Attack to Cancel
Culture," *Washington Post*, August 22, 2022, https://www.was
hingtonpost.com/business/stop-linking-rushdie-attack-to-can
cel-culture/2022/08/21/00c036f6-2152-11ed-a72f-1e7149072f
bc_story.html.

113 Derek Scally, "High-profile death prompts backlash against
#MeToo in Sweden," *The Irish Times*, March 30, 2018, https://
www.irishtimes.com/news/world/europe/high-profile-death-
prompts-backlash-against-metoo-in-sweden-1.3444849.

114 Marie Le Conte, "The Eye of the Storm," *The Critic*, July/August
2020, https://thecritic.co.uk/issues/july-august-2020/the-eye
-of-the-storm/.

115 Alona Ferber, "Judith Butler on the culture wars, JK Rowling
and living in 'anti-intellectual times'," *The New Statesman*,
September 22, 2020, https://www.newstatesman.com/long-re
ads/2020/09/judith-butler-culture-wars-jk-rowling-and-living
-anti-intellectual-times.

116 Ruth Hunt, "Our work for trans equality is at the heart of our
mission for acceptance without exception," Stonewall, October
4, 2018, https://www.stonewall.org.uk/node/100426. See also

Haroon Siddique, "Stonewall is at centre of a toxic debate on trans rights and gender identity," *The Guardian*, June 5, 2021, https://www.theguardian.com/society/2021/jun/05/stonewall -trans-debate-toxic-gender-identity.

117 Chris Hedges, "Chris Hedges: Cancel Culture, Where Liberalism Goes to Die," *Scheerpost*, February 15, 2021, https://scheerpost .com/2021/02/15/hedges-cancel-culture-where-liberalism-go es-to-die/.

118 Jeffrey M. Berry and Sarah Sobieraj, *The Outrage Industry: Political Opinion Media and the New Incivility*, Oxford University Press, 2014, p. 5.

119 Ibid., p. 9.

120 Eric Kaufmann, "The Threat to Academic Freedom: From Anecdotes to Data," *Quillette*, March 12, 2021, https://quillette .com/2021/03/12/the-threat-to-academic-freedom-from-anec dotes-to-data/.

121 Kate Manne and Jason Stanley, "When Free Speech Becomes a Political Weapon."

122 Nesrine Malik, "The myth of the free speech crisis."

123 "Roe v Wade: What is US Supreme Court ruling on abortion?," BBC News, June 24, 2022, https://www.bbc.co.uk/news/world -us-canada-54513499.

124 Nesrine Malik, "The myth of the free speech crisis."

125 Chris Hedges, "Chris Hedges: Cancel Culture, Where Liberalism Goes to Die."

126 Jeffrey M. Berry and Sarah Sobieraj, *The Outrage Industry*, p. 7.

127 Chris Hedges, "Chris Hedges: Cancel Culture, Where Liberalism Goes to Die."

Chapter 5: Toward a New Progressive Left

1 Alicia Garza, *The Purpose of Power: How We Come Together When We Fall Apart*, One World, 2020, chapter 6 ("Trayvon, Obama, and the Birth of Black Lives Matter").

2 John H. Richardson, "Michael Brown Sr. and the Agony of the

Black Father in America," *Esquire*, January 5, 2015, https://www
.esquire.com/news-politics/interviews/a30808/michael-brown
-father-interview-0115/.

3 "Herstory," https://blacklivesmatter.com/herstory/.

4 Alicia Garza, *The Purpose of Power*, chapter 7 ("Rebellion and Resistance").

5 Ibid.

6 Monica Davey and Julie Bosman, "Protests Flare After Ferguson Police Officer Is Not Indicted," *The New York Times*, November 24, 2014, https://www.nytimes.com/2014/11/25/us/ferguson-dar
ren-wilson-shooting-michael-brown-grand-jury.html.

7 Alicia Garza, *The Purpose of Power*, chapter 7 ("Rebellion and Resistance") and chapter 5 ("Unite to Fight").

8 Darnell L. Moore, "Two Years Later, Black Lives Matter Faces Critiques, But It Won't Be Stopped," *MIC*, November 8, 2015, https://www.mic.com/articles/123666/two-years-later-black-liv
es-matter-faces-critiques-but-it-won-t-be-stopped.

9 Alicia Garza, *The Purpose of Power*, chapter 7 ("Rebellion and Resistance").

10 "Patrisse Cullors: Black Lives Matter co-founder resigns," BBC News, May 28, 2021, https://www.bbc.co.uk/news/world-us-ca
nada-57277777.

11 Darren Sands, "What Happened To Black Lives Matter?," Buzzf
eed.News, June 21, 2017, https://www.buzzfeednews.com/article
/darrensands/what-happened-to-black-lives-matter.

12 Arwa Mahdawi, "Black Lives Matter's Alicia Garza: 'Leadership today doesn't look like Martin Luther King'," *The Guardian*, October 17, 2020, https://www.theguardian.com/world/2020
/oct/17/black-lives-matter-alicia-garza-leadership-today-doesnt
-look-like-martin-luther-king.

13 Nate Cohn and Kevin Quealy, "How Public Opinion Has Moved on Black Lives Matter," *The New York Times*, June 10, 2020, https://www.nytimes.com/interactive/2020/06/10/upshot/black
-lives-matter-attitudes.html.

14 Juliana Menasce Horowitz, "Support for Black Lives Matter

declined after George Floyd protests, but has remained unchanged since," Pew Research Center, September 27, 2021, https://www .pewresearch.org/fact-tank/2021/09/27/support-for-black-lives -matter-declined-after-george-floyd-protests-but-has-remained -unchanged-since/.

15 Kim Parker and Kiley Hurst, "Growing share of Americans say they want more spending on police in their area," Pew Research Center, October 26, 2021, https://www.pewresearch.org/fact-ta nk/2021/10/26/growing-share-of-americans-say-they-want-more -spending-on-police-in-their-area/.

16 "Herstory," https://blacklivesmatter.com/herstory/.

17 Alicia Garza, *The Purpose of Power*, chapter 4 ("The First Fight").

18 Carrie N. Baker, "For Equality, Loretta Ross Argues We 'Call In,' Not 'Call Out': 'There's Too Much Infighting in the Feminist Movement'," *Ms.*, May 20, 2021, https://msmagazine.com/2021 /05/20/loretta-ross-feminist-social-justice-callout-cancel-cultu re-woke/.

19 Alicia Garza, *The Purpose of Power*, chapter 4 ("The First Fight").

20 Ibid., chapter 7 ("Rebellion and Resistance").

21 Ibid., chapter 4 ("The First Fight").

22 Deepa Shivaram, "5th Women's March focuses on reproductive rights after new Texas abortion law," NPR, October 2, 2021, https://www.npr.org/2021/10/02/1042707939/womens-march -abortion-protests-washington-texas.

23 Alicia Garza, *The Purpose of Power*, "Introduction."

24 Ibid., chapter 16 ("United Fronts and Popular Fronts").

25 Ibid., chapter 9 ("Unity and Solidarity").

26 Kimberlé W. Crenshaw, "Mapping the Margins: Intersectionality, Identity Politics, and Violence against Women of Color," *Stanford Law Review*, 43 (6), 1991, pp. 1241–99, https://doi.org /10.2307/1229039.

27 Ibid., p. 1242.

28 Alicia Garza, *The Purpose of Power*, chapter 8 ("The Meaning of Movement").

29 Ibid., chapter 16 ("United Fronts and Popular Fronts").

30 Ibid., chapter 12 ("The Power of Identity Politics").

31 Abby Ohlheiser, "Why 'social justice warrior,' a Gamergate insult, is now a dictionary entry," *Washington Post*, October 7, 2015, https://www.washingtonpost.com/news/the-intersect/wp/2015/10/07/why-social-justice-warrior-a-gamergate-insult-is-now-a-dictionary-entry/.

32 Cited in ibid.

33 Ibid.

34 Douglas Murray, *The War on the West*, HarperCollins, 2022, "Conclusion."

35 "social, adj. and n." *OED Online*, Oxford University Press, September 2022, www.oed.com/view/Entry/183739.

36 Charles Taylor, "The Politics of Recognition," in Amy Gutmann (ed.), *Multiculturalism: Examining the Politics of Recognition*, Princeton University Press, 1994.

37 Ibid., p. 25.

38 Nancy Fraser and Axel Honneth, *Redistribution or Recognition? A Political-Philosophical Exchange*, Verso, 2003.

39 Nancy Fraser, "Why Overcoming Prejudice Is Not Enough: A Rejoinder to Richard Rorty," in Nancy Fraser (edited by Kevin Olson), *Adding Insult to Injury: Nancy Fraser Debates Her Critics*, Verso, 2008.

40 United Nations, "Universal Declaration of Human Rights," https://www.un.org/en/about-us/universal-declaration-of-human-rights.

41 "participation, n." *OED Online*, Oxford University Press, September 2022, www.oed.com/view/Entry/138245.

42 Nancy Fraser, *Scales of Justice: Reimagining Political Space in a Globalizing World*, Columbia University Press, 2009, p. 17.

43 Charles Taylor, "The Politics of Recognition," p. 62.

44 Nancy Fraser, "Social Justice in the Age of Identity Politics: Redistribution, Recognition, and Participation," in Nancy Fraser and Axel Honneth, *Redistribution or Recognition? A Political-Philosophical Exchange*, Verso, 2003, pp. 26–30.

45 Wendy Brown, "Neo-liberalism and the End of Liberal

Democracy," *Theory & Event*, 7 (1), 2003, https://doi:10.1353/tae
.2003.0020.

46 Wendy Brown, *In the Ruins of Neoliberalism: The Rise of
Antidemocratic Politics in the West*, Columbia University Press,
2019, p. 8.

47 Ibid.

48 Frank Hobson and Aaron Kulakiewicz, "Potential merits of a
universal basic income," House of Commons Library, Debate
Pack, June 13, 2022, Number 2022-0104, https://researchbrie
fings.files.parliament.uk/documents/CDP-2022-0104/CDP-20
22-0104.pdf.

49 Lars Trägårdh, "Scaling Up Solidarity from the National to the
Global: Sweden as Welfare State and Moral Superpower," in
Nina Witoszek and Atle Midttun (eds.), *Sustainable Modernity:
The Nordic Model and Beyond*, Routledge, 2018, pp. 82–5.

50 "Interview, William Julius Wilson," PBS Frontline, Spring 1997,
https://www.pbs.org/wgbh/pages/frontline/shows/race/intervie
ws/wilson.html.

51 Lars Trägårdh, "Scaling Up Solidarity from the National to the
Global," pp. 88–92.

52 Nancy Fraser, *Scales of Justice*, pp. 13–14.

53 Ibid., p. 24.

54 Lars Trägårdh, "Scaling Up Solidarity from the National to the
Global," pp. 96–8.

55 Esteban Ortiz-Ospina and Max Roser, "Trust," Our World in
Data, 2016, https://ourworldindata.org/trust. See also "The
Inglehart-Welzel World Cultural Map 2022, World Values
Survey 7," https://www.worldvaluessurvey.org/wvs.jsp.

56 Arlie Russell Hochschild, *Strangers in Their Own Land: Anger
and Mourning on the American Right*, The New Press, 2016,
chapter 1 ("Traveling to the Heart").

57 "6 Books to Help Understand Trump's Win," *The New York
Times*, November 9, 2016, https://www.nytimes.com/2016/11
/10/books/6-books-to-help-understand-trumps-win.html.

58 Ian Haney López, *Merge Left: Fusing Race and Class, Winning Elections, and Saving America*, The New Press, 2019, p. 59.

59 Daniel Cox, Rachel Lienesch, and Robert P. Jones, "Beyond Economics: Fears of Cultural Displacement Pushed the White Working Class to Trump | PRRI/The Atlantic Report," PRRI (Public Religion Research Institute), September 5, 2017, https://www.prri.org/research/white-working-class-attitudes-economy-trade-immigration-election-donald-trump/.

60 Alicia Garza, *The Purpose of Power*, chapter 4 ("The First Fight").

61 Arlie Russell Hochschild, *Strangers in Their Own Land*, chapter 15 ("Strangers No Longer: The Power of Promise").

62 Laura Favaro, "Researchers are wounded in academia's gender wars."

63 Kate Manne, *Down Girl: The Logic of Misogyny*, Oxford University Press, 2018, p. 290.

64 Maggie Doherty, "The Philosopher of #MeToo," *The Chronicle of Higher Education*, November 13, 2019, https://www.chronicle.com/article/the-philosopher-of-metoo/.

65 Ian Haney López, *Merge Left*, p. 83.

66 Ibid., p. 86.

67 "The Race Class Narrative," We Make the Future, https://www.wemakethefuture.us/history-of-the-race-class-narrative.

68 Ibid., p. 6.

69 Ibid., p. 7.

70 Ibid.

71 Raquel Jesse, "The UK Race Class Narrative Report," CLASS (Centre for Labour and Social Studies), May 17, 2022, https://classonline.org.uk/pubs/item/the-uk-race-class-narrative-report. See also "The Race-Class Narrative Project," Demos, May 21, 2018, https://www.demos.org/campaign/race-class-narrative-project.

72 Jean Wyllys and Julie Wark, "Brazil, Amazon, World: Being Black," *CounterPunch*, July 21, 2022, https://www.counterpunch.org/2022/07/21/brazil-amazon-world-being-black/.

73 Loretta J. Ross, "Ritualizing Social Justice – Dred Feminist Rant #9."

Epilogue

1 George Orwell, "The Freedom of the Press," The Orwell Foundation, https://www.orwellfoundation.com/the-orwell-fo undation/orwell/essays-and-other-works/the-freedom-of-the -press/.

2 Arlie Russell Hochschild, *Strangers in Their Own Land*, chapter 15 ("Strangers No Longer: The Power of Promise").

3 Cornel West, Twitter, @CornelWest, July 13, 2021, https://twit ter.com/CornelWest/status/1414765668222869508?s=20&t=T Vy8ihkCrdqMA-kIwtXgmA.

4 Benjamin Wallace-Wells, "How a Conservative Activist Invented the Conflict Over Critical Race Theory," *The New Yorker*, June 18, 2021, https://www.newyorker.com/news/annals-of-inquiry /how-a-conservative-activist-invented-the-conflict-over-critical -race-theory.

5 Jacob Sarkisian, "A best-selling children's author was sacked by her publishers after tweeting her support for JK Rowling," *Insider*, July 6, 2020, https://www.insider.com/gillian-philip-chil drens-author-sacked-tweeting-support-jk-rowling-2020-7.

6 Samantha Kamman, "Canadian nurse facing disciplinary hearings for supporting JK Rowling, believing there are only 2 sexes," *The Christian Post*, September 26, 2022, https://www.christian post.com/news/canadian-nurse-faces-hearings-over-views-on -trans-issues-biology.html.

7 Philip Bump, "That Giorgia Meloni speech captivating the U.S. right doesn't make sense," *Washington Post*, September 27, 2022, https://www.washingtonpost.com/politics/2022/09/27/meloni-i taly-united-states-far-right/.

8 Paulina Neuding, "Two Bombings in One Night? That's Normal Now in Sweden," Common Sense, https://www.commonsense .news/p/two-bombings-in-one-night-thats-normal. See also "Sprängningar och skjutningar – polisens arbete," Polisen,

https://polisen.se/om-polisen/polisens-arbete/sprangningar
-och-skjutningar/.

9 "Russia–Ukraine war 2022 – statistics & facts," Statista, October
   4, 2022, https://www.statista.com/topics/9087/russia-ukraine
   -war-2022/#dossierKeyfigures.

10 "Canada's first Federal 2SLGBTQI+ Action Plan . . . Building our
   future, with pride," Government of Canada, https://women-gen
   der-equality.canada.ca/en/free-to-be-me/federal-2slgbtqi-plus
   -action-plan.html.

11 "10 Stunning Amazon Rainforest Deforestation Facts to Know
   About | Earth.Org (2022)," https://himbat.ngontinh24.com/ar
   ticle/10-stunning-amazon-rainforest-deforestation-facts-to-kn
   ow-about-earth-org.

12 Patrick Greenfield, "More than 1,700 environmental activists
   murdered in the past decade – report," *The Guardian*, September
   29, 2022, https://www.theguardian.com/environment/2022/sep
   /29/global-witness-report-1700-activists-murdered-past-decade
   -aoe; Max Roser, "Global poverty in an unequal world: Who is
   considered poor in a rich country? And what does this mean
   for our understanding of global poverty?," Our World in Data,
   March 5, 2021, https://ourworldindata.org/higher-poverty-glo
   bal-line.

Index